MURPHY'S LAW

MY JOURNEY FROM ARMY RANGER AND GREEN BERET TO INVESTIGATIVE JOURNALIST

JACK MURPHY

Threshold Editions

NEW YORK LONDON TORONTO SYDNEY NEW DELHI

Threshold Editions
An Imprint of Simon & Schuster, Inc.
1230 Avenue of the Americas
New York, NY 10020

First Threshold Editions hardcover edition April 2019

THRESHOLD EDITIONS and colophon are trademarks
of Simon & Schuster, Inc.

For information about special discounts for bulk purchases,
please contact Simon & Schuster Special Sales at 1-866-506-1949
or business@simonandschuster.com.

The Simon & Schuster Speakers Bureau can bring authors to your
live event. For more information or to book an event, contact
the Simon & Schuster Speakers Bureau at 1-866-248-3049
or visit our website at www.simonspeakers.com.

Interior design by Paul Dippolito

Manufactured in the United States of America

1   3   5   7   9   10   8   6   4   2

Library of Congress Cataloging-in-Publication Data is available.

PHOTO CREDITS
Courtesy of the author: 1, 2, 3, 4, 5, 6, 7, 8, 9, 10, 11, 12 ,13, 14, 15, 16, 17, 18,
19, 20, 21, 22, 23, 24, 25, 26, 27, 28, 29, 30, 31, 32, 33, 34, 35, 36, 37, 41, 42
Courtesy of Joey L.: 38, 39, 40

ISBN 978-1-5011-9124-4
ISBN 978-1-5011-9126-8 (ebook)

FOLLOW JACK MURPHY

Facebook: Facebook.com/jackmurphyauthor
Twitter: @JackMurphyRGR
Instagram: @JackMcMurph

Dedicated to SSG James Hupp and SGT Joe Barnes

AUTHOR'S NOTE

Writing about the army and warfare goes almost hand in hand with the use of obscure acronyms. In this book, I have done my best to limit their use or properly explain what they mean. A glossary is provided at the end of the book as well.

Certain names of individuals mentioned in this book have been changed, whether or not so noted in the text.

CONTENTS

Prologue   1

PART I

1. No Plan Survives First Contact with the Enemy   5

2. Friendly Fire Isn't   23

3. Anything That Can Go Wrong, Will Go Wrong   45

4. Ranger Days and Time-sensitive Targets   56

5. If Enough Data Is Collected, a Board of Inquiry
   Can Prove Anything   62

6. Luck Can't Hold Out Against Murph   80

7. For Every Action, There Is an Equal and
   Opposite Criticism   91

8. The Wedding Crashers   109

9. The Firepit   131

PART II

10. Anything You Do Can Get You Killed, Including
    Doing Nothing   155

11. Covering Conflict: Switzerland to Syria   167

CONTENTS

12. Flapping in the Breeze 178

13. Dark News 198

14. Humvees and IEDs 221

15. Another Surreal Journey: Meeting President Assad
    in Damascus 232

16. No Matter Which Way You Have to March, It Is
    Always Uphill 242

17. Controversy and Upsets 250

    Epilogue 257

    Glossary 263

    Acknowledgments 269

MURPHY'S
LAW

PROLOGUE

"HAVE YOU EVER BEEN SHOT AT?"

I hesitate before answering. "Yeah."

Sure, I've been shot at. Some memories start to come back to me. Bits and pieces of things I put behind me, or thought I did. Machine gun fire in the streets of Mosul as I choke on diesel exhaust. A female Kurdish sniper leans against the side of a stairwell inside an abandoned apartment building and smiles. Someone walks into the middle of the street in the city of Khost, Afghanistan. They shine their flashlight in my direction, nearly whiting out my night vision optics as I pivot. Are these the kinds of memories that the Vietnam vets call flashbacks? I don't know.

I snap back to the present after this brief temporal displacement. I'm sitting on a tree stump in Texas, two television cameras in my face, while a producer interviews me. After the army, I became an investigative journalist focusing on special operations and the intelligence community, so I have done plenty of TV news spots over the years, covering desperate firefights from Benghazi to Niger. This is the first time I've ever done an actual television show.

"Did you return fire?" the producer asks.

His name is Chris. He has a short beard, his daughter's name is tattooed on his neck, and he seems like the type of dude who never runs out of energy—a great trait to have in his line of work. I pause at this question, too, as I recall the entire world coming down on top of me on

1

a lonely mountainside in Afghanistan. It brings up a conflicted and confused churn of emotions. I can tell you that feeling lonely in a firefight can't even begin to compare to the loneliness that comes with taking responsibility for the decisions you've made in combat. In the end, you walk that road alone.

"Yeah, I returned fire."

I'm thirty-four years old. When my good friend and fellow Special Forces veteran Jim West finally convinced me to go talk to someone at Veterans Affairs, the psychologist asked me if I felt older than I really was. I said it wasn't that so much as it was that I never felt young in the first place. The stories I could tell. The stories so many young men of my generation of soldiers could tell, if only anyone would believe them.

You may have heard of Murphy's Law, which states that anything that can go wrong will go wrong. With my last name, I kind of stood out among some of my peers. You know you might be in trouble when a dude named Murphy is on your team.

I had rejected the notion of writing a book about myself for a long time. It seemed like kind of a douchey thing to do. I mean, who am I, really? I've written hundreds of articles, interviewed countless people, written about mass graves in the Philippines and dirty wars in Syria, and dodged IEDs while reporting on the ground in Iraq. Sitting in a crappy Mexican restaurant in Manhattan one day, I told Jim that I felt as if I've written everyone else's story except mine. "You're avoiding it," Jim told me. "That's because of PTSD. You don't want to confront what you've been through."

But tonight, during the interview, I'm in Texas, not Manhattan, not Afghanistan. I look right into the camera and tell the world that I've been fired upon and that I've returned fire in combat. Writing about the combat experiences of our soldiers and our allies has been an honor and privilege, but I now understand that it has also been a way for me to selfishly gain some leverage against the horrible experiences of war. It has been my way to try to understand combat, to conquer it. Deep down, I know there is no taming that beast. But I'm intoxicated by the horrible reality of war and always have been.

And so, yes, I've told everyone's story but mine.

Until now.

CHAPTER 1

No Plan Survives First Contact with the Enemy

SOME OF MY EARLIEST MEMORIES ARE OF WATCHING THE Gulf War on television.

I was seven years old, staring at CNN on the screen. News coverage was nowhere near as comprehensive or instantaneous as it is today. CNN would just play the same clip of an American soldier bounding forward, filmed through a night vision scope, with tracer fire skipping overhead. For all I knew, it could have been training footage and they ran it because it was the only action shot they had of the war. It didn't matter. I was hypnotized by the images on the screen.

Years later, the Harrison Ford movie *Patriot Games* came out on video. I was watching it with my mom. There is a scene in the movie where the SAS launches a surprise attack against a terrorist camp in the desert. As a kid, I struggled to understand what I was watching. This wasn't a war, not really. It wasn't like the old movies I had seen about World War II. I expressed this confusion to my mom. What was this if not a war?

"Secret mission," my mom replied.

"Really? Can they do that?"

"Of course they can."

My mom was no doubt aware of things that had appeared in the press over the last few decades, from the Church Committee hearings to

Iran-Contra. But this was all new and exciting information to me. Secret missions? Holy shit, I was sold.

I grew up in a house that was over a hundred years old, near Beekman Avenue, in what was then North Tarrytown, New York. My mom worked as a waitress, and my dad was a carpenter, electrician, plumber, pretty much whatever was needed. While my dad worked to fix up our new house in North Tarrytown, after we moved out of Irvington where we lived for that first year after I was born, my mom kept me in a basket in the living room with a space heater. I have scattered memories of this time, as I was very young. I do recall when my dad installed all the new cabinets in the kitchen and when he lifted the big stone slab in the front yard with a pry bar and we found a huge brick-lined well underneath. I recall my parents coming home with my little sister, and I recall holding her in my arms all those years back.

Sadly, this was not to be our childhood, as my father was diagnosed with lung cancer and died when I was seven and my sister was three. Meanwhile, my mother came down with what we now know today to be Lyme disease. Back then, the doctors thought she was just depressed because her husband had died. Meanwhile, she was getting sicker and sicker. I believed that my mom was going to die as well, and then who knew what would happen to me and my sister. It was many years before my mom found a doctor who understood what she was going through and began to treat her for Lyme.

My mom eventually remarried, and we moved to North Salem, New York, when I was about fourteen. My stepdad, Irv, has been with us ever since. He was a floral shop owner and now works as a general contractor. My mom went on to work as a teacher's assistant for a while and then got her degree and works to this day as a social worker.

I guess middle school and high school are tough for a lot of kids, but

I found them to be insufferable. I never really felt like a kid; I felt like a grown-up trapped in a kid's world. I couldn't relate to kids my own age. Despite going to high school in an affluent area where no one even dreamed of joining the military (that was for losers), I was still interested. I was plotting my escape from the dreary boring world that I had been trapped in.

In the meantime, I filled my mind with books about the type of life I wanted to lead. I read every book I could find about Long Range Reconnaissance Patrols, or LRRP/Rangers, in Vietnam. I read about Navy SEALs, Special Forces, marines, everything I could find. I was amazed by stories about small teams of Rangers or marines patrolling through the jungle.

I also delved into fiction. I read Robert E. Howard's *Conan the Barbarian,* H. P. Lovecraft's short stories, Robert A. Heinlein's *Starship Troopers,* and best of of all, Don Pendleton's Mack Bolan series. The Internet was just coming into the homes of Americans, and information about the military was harder to obtain than it is today. All I had to rely on was accounts from Vietnam-era soldiers. I also took an interest in computers and learned how to build them, so it wasn't long before I was tearing up PC games like *Half-Life* and *Deus Ex.*

North Salem High School was not quite sure what to do with me. This became pretty clear when one school advisor called me into the office and asked me about applying to colleges.

"No need," I told her. I was going to join the military and become a sniper.

"Oh, well . . . follow your dreams," she said, smiling. A social worker at our school came to talk to us in my English class one period. He knew I was interested in joining the military, and he remarked, "Jack is going to come to class with an AK-47 and shoot all of us." Even as a teenager, I found his comments revolting.

After Columbine happened, I guess he didn't find his own joke so funny anymore; he approached me on the way to class one morning. He said that I had made a comment in class one day about shooting everyone with a rifle. I corrected him, pointing out that he was the one who had made that comment. I would never say such a thing. He went away after that.

As time went on, it seemed like not much was going on in the world for a soldier to do. I followed events as closely as I could, such as the 1999 Kosovo conflict, the atrocities in Sierra Leone, and the capture of PKK leader Abdullah Öcalan. Other than war criminals being chased around Bosnia or the occasional firefight in Somalia, not much was going down. By my senior year of high school, I was thinking that in order to lead the life of adventure, I would have to join the French Foreign Legion, which is known to take in foreigners looking for some action.

Then one day in computer class, Mr. Greer came walking into the room with a worried expression on his face. "I don't want to alarm anyone," he said. "But a plane just flew into the World Trade Center."

At that moment, I don't think any of us teenagers took the words too seriously. It sounded like an accident to me. I had read about small planes flying into buildings before, including the Empire State Building, so I figured it was something like that. But not long after, we learned that a second plane had flown into the World Trade Center. At that moment, everyone in America realized that something was seriously wrong.

A few years before, I had visited an older friend at his college campus in Hoboken, New Jersey. After getting off the PATH train, we'd paused as we walked uphill to his school and stared across the Hudson River at the Twin Towers. "Worth it for the view, huh?" my buddy had commented.

Now the towers were burning.

I still remember all the rumors swirling around that day. There were reports that the State Department had been bombed, which it hadn't. There were reports of an explosion at the Pentagon, which of course was true. It was like the plot of a Mack Bolan novel come to life. Parents were picking their kids up early from school because they were so scared.

Driving to school the next morning, I was in the only car on a highway that was normally packed during the morning rush. It was just me and a police cruiser with two police motorcycles in front and two more in the back. America was changing, and the media was already hot and heavy with speculation over which country we were about to invade in retaliation. For me, it cemented the idea that I needed to join the military. My generation was going to war.

When I walked into the recruiting office, I went straight to the Marine Corps. I told the recruiter that I wanted to be a marine infantryman, and eventually try out for force recon, and was ready to sign on the dotted line. Rather than sign up a young man, he seemed like he was trying to intimidate me into signing, trying to hard-sell me. I got sick of his bullshit, went down the hall, and told the army that I wanted to be a Ranger.

The big day came in October 2002. I had been closely following developments in our new war on terror in Afghanistan. Special Forces was over there kicking some Taliban ass. I just hoped that they'd have left some for me by the time I got there. My parents gave me a hug in the parking lot of the recruitment office in Peekskill, New York, and then I was off on a flight to Atlanta, Georgia. I was nervous as hell but ready. The bus ride to Fort Benning with the other recruits was a quiet one. I had an Option 40 contract, meaning that I would spend eleven weeks in infantry basic training, then three weeks at airborne school, then I would get my shot at joining the Ranger regiment by going to the Ranger Indoctrination Program (RIP). Is the acronym intentional or just a happy coincidence? You be the judge.

Back in those days, RIP was designed to smoke the shit out of soldiers and see what they were made of. I rather enjoyed it, because the shitbags who didn't take soldiering seriously were dropping like flies. The cadre didn't mess around at all—they kicked guys out of the course for a minor infraction like losing a canteen because it showed a lack of attention to detail. Back then, privates could still get drop-kicked for not paying attention—unfortunately, the army has taken a lot of these disciplinary tools away from our soldiers.

But don't get me wrong, RIP broke me off, too.

During the twelve-mile road march, I simply could not keep up. They retested the failures, and again, I simply could not keep pace. I was not meeting the standard. It was frustrating because I had done a lot of physical training on my own and knew that I could complete the task. My body just wouldn't let me do it for some reason. I had joined the army for the express purpose of going to war with a special operations unit and had zero interest in failing RIP and getting sent to a conventional unit.

After failing the road march twice, I was sent to the holdover platoon to receive a grilling from Staff Sergeant Phipps. As the Non-Commissioned Officer In Charge, or NCOIC, of the holdover platoon, Staff Sergeant Phipps was responsible for getting guys ready for RIP, or at least setting them on the right track. He was hard but fair.

"Do you want to recycle, Murphy?" he asked me on the field in front of the RIP barracks, the identical-looking concrete buildings that dotted most military bases.

"Roger, Sergeant."

"Why do you want to recycle? You failed the twelve-mile road march. The next RIP class starts on Monday." That was in three days. "What is going to change between now and then?"

"I think I should go to sick call, Sergeant," I said. "I'll be ready on Monday."

Sergeant Phipps looked dismissive of my claims but instructed me to fall into his holdover formation. They were about to do afternoon PT, and then I could go to the troop medical clinic and see someone. We jogged down the road and did a practice PT test in preparation for the RIP PT test on Monday. After we jogged back to the barracks, I peeled off my bloody socks and went down to the TMC. The nurse said that it sounded like one of my lungs was halfway filled up with fluid, which would explain why I was short of breath and could not keep up on a road march.

She tried to prescribe me a week's worth of antibiotics, but I told her that wouldn't work; I could not be on any prescription drugs when I started RIP. She sighed and handed me a three-day treatment of pills. I took them and, as planned, started RIP on Monday to go through the course all over again, including the dreaded trip to Cole Range.

Cole Range was where RIP students conducted their land navigation testing with a map and compass. It was also where the cadre smoked the shit out of the students with physical exercises. My most vivid experience from RIP was one of those two a.m. smoke sessions in which the super-strict Sergeant Straight was having his way with us, making us do flutter kicks while we held our rucksacks in the air and all kinds of other exercises that only a true sadist could dream up.

Straight tapped out and switched places with another cadre member who was known to be a little more relaxed. This cadre told us to lie down on the ground with our faces in the dirt so that we could not see one another. I was expecting some new type of smoke session to ensue, but instead, the RIP cadre began to give us a speech about what it meant to be an American. "Listen, men, you don't have to be a Ranger to be a good American. You can go to a conventional unit and serve your country there. There is nothing wrong with quitting, you can still be a good American, you can still be a good soldier. Your buddies can't even see you quit now. Just stand up, quit, and you can go sit by the fire and eat an MRE."

He stuck to this theme for maybe fifteen minutes, telling us how we could be good American patriots in some other unit. I heard the RIP students to my left and to my right stand up and walk over to the firepit and quit the course. Holy shit, I thought, this is the real deal: It is the psychological uncertainties that lead people to quit more than the physical stress. Being a Ranger requires you to be self-motivated, confident, and trust your teammates, which is possible because we all had to suck it up through some shit in training.

When it came time for the twelve-mile road march, I ran the entire twelve miles. When I arrived at the end, a cadre came walking up to meet me as if he hadn't expected to see anyone yet. "Are you the first one back, Murphy?"

I looked around and didn't see anyone. "I guess so, Sergeant."

I was assigned to 3rd Ranger Battalion, just down the road from the RIP barracks, located behind a notorious brown fence that no one could see through. Other units on post knew not to go inside. Down the street at airborne school, the instructors would warn the students to stay away from us because we were violent and dangerous. We took this as a compliment.

Waddling down the sidewalk to 3rd Ranger Battalion, 75th Ranger Regiment, abbreviated as 3/75, with my duffel bags, I was assigned a barracks room and placed in the anti-tank section in Alpha Company. We were the "goose gunners" who employed the 84mm Carl Gustaf recoilless rifle. These were Ranger days, an exciting time for a new private in an elite unit. Every day was something new, every day a competition with everyone else.

You were subject to no shortage of being broken in as the new guy. These days they would probably call that hazing and harassment, and a guy from today's video game generation of kids would run to his congressman to complain about how his squad leader was triggering him with micro-aggressions. The reality is that building soldiers is an ancient task, one that does not require modification for the sake of political correctness. Young soldiers need tough training, discipline, and strong leaders. I was very fortunate to have all three in spades.

That summer we flew around in MH-60 helicopters, doing false insertions in the wood line before fast-roping on top of buildings at the urban training range, blasting objectives with the Carl Gustaf out at Kilo 22, doing stress shoots all over Benning with our rucksacks and rifles, then locking and loading when we arrived at the range and shooting at cardboard targets that look like a human silhouette called E-Types. For me, it was a dream come true. I was drinking from the firehose, as they say, learning about infrared laser night sights, parachuting out of a plane with an anti-tank weapon, and as funny as it seems to me now, using the focus knob on my night vision optics. I was a kid and didn't know shit!

All the other guys in my company had just gotten back from the invasion of Iraq. Three Rangers had been lost, and the stories I was told brought home how real all of it was. My team leader teared up a little while talking about how he had used his jacket to smother the flames on his squad leader's body after an IED went off. I could sense that the guys had been traumatized by the Iraq deployment, but no one wanted to talk about that. They were Rangers, and their concern was for the next mission. It was a quiet type of mourning that no one really wanted to acknowledge.

We were gearing up for a training deployment to Thailand, which seemed cool as hell to me, but it was not to be: 3/75's sergeant major was upset that our battalion was not sending enough privates to Ranger School. A lot of people confuse the unit and the school. Both serve a purpose but completely different ones. The Ranger regiment is a special operations combat unit, and Ranger School is a course open to the whole army that teaches tactics and leadership. To hold a leadership position in the Ranger regiment, you have to pass the school, so for us, it was graduate or get kicked out of our unit.

Due to the small number of guys from my unit going to Ranger School at that time, the company first sergeant dictated that all privates would take a pre-Ranger PT test, and the men with the highest scores would go to Ranger School. I took the PT test, did well, and to my horror, was on my way to Ranger School. It wasn't that I didn't want to go, I just knew that I was about as green as they come. Usually, Rangers spend a year or two in the regiment before going to the school; I had been there a few months. However, this was not an opportunity you turned down. Until I had my Ranger tab, I would be just a Ranger private. With that said, I was off to pre-Ranger at the Ranger Training Brigade, where RIP was located. More than a few instructors looked at me and asked what the fuck I was doing back there.

After a few weeks of pre-Ranger training (including another trip to Cole Range), I departed for Ranger School where I promptly got recycled as a land navigation failure. It was kind of fucked up how I failed that event. At each point you use the hole punch strung to the pole on your test sheet to prove that you were there, then write down the number on the point. It was raining, so although I had the correct punch on my test sheet, the ink bled to the point that it was illegible, which meant that I had failed the event since the instructor could not read the number. I was given the option to recycle and took it.

I want to take a moment here to point out that, as you may have surmised, I was no Captain America. Though I failed in some of my endeavors, the army is pretty good about rewarding perseverance, which is a quality I think they intentionally cultivate. Standards are not lowered, but you are given the opportunity to retest. However, quitters are banished in the Ranger community. For Rangers, there is nothing worse you can be in life than a quitter.

Christmas was coming up, so I was placed in Vaughn's platoon (the recycle platoon) to do details around the Ranger Training Brigade for about a month, then sent home on Christmas exodus, then back to Benning to start Ranger School again. I was in that goddamn Vaughn platoon for so long that I thought they would rename it Murphy's Platoon.

I could tell Ranger School stories all day. I was totally lost in the sauce. I didn't understand basic infantry tactics and had essentially zero leadership ability. I was a private second class who had been promoted to private first class just so I could attend the school. In other words, I was a dope who didn't know a damn thing. Ranger School was a great experience for me—I learned a lot about infantry tactics, mission planning, and leadership, because we repeated the mission-essential tasks over and over until they became second nature.

One moment that stands out for me was in Mountain Phase, which takes place in Dahlonega, Georgia. I was humping the M240B machine gun once again. Like everyone else, I was exhausted and sleep-deprived, and the local ambience that day just made things so much worse. Many of our patrols took place along the Appalachian Trail, where there are loads of trail hippies; as I came to find out, some of them take up trail names.

Our patrol moved in a single-file column between two trail hippies having a conversation. As I walked between them, I heard a snippet of conversation.

"My name is Ziggy, I didn't catch yours."

"My name is Geo. For Geochemistry!"

He sounded like that fat nerdy kid on *The Simpsons*. That was all it took—my morale plummeted. Listening to these two hippies wax poetic was just more than I could take. I don't know how I talked myself out of quitting Ranger School that day. But somehow I made it through Mountain Phase in January, went on to Florida Phase, and graduated with Class number 04-04, meaning it was the fourth graduating class of the fiscal year of 2004.

After Ranger School, I had two weeks of leave. Feeling like a big old twenty-year-old badass, I went backpacking and scuba diving by myself in Costa Rica. I ended up walking about thirty miles through the jungle out of Drake Bay. It was an amazing trip, my first time outside of the United States, and it cemented the idea that I was heading for some exciting adventures in life.

When I arrived back at my company in 3rd Ranger Battalion, my unit was deployed to Afghanistan. Yes, I was pissed, as I'd missed out on both Thailand and a combat deployment so I could freeze my balls off in January on the Tennessee Valley Divide in Dahlonega, Georgia. However, we had a new squad leader in Alpha Company, or A/co, whom I got to talking to. He asked me if I would have any interest in going over to the sniper section. Hell yeah, I would. He walked me next door to Headquarters and Headquarters Company (HHC), where I met Staff Sergeant Jared Van Aalst and one of my pre-Ranger cadre, Sergeant First Class Randy, who was now helping stand up our new reconnaissance, or recce, detachment, which would act as scouts for our battalion and gather intel on Ranger objectives prior to raiding them. They asked me to come back for an interview, which I did. Afterward, they allowed me to join the sniper section.

Sniper section had an odd dynamic. Sniper section liked to sell itself as being a more relaxed adult environment than the line squads, but that really wasn't the case. I got to suffer the harassment of being the new guy all over again, and this time without the coaching, teaching, and mentoring that I had experienced in Alpha Company. I was never given any real instruction other than at the very last minute, when we were out at a range. I felt ignored until I went to sniper school in the summer of 2004 and learned how to shoot at long range. I graduated the course that summer, spending every day sweating through my uniform.

In time, I began to feel quite a bit of resentment toward Van Aalst and some of the other leaders in the section. It struck me that their passive-aggressiveness was an attempt to gloss over a lack of combat experience. VA was the type of guy you could say hi to and he would walk right past you as if you didn't exist. While other Rangers were deploying to war, Van Aalst had been at the Army Marksmanship Unit, shooting on the flat range. Now he was substituting crappy corporate tactics that kept his subordinates perpetually scared of losing their jobs in place of actual leadership. I quickly learned that I was never going to fit in with this crew personality-wise. I will never dispute the amount of talent in that sniper section, including Van Aalst, arguably one of the best shots in the army, but because of his idiosyncratic leadership style—you never knew where you stood with him—I never felt that I could trust him.

After the Fort Benning sniper course, it was a relief to deploy. I would be partnered up with Joe and deployed with Charlie Company to Khost, Afghanistan. Joe had graduated from the Benning sniper course, the Special Operations Target Interdiction Course, and the Marine Corps Scout Sniper School, and had his hog's tooth around his neck to prove it. The hog's tooth is a 7.62 bullet strung on a piece of nylon parachute cord that is worn like a necklace by graduates of the scout sniper course. For the Marines, this is a really big deal. Joe was a short guy who could run like the wind. He had spent a significant amount of his life living abroad before joining the military.

Joe knew his stuff and really took me under his wing to teach me how to be a Ranger sniper. In the army, you get to learn real, practical skills, and you see the results. Steady body position, proper trigger control, and correct sight alignment end with rounds on target. Of course, there is a bit more to it than that, as snipers have to calculate for the effects of wind, gravity, and a number of other environmental frictions, but you get the idea.

Another thing you should understand about the Ranger Battalion is that it is a closed culture and generally very insular. With its own unique culture and traditions, as well as a huge distrust of outsiders, the Ranger Battalion is almost like a cult. Many Rangers are going to be quite mad at me for writing this book; others have ostracized me in the past for sharing parts of our Ranger culture. One thing I've avoided writing about is operational security (OPSEC, relating to specific tactics, techniques, and procedures used in combat), which is seen as paramount.

That's why it seemed a little weird when our battalion commander mounted a podium with a microphone rigged to loudspeakers behind our battalion headquarters to give us a rousing war speech. He addressed each platoon in the battalion, saying things like "First Platoon, you will be deploying to Baghdad and working with the British SAS! Alpha Company, you will be working with Delta Force in Mosul!" You could hear his voice echoing across Fort Benning. We all kind of looked at each other, wondering what the fuck we had just witnessed. It must have been the biggest OPSEC violation in Ranger regiment history.

Joe and I boarded a C-17 aircraft with elements of Charlie Company and flew to Afghanistan. The ramp lowered when we were still taxiing on the tarmac in Bagram, and we could see the snowcapped mountains beyond. We were only in Bagram for maybe a day, which suited me just fine. The special operations compound at Bagram looked like Auschwitz, and the guys there were treated like dirt. There were rules posted everywhere for everything. Rules for the coffeemaker, rules for the showers, rules about which days of the week you are allowed to jack yourself off, it seemed. I later found out that things were so bad there that a lot of squad leaders ended up coming home on antidepressants. The deal with Bagram was that the guys there were on 24/7 standby to go roll up Osama bin Laden once intel figured out where he was, so they were just training in Afghanistan every day, waiting for the word to stand by. It was a miserable existence for those dudes, and they rightfully hated it there.

We loaded up on ammo and frags, then boarded a C-130 aircraft bound for Forward Operating Base (FOB) Salerno in Khost Province. At FOB Salerno, we Rangers had a small compound within a compound. As snipers, Joe and I were put in a tent with our battalion's brand-new recce teams. For years, the Ranger Reconnaissance Detachment had done the recon work for Ranger Battalions, but now they were getting absorbed into Joint Special Operations Command (JSOC) operations and expanding into a company-sized element called the Ranger Reconnaissance Company or RRC, which would keep them doing recce missions for

Delta Force or whoever else. Years later, I found out that they took part in the Omega Program, in which RRC seconded Rangers to the CIA, but I knew nothing about that at the time. So now each of our three battalions needed its own recon team. This was the first deployment for our recon teams. It was mine, too.

The tents we were in were called GP mediums, the GP standing for General Purpose. They are just OD green canvas tents that we were crammed into on cots alongside our rucksacks, black tough boxes, rifles, and the occasional portable DVD player or game console scattered around. I had brought about a dozen books with me, planning to read up on Alexander the Great and the Nepalese Gurkhas, both of which had history in this part of the world. The boys soon scored a bootleg copy of *Team America: World Police,* and I shit you not, they watched it several times a day.

The other new thing about us was our facial hair. Rangers were notorious for their spit-and-polish image. We had a little blue book filled with Ranger standards that were followed to the letter; it had to be kept in our uniform pocket at all times. This wasn't Special Forces (Green Berets); there was no room for deviation. (Go figure, the regiment is very regimented.) Anyway, we had a "high-and-tight" haircut that had to be fresh every Monday morning. Frankly, it was a stupid-looking haircut that made us look like giant penises. All that was changing now. Our regimental command sergeant major rightly pointed out that our distinctive Ranger haircuts were an OPSEC violation in and of itself: You can take the patches off your uniform, but when a whole battalion of dudes with high-and-tights shows up, everyone knows they are Rangers. Furthermore, recce and snipers were expected to do low-visibility work, sometimes dressed in indigenous garb. All recce and snipers were ordered to grow out their hair and beards. Having a beard was also kind of a status symbol in special operations; it meant you were one of the "cool guys." This led to quite a bit of consternation in the regiment. The old guard just could not let go of their high-and-tight haircut.

Randy, who was the recce platoon sergeant, was already on the ground when we arrived, as he had deployed with the advanced party. He helped us get off to a good rolling start as we relieved 2nd Ranger Battalion, who were now heading home. We had to get familiarized with our NSTVs, or nonstandard tactical vehicles. These were Toyota Hilux pickup trucks that had been modified with some improvised armor: chest plates strapped in the doors; racks installed for radios; tow straps prepositioned; generally packed with spare magazines and hand grenades. The recce guys were to use them for close-target reconnaissance, and I often found myself riding with them.

When my first live operation happened, Joe and I split up on the objective. Some of you have this vision of a sniper/spotter team formed from the Vietnam experience, Carlos Hathcock in Elephant Valley. Yeah, I read that book, too, but this wasn't 'Nam. As Ranger snipers, we normally worked in a direct action capacity, supporting the assault elements on the ground. My first operation was an example of this.

Our ground assault force convoy pulled up to the objective. I jumped off the Humvee I was in and dashed up a cliff. I had an idea where I was going from looking at the maps and other imagery products we had during mission planning. At the top of the hill, I found a small shrub that would serve as concealment but not cover. I pretty much got into position just after the assault force hit the compound. From my vantage point, I was able to scan ahead of the assault teams with the high-powered optics on my SR-25 as the Rangers below leapfrogged from building to building. Once the compound was announced to be secure, I turned around and pulled security on our perimeter.

The mission went down without a hitch, though I don't recall that we found any bad guys. This was 2004, and the U.S. military was in the eye of the storm. American military forces had shocked and awed the Taliban and Al-Qaeda, sending them fleeing for Pakistan, if they were lucky. A lot of them were just killed outright. My battalion conducted a combat jump on an airfield in Afghanistan during that first deployment. Now we were looking for Taliban holdouts and Al-Qaeda foreign fighters.

What the larger plan for Afghanistan was, if one existed, was never articulated to me. Our instructions were to keep up the pressure on the Taliban and the Haqqani network. Our regimental commander visited at one point and said he didn't care if we hit dry holes to keep the pressure on the enemy. That never made much sense to me, because if it is a truly dry hole you are hitting, all you are doing is pissing off the locals and missing the enemy by a mile. How that keeps pressure on them is difficult to understand.

My second mission with Charlie Company came perhaps a week later. I found myself laying my SR-25 on the hood of one of our Humvees and pulling security. This was early on in the war in Afghanistan. The Taliban had been roused during the initial invasion and were still on their heels, trying to get their shit together. Sometimes we would go weeks in between missions. Joe and I made use of our spare time to train: We often went out to the range and fired our sniper rifles, practiced range estimation, reconfigured our gear. Joe taught me how to shoot a pistol, which I had really sucked at up until his instruction. On other occasions the recce teams would do ad hoc training missions in which one team had to recce out a target designated on our FOB while the other team acted as the enemy aggressor. Sometimes these training missions could be a lot of fun and all kinds of hijinks would ensue.

Charlie Company had their fun, too. I remember young Leo Jenkins, one of the company medics, participated in a classic Ranger birthday tradition. He and a few other guys flex-cuffed a Charlie Company Ranger to the fence that surrounded our compound and covered him in shaving cream; they left him out there and went back to their tent to watch episodes of *Friends* on DVD. Eventually, someone came over and set him loose. On one of my birthdays, the guys got me good back at Benning. They flex-cuffed me, covered me in shoe polish and shaving cream, then threw me in the shower. While I was walking back to the barracks to clean myself up, several groups of Rangers waved and wished me happy birthday.

Another mission came down to us: to go and capture a Taliban intelligence officer named Jamal Adin. We hit the compound at night, and ol' Jamal and his pals were marched outside the front gate blindfolded and flex-cuffed. I noticed that all of our prisoners were shaking like French soldiers. That was when I realized that these Taliban goons were not used to dealing with American soldiers who follow a code of conduct. They thought we would behave the way they did, or perhaps like the Russian troops who had been in Afghanistan in the seventies and eighties. These dudes thought we were about to execute them. Of course, this was not to be the case. We also found a decent-sized cache of weapons and ammunition on the compound, which was at the top of a hill. I got to carry one of those wooden crates down the hill on my shoulder. Soon we were off on another midnight ride through dusty streets, navigating through the green tint of night vision goggles. Jamal Adin was released a few weeks later due to lack of evidence.

Afghanistan was a frustrating experience in many ways. It was 2004 and no one was sure if we had won the war or not. No one thought we would be in that country a decade and a half later.

CHAPTER 2

Friendly Fire Isn't

AFGHANISTAN IS A DIFFICULT PLACE TO EXPLAIN IF YOU haven't been there. It is beautiful, deadly, and beyond maddening all at the same time, but this has always been the case for soldiers in that country since time immemorial. Alexander knew this. The Russians knew this. We should have known better.

The terrain reminded me of Robert Howard's fictional Afghulistan in his Conan novels: sharp crags withered away by centuries of cold and wind, jagged ridgelines, flat expanses that look like the surface of the moon. You might believe you are on a different planet. Kids walk up to you with wide eyes, curious but standing off at a distance, just watching. Nomads pass leading a camel. Men with broken teeth sit around for days at a time picking at their feet. Afghans feud with one another and hold grudges for decades if not longer. I learned early that local conflicts involve local people, and the fighting often happens regardless of American troops in the area. We're not always as important to the local people as we might like to believe we are.

In subsequent years, various Afghan expats and other apologists have pointed to some mythical era in 1960s Kabul when liberated chicks wore skirts and attended college. Afghanistan was a nature preserve for bunny rabbits until evil Western colonial powers showed up, or so they say. This is a load of bullshit. Sure, Kabul was okay for a certain class of people for a brief period of time, but Afghanistan has always been tribal, primitive, and ungovernable. If you took away the cell phone, the automobile, and the AK-47, then the people of Afghanistan would be indistinguishable from those living in the times of Jesus, all flip-flops and man pajamas.

But Afghanistan also offered an allure to a young man like me. In each valley was the unknown, a new adventure, something that few had ever laid eyes on or, if they had, probably hadn't lived to tell the tale. This was very much the opposite of the dreary predictable lives that we had back home, where every day was exactly the same, where we were all expected to fall into sequence, where we followed a predictable life trajectory as dictated by social norms that someone we'd never met laid down a long time ago. From my perspective, combat would prove that I existed.

It was my feeling that our lives were just a series of false faces, unrealities projected on one another because we were so afraid of the truth. But in combat, one could see and experience the truth, because when the bullets started flying, there was no place to hide.

As I've grown older, I have not really changed my mind about this. It seems that spending your youth fighting and dying alongside other young men in combat is a much more powerful and important experience than that had by others of my age who attended college and led comfortable lives. They got to fall in love with the cute girl in the school library while my peers and I were fighting in Afghanistan and Iraq, but it is truly those most difficult times that come to define who you are as a man.

Back then, I had no idea how true that would be.

Some of the coolest missions were the ones that never went down, although you might argue that this was for the better, considering the risks that were often involved.

In one instance, we were all given these massive horse pills to start taking, which would supposedly help fight altitude sickness when we were scheduled to be inserted into the Hindu Kush Mountains to take down some Iranian Al-Qaeda member. Snipers and the recce teams were to insert ahead of the main assault element while pre-assault fires from U.S. fighter aircraft would be ongoing. Due to the high altitude, there would only be two or three guys on each MH-60 helicopter. After high winds and a little math were taken into account, it became clear that long-range sniper shots would be out of the question. While we got eyes on target, the Ranger element in Bagram would fast-rope in from MH-47 helicopters. In the end, the whole mission got scrubbed.

In another instance, "Other Governmental Agency," or OGA, asked Joe and me to provide sniper support for one of their operations. The CIA's paramilitary component is called Ground Branch, and they worked with indigenous commandos whom they trained out of the nearby FOB Chapman. We were going to go in and hit a series of three compounds and provide sniper support, but that one ended up not getting the green light. I never found out why, but this isn't uncommon. Maybe the target moved, maybe the intel just never panned out.

In another strange would-be mission, Joe and I were told that a "non-American" entity was holding an Al-Qaeda leader's family who had divulged his location. After we bombed the living hell out of the target, Joe and I were tasked to mop up whoever was left standing. But military planners could not make sense of the information until they realized that they were looking at the wrong valley—it was actually the next valley system up on the map they had. Just another mission that never ended up happening for reasons that were never really explained.

Others did get the green light. Charlie Company hit three targets in one night, taking down an illicit passport-making operation. Joe and I provided sniper support. By now I had taken to carrying an AK-47 with me in the vehicle in case of an ambush or other short-range engagement in which my SR would be unwieldy.

Things took on a new level of cool when Little Bird helicopters showed up at our FOB one night. We were going to have one night of training for an aerial platform support mission, then, during the next period of darkness, we were going hot for a high-value-target strike against a Taliban leader. Remember, I was a twenty-one-year-old Ranger. I was living out every special operations dude's dreams. In the past, this was stuff that probably only seasoned Delta Force operators got to do. Since 9/11, things had changed. Everyone was expected to step up to the mission before them.

Since I had never fired a sniper rifle, or any weapon, from a helicopter, I asked Joe if he could give me a little class on how to go about it. Joe was a sniper god, as far as I was concerned, and knew his precision marksmanship forward and back. He was a shorter guy with sandy-colored hair and a long red beard, which was why we would joke that he looked Chechen. In conversation, I learned that he had grown up all over the world and had a pretty rough upbringing prior to joining the army. Joe was a tough customer, and this definitely wasn't his first rodeo.

"It's simple," Joe replied. "You know how you have to lead a moving target?"

"Sure."

When you fire a bullet at long range, depending on the range and the type of bullet, it could take a second or a second and a half before your bullet impacts its target. This is called time of flight. When you are shooting at a moving target, you need to lead him—that is, fire in front of where he is when you pull the trigger, so that he walks into the bullet by the time it arrives at his location. You are shooting where your target will be rather than where he is.

"So, it is just the opposite: You are the moving target, because you are on a helicopter," Joe replied matter-of-factly. "So you just use a reverse lead and fire behind the target."

Wait.

What?!

Eventually, I got up to speed on how to snap-link myself to the exterior pod on the Little Bird so I didn't fall off (that's important), how to snap-link my SR-25 to myself so I didn't lose it in flight (that is also important), and how to fire at any enemy combatants. The safety aspect isn't a joke. One time a Little Bird landed on an incline. The Delta operator on the pod got off and moved out, not realizing that the pitch of the rotors was tilted due to the incline. The rotor blades took off the top of his head. His teammates found the top of his helmet with the top of his skull inside it, sheared off in a perfect straight line.

It was actually pretty straightforward. I would straddle the pod as if I were riding a horse, John Wayne–style. The SR would just lie in my lap, and I would use my infrared laser—which I could see with my PVS-14 night vision goggles—to shoot any bad guys. At night, the pilots walked us through a familiarization of their aircraft before we got started. The Little Bird is like a little black egg of death, one that can deliver troops on target or be specially outfitted with machine guns and rocket pods.

Targets were set up on a nearby range for us that night. We snapped into the pod on the Little Bird, gave the pilots a thumbs-up, and lifted off. So, do you think riding outside a helicopter in flight, during the night, under night vision, and shooting guns from it sounds cool? Well, I won't lie to you. It fucking is. Joe and I lit up some targets that night as the Little Birds took us overhead on several passes. The SR would chirp in my lap as I oriented the IR laser onto the targets and squeezed the trigger again and again. Then the pilot would bank and peel off, with me suddenly looking straight down at the ground below.

The following night, we were waiting around for the green light for our mission, and I got to talking to the pilot. He seemed like a super-cool dude. He told me that this was his last combat operation before he went home to run the flight simulator and train new pilots. Needless to say, he was hoping to go out with a bang and really wanted the assault force from Charlie Company to get their man. Before long, word came down from higher. Charlie Company had launched their ground assault force in Humvees. We waited back at the FOB, timing our departure so that the air and ground elements would arrive on target at the same time. These dudes definitely knew what they were doing. If you read about the history of special operations forces, you will notice that 160th was created after the Desert One debacle in Iran. In 1980, the newly established Delta Force was tasked to rescue American hostages held in Iran, but the mission was a failure, largely due to conventional helicopters being used; America simply did not have a special operations aviation capability back then. Afterward, this very special helicopter unit was formed to undertake the most dangerous missions in the most adverse conditions.

After an hour or so, the pilots cranked their engines and we lifted off. It was winter in Afghanistan, and I had come prepared. I wore a heavy Columbia winter jacket over my plate carrier. Under that I had on more snivel gear, because I was expecting to be turned into an icicle on the side of this Little Bird. I was excited and ready to roll. Once the pilot brought his helicopter around and nosed us in the proper direction, he hauled ass. I was John Wayning it on the pod, which became an endurance event for my abs due to the wind pushing me backward. We blasted over mountains, dusty dirt roads, valleys, and walled compounds that looked empty aside from the faint traces of light that you could see only under night vision.

After about half an hour of flying, we arrived at the target compound just as Charlie Company was pulling up. The Ranger assault force departed their vehicles and prepared to make entry. We hovered overhead, watching for "squirters," or bad guys trying to run away. The 160th pilots spotted someone on the compound trying to walk out and decided to keep the pressure on them, you know, give them a little something to think about instead of escaping. Through my night vision optics, I watched the Little Bird that Joe was on do a dive-bomber run on the compound. The pilot expertly dove right into the center of the compound before pulling up at the last second, stirring up a blast of rotor wash inside the compound walls before disappearing back into the darkness of the night.

Charlie Company made entry, and before long they radioed a code word: "Jackpot." It meant that they had secured the Taliban leader we were after.

"Yeah!" the pilot exclaimed in my headset.

That was a hell of a good mission, but they didn't all go down so smoothly. On another operation, Charlie Company shot and killed a sixteen-year-old kid while clearing his bedroom. Randy later told me that the kid had jumped on our air force JTAC, or Joint Terminal Attack Controller, and attacked him, leaving the Rangers with little choice.

On yet another operation, I was in a Charlie Company convoy, heading out to a location near the Pakistan border. Joe had kitted up and departed a few days earlier with one of the recce teams. He was a hell of a good sniper partner who had taught me a lot, and he trusted me to do my job when I was left without his supervision. Joe was an intense sort of dude, but we understood each other and worked well together.

Joe and the recce guys had linked up with a dude from Task Force Orange, also known as intelligence support activity (ISA), or one of many constantly changing code names. This guy was a signals intelligence dude who was listening to commo traffic across the border. I'm sure he was listening for someone specific (I was never told whom) to come over the net so that he could call in the Rangers to detain them.

The recce team had conducted a route reconnaissance on their way out there and transmitted it back to our FOB, but for some reason, the Charlie Company guys never got that. Convoying it out there became a bit of a mess, as we made several bad turns and had to turn around.

Afghanistan isn't exactly the best mapped or easiest to navigate country in the world, so I can see why we got turned around a few times. We started driving out during the day, and as with every road in Afghanistan, the dust became overwhelming. Because of the amount of dust, one driver could not see a bend in the road in front of him. The vehicle went over a ledge and rolled over. Sadly, the .50-cal Ma Deuce machine gunner sitting in the turret was crushed. His name was Corporal William Amundson.

The rest of the convoy stopped. I got out with the other Rangers to establish 360-degree security, wondering what was going on. Charlie Company got a nine-line medevac order back to our FOB, and a helicopter was eventually dispatched. From my perspective, it seemed like it took forever. Maybe a faster response wouldn't have made much of a difference. Tragically, Sergeant Amundson died from his wounds. I had crossed paths with Amundson, since we were both in HHC, but we didn't really know each other. In retrospect, I wish I did. In a Ranger Battalion, there is no telling who might not be around the next day.

With his remains evacuated by helicopter, it was left to us to continue on and accomplish the mission. We were in a state of shock at the time and didn't really talk about what had just happened. Finally, we made it out to where Joe and the recce team were located. The previous night they had holed up in a draw coming down off a hill where a castle stood, which now served as a base for Afghan border guards. There was a quiet frustration among the Charlie Company guys over the unexpected loss of a man. Their company commander appeared to be in a daze, lost in his own thoughts. But you have to find a place to sleep, and as it began to lightly rain, I crawled underneath one of the Toyota Hiluxes and went to sleep on the rocks.

First Sergeant Sealey was also out there, and he was trying to keep things lighthearted the next morning as we stood around a small fire we had made. The Charlie Company first sergeant was a large black man who was much loved by his men; he was fun to be around but certainly not someone to be fucked around with. Something popped off in the fire and exploded, a piece of shrapnel buzzing right past my right ear. "That was your momma praying for you to make it home, Murphy! She saved your life!" Then he launched into another joke about how I looked like Jeremiah Johnson with my beard. Sealey was a hell of a good guy, and I knew he wanted all of us to laugh, because if we didn't, a lot of dudes would have been crying.

Back at the FOB, there was more training. Recce had been asked to begin training the local Khost police as some kind of SWAT-type element, which they did once a week. I also got to participate in call-for-fire training, calling in air strikes from Cobra gunships. Another time the mortar crew showed us how to fire 81mm and 60mm mortar systems.

On another occasion we got an aerial platform support mission, this time flying with marine Hueys. The marines had tons of restrictions on what they (and we) could and could not do, but we all did our best to make it work. I was on a Huey with the Charlie Company executive officer (XO) as we orbited the target area for what seemed like hours. He ended up puking in an MRE bag. By the time we made it back to the FOB, I don't think I was far behind him. We had been flying circles around the objective area for hours, and when we landed my legs were wobbly.

About halfway through the deployment, we got word that we were to prepare for a new recce mission, one that had special significance for the Ranger regiment. We were to recon the compound harboring the suspected Taliban leader who'd planned the Pat Tillman ambush, so that it could be assaulted by a Ranger strike force. Pat had been an NFL player who'd quit his high-paying job as a professional athlete to become a Ranger, making national headlines by doing so.

I had never actually met Tillman; he was maybe one or two cycles ahead of me in training. I saw him once in the Ranger regiment chow hall, but that was about it. I did speak to guys in his battalion when I was in pre-Ranger, getting ready for Ranger School, and they told me that Pat Tillman was a good guy, the real deal. So I was shocked when, after Ranger School, I went into an Internet café in a small town where I was backpacking in Costa Rica and saw on the front page the news of the day: Pat Tillman had been killed in Afghanistan. Initially it was reported that he was killed by the enemy in a firefight, but later on it came out that Tillman had been killed by friendly fire. Fast-forward to the winter of 2004–05: Now we were looking for the guy behind it.

I worked with Paul, the assistant recce team leader, and Grant, the recce team leader, and their recce team on immediate action drills, rehearsing what we would do if we got ambushed, if a vehicle was disabled, if both vehicles were disabled, and other contingencies, down to simple things like changing a tire. We got our desert tiger-stripe uniforms and pakol hats, which have flat tops and a roll of fabric that goes around the top of your head, to disguise ourselves as Afghan paramilitary soldiers. The plan was to drive our vehicles down to the Pak border and link up with the paramilitaries at their border control point (BCP). From there we would team up and accomplish our mission of laying the groundwork for Charlie Company to conduct a direct action raid and police up this guy who had been involved in the Tillman ambush.

The recce team rolled out with two attachments, me as the sniper and an air force JTAC. We began the long drive down to the Pakistan border and the Afghan BCP, passing through the Khost bowl, a large flat open area surrounded by mountains on all sides. Nomads—or Kuchis, in the local language of Dari—lived in what looked like gypsy camps out on the flat expanse. From there, we entered more remote, untamed areas, driving through dangerous switchbacks and steep valleys. As I mentioned, there were times when it truly felt like you were on another planet.

We drove across golf ball–sized stones at the bottom of a narrow valley and rounded a bend. A stream ran through the valley, and a woman wearing a burka knelt beside it, washing her dishes in the water. Ancient terraces rose up on either side of the valley, making use of a complicated system of irrigation to grow crops. Toward the top of the valley were adobe huts that seemed like they were built right on the rock face.

Around another bend, we entered a forested area with thick pine trees, eroded ledges, and undergrowth pouring out toward what passed for a road. A lone man wearing a pakol and a vest stared at us and walked away. We descended into canyons with marijuana plants growing on both sides in thick fields. We climbed up the side of mountains, narrowly passing by flatbed trucks loaded with lumber cut from the surrounding areas. On several occasions, we drove through valley passes that were so narrow that our Hiluxes barely made it through. There was no way that the wide-framed U.S. Army Humvees could make it through this terrain. One pass looked like it had been dynamited open not that long ago. It was easy to see how the Afghans trapped invaders inside mountain pass after mountain pass, wearing them down by attrition with ambush after ambush.

We arrived at the BCP, which looked like a Vietnam-era firebase surrounded by sandbagged positions and concertina wire. We occupied the CIA team house, which was empty at the moment. We had brought two mortar men, who went about setting up their 81mm mortar and their fire direction center to help support our recon mission. Afghan paramilitaries were . . . curious. In that part of the world, the locals would vigorously deny that they were homosexual, but they would grab each other's dicks right in front of us, giggle, and cuddle. One of the younger recce guys told me that they were just trying to see how we'd respond.

The first day, I was left behind at the BCP; there was not enough room in the Hiluxes for all of us plus the Afghan translators. That night when the guys came back, I ate an MRE and had a really bad stomachache. When it was my shift on radio guard, I remained awake after my hour was up and manned the radio just because I knew I wouldn't be able to sleep—I figured the other guys could continue to rest. Eventually, I woke up Grant, who was next on the rotation, and I think I drifted off for an hour or two.

The next morning, the recce team was going back out, and it seemed like I would be left behind again, but one of the mortar guys suggested that I ride in one of the Afghan vehicles. I brought this up to Grant, and he said, "Well, as long as you don't mind riding with them, sure, no problem." It wasn't an issue for me. The Afghans were actually pretty good drivers; it was their home turf, after all. Their Hiluxes were set up as technicals, meaning there was a machine gunner standing on the bed of the truck or sitting in a chair bolted to it, and the truck I rode in had an old vinyl car seat bolted to the back for a PKM machine gunner to sit in.

We rolled out at around nine in the morning and drove up along the spine of a ridge to conduct our recon mission. When we hit the location we wanted to stop at and use as a mission support site, Grant took his recon team and departed.

I was exactly where I wanted to be, doing exactly what I wanted to do. The day was absolutely perfect with not a cloud in the sky. Small pine trees covered the mountains, stretching out into forever in every direction. I was in the Hilux with my SR-25 sniper rifle at my side, disguised in the desert tiger-stripe uniform and pakol hat worn by the two CIA-trained Afghan paramilitary troops in the front seats.

I had no idea what I was in for.

The vehicles stopped at the top of the ridgeline, and I got out of the truck to rejoin my teammates. I met with the recce team leader, and we quickly covered the five W's—the who, where, when, what, why—which explained where he was going with six other recce members and what we were to do in case of enemy contact, which was standard operating procedure when a unit separated into two elements. I would be left behind with the Afghan counterparts and a couple other Rangers.

Our mission was to get eyes on an enemy compound and then get away unobserved. The team leader tasked us to look for landing zones

(LZs) where helicopters could land or Rangers could fast-rope onto when the raid against our target was launched.

Marine Corps helicopters buzzed overhead before leaving us in an eerie silence. It was all part of the plan: Desensitize the locals to the sound of helicopters so that when the real thing went down and Rangers got boots on the ground, the locals would just think it was another routine helicopter pass.

When the six-man recce team departed on foot, Val, another Ranger assigned to the recce team, and I left to go scout out some LZs. We left Alec, our team member manning the radio at the mission support site, where the vehicles were lined up on the lonely dirt road. The terrain here looked more like Colorado than how we usually think of Afghanistan, as it was covered in pine trees. The Afghan paramilitary troops drove us a few minutes away to a large open area. I plunged right into a cluster of pine trees without hesitation, looking to see what, if anything, was hiding in there.

We moved out light and stayed agile. Over my uniform I wore a chest rig with four additional magazines loaded with 7.62 LR (long-range) rounds specially made for sniper rifles. I had a map inside a plastic case that I wore around my neck on a piece of parachute cord, which was then tucked under my shirt. I had some water, a PVS-14 night vision monocle, and a small survival kit. A 9mm Beretta M9 pistol hung from my hip in a drop-leg holster. I carried two Dutch-made mini-fragmentation grenades the size of golf balls, which our team had acquired from the CIA. My SR-25 was my baby, with all the bells and whistles. A 3.5-10 power scope, infrared laser, suppressor, and I was a pretty good shot with it, if I do say so myself. And I had training: Ranger School, sniper school, and a lot of exercises at my unit prior to being deployed to Afghanistan. I was confident, perhaps dangerously so.

"Hold on, Murph!" Val shouted to me. I was pushing through the trees too quickly, and he was telling me that we were going too deep into the forest. It was just us, after all. We turned around and went back to the clearing. From there we cleared along the top of the mountain. Spotting some lean-tos up against the slope of the mountain, I slung my SR and drew my pistol in case I had to shoot someone at close range. My hands tightened around the grip of the pistol, ready to fire, but the lean-to was empty and did not appear to have been used recently.

We continued around the open area, eventually arriving on the other side. Up on top of a rocky outcropping, Val and I looked down into the adjacent valley. We couldn't see anyone below, but we could hear a full-on firefight—individual shots as well as machine gun fire and the occasional *CRUMP* that signaled mortar fire. We had been told that this was infighting between two rival families by the Afghan paramilitary troops.

That was when Val got a call over his Multiband Inter/Intra Team Radio (MBITR). The transmission was scratchy and difficult to make out, but it was the team leader telling us that they had gotten eyes on an enemy patrol heading in our direction: about ten men, heavily armed with RPGs and recoilless rifles. Were they Taliban? Al-Qaeda? Or just one clan going to fuck up another in those desolate Afghan mountains? No way to know, really. We got back in the Hilux and raced for the mission support site. Alec was at the MSS, and we didn't want him to be there by himself if the enemy showed up to party.

When we arrived, we found Alec still monitoring the radio. Val and I decided that rather than just wait around for the bad guys, we should seize the initiative and establish a hasty ambush down the road to cut them off before they arrived at the MSS. Meanwhile, we tried to get in touch with the recce team leader, who was still out with his patrol, but comms were in and out. We gathered about a dozen Afghans into their vehicles and sped down the road, unsure whether we were about to run smack-dab into the enemy. About five hundred meters down the road, we cached the vehicles, and I led everyone into the wood line, paralleling the dirt road.

According to the doctrine I had learned in training, a hasty near-ambush like this was tactically sound but about as dangerous a maneuver as you could possibly attempt. We were on a decline, which looked about right to me, since we would command the high ground above the road that the enemy was coming down. On the other side of the road, the mountain ridge rose again, meaning that if the enemy tried to flee, they would have to run uphill. We had a strong terrain advantage, with plenty of trees to use as cover. I shook the Afghans out into a rough assault line. They didn't want to go into the prone or use cover as they prefer to squat for some reason, but I insisted, moving from person to person with an interpreter who relayed my instructions. I told them they could blow me off and use the squat position they favored and spray rounds on full auto, but it was on them at the end of the day if they caught a bullet to the face. However, there was one instruction that was not optional: No one fires before I do. I had taken charge of the ambush and was responsible for it. The patrol leader initiates the ambush when the enemy is inside the kill zone, end of story. After setting everyone in position, I found some cover behind a tree and lay down in the prone beside it. I pulled down the bipod legs of my rifle and set them in the dirt, trying to acquire a decent sector of fire. Val was off to my right, wearing a kaffiyeh around his head, with an M4 rifle in one hand and his MBITR radio in the other. We still had shitty comms with the recce patrol leader. We also had no idea when the enemy would show up; it could be any second.

I took a few seconds to make sure I had my field of fire, then the ambush was set: We were as ready as we could be on short notice. Now I had time to think. We were about twenty meters away from the road. There was sparse vegetation aside from the thin pine trees, and we could easily be spotted by the road. We were relying on the element of surprise, but we could easily be compromised. The enemy might see us, they might outflank us, the Afghans with me might turn tail and run, a million things could go wrong.

Then I was scared. I don't know how to describe it to someone who has never been in a situation where he knows he's walking into a situation that will spell his violent death. I was going to die this day, I understood that. The only person I knew I could really count on was Val; everything else was a coin toss. In a close-range firefight like this, we were going to get wasted, no question in my mind. This was a very real, very deep kind of fear that washed across my body. In this scenario, it isn't just that you intellectually know you're going to die, it's your body having a physiological reaction, warning you of impending doom. I almost started shaking. Almost. Then I resigned myself to this fate and decided that I was going to take with me as many of these motherfuckers as I possibly could. What is, is. I wasn't afraid anymore.

All of these thoughts passed through my mind in seconds. I couldn't tell you how long I was lying in the prone before I heard the enemy coming down the ridgeline opposite us. Maybe it was just a few minutes. Rocks were rolling down the hill as the enemy crept forward, but they were not on the road, they were bypassing our entire kill zone. Things had just gotten even more complicated.

I shifted my angle of attack, changing the position of my body on the ground and adjusting the direction that the SR-25 was pointing in. We would all have to adjust, since the enemy was walking right past where we'd projected them to be. If we let them slip through our net, then what? Ten bad guys walk right into the MSS where Alec is hanging out with three or four Afghans. If we let these guys get past us, we're basically handing A his death sentence. I couldn't let that happen.

The Afghans, to their credit, were holding their fire. Waiting. Waiting for me.

I spotted the first enemy in the order of movement. He was just a silhouette moving through the trees. He moved in and out of the scope of my rifle too quickly for me to get a bead on him and fire. Then the second in the order of movement came into my view. He walked with a rifle held at his side, a pakol cap on his head. Tell you the truth, it was a shit shot. There were tree branches I had to shoot through, I was at an odd angle, it sure as hell wasn't the kind of thing you do on the flat range at Fort Benning. But I knew that it was now or never. I lined up my crosshairs on the target, leading him slightly. I estimated the range to be at under a hundred meters. Should be a nice clean kill.

As the silhouette moved, my finger tightened around the trigger. Not only did I have to kill the enemy, I had to initiate the entire ambush so that we could kick off the firefight before the MSS got hit. I squeezed the trigger. The gunshot was a snap through the forest, the sound dampened by the suppressor. The gun jumped slightly in the pocket of my shoulder. Everything seemed to hang in suspended animation for a moment, the space of the mountain left quiet, empty, barren.

Then the entire world exploded around me.

Bullets were slamming into the tree I had taken cover behind, raining wooden splinters down on me. Little geysers of dirt were kicked up right in front of my face. The Afghans in my ambush line opened up on full auto, shooting from the hip. Bullets were whizzing everywhere like angry hornets. I could not visually identify any more targets, so I fired my SR-25 at likely and suspected targets. I did not realize it at the time but was told later that several grenades went off behind me. To my right, Val was also returning fire, blasting through a couple magazines with his M4.

Then one of the Afghans started shouting and waving, with his walkie-talkie in one hand. "No shoot, no shoot!"

We got the message: Something was wrong. There was no more incoming fire. I gave the order to cease fire but also told everyone to stay down. The Afghans were excited and gesticulating in all directions.

"Do not stand up," I said to Val. "Do not get up."

You never, ever stand up in an ambush, regardless of what you think is going on. That's how you get dead. But something was definitely wrong. Clearly, the Afghans did not believe that we had ambushed an enemy force. Had we accidentally ambushed some Afghan police officers or soldiers? Had an American unit not made us aware that they would be in the area and stumbled into our kill zone? What the fuck was going on?

Well, clearly, as the patrol leader for this ambush, I had to establish what the fuck was going on. There was really only one way to do that. I had to stand up in an ambush, walk down into the kill zone, liaise with whoever was down there, and try to negotiate the situation.

"I'm going down there to sort this out," I told Val.

I took a deep breath and stood up, positive that I was about to eat a round in my face. But that bullet didn't come. I flicked the selector on my SR-25 back to the safe position and shuffled down the embankment toward the dirt road. As I neared the road, I came face-to-face with Paul, the recce assistant team leader, who was about thirty feet away. The horrible reality of what had just happened dawned on me: I had just ambushed our own recce team.

"Murph?" Paul said.

I really can't remember what I said to Paul, exactly. I think I asked him what the hell had just happened. I went back to Val and told him to get the Afghans to set up a security perimeter while we figured out what was going on. It seemed that we had just hit our own guys.

I went back down the embankment and walked to where I had shot at the guys I now knew were my teammates. Grant was on his hands and knees. His shirt was off, and a recce member was applying bandages to his back. I thought he had been shot between the shoulder blades at first, but the recce member was informing Grant that he would be okay. It was a grazing shot that mostly cauterized the wound as it passed through his flesh.

When Grant looked up and saw me, he immediately asked, "Who shot me?"

"I don't know," I replied. I really didn't at that moment, although it could have been me. My mind was racing.

The JTAC called in air support, and a couple marine Cobra attack helicopters were orbiting overhead in minutes. Meanwhile, we moved up to the open area that Val and I had marked as a potential LZ for the Charlie Company mission. Now we needed it to evac our own team leader after a friendly-fire incident, one I was responsible for. I got up on the perimeter and pulled security, my mind a mess of different emotions as Grant was loaded onto a medevac bird and taken away.

I was horrified by what had just happened. Disgusted to my core by it, in fact. I was in a state of shock at how Grant had nearly been killed. I was proud of the recce team members and how professionally they had acted in the aftermath of the firefight, keeping their cool and doing their jobs. Beneath all of those feelings, I was fucking pissed off that we had been cheated out of what should have been a righteous firefight.

Paul assumed control of the patrol. We got back in our vehicles and headed out to the TCP. Once we arrived, we all sat down and conducted an after-action review, going over everything that had happened. In some ways, it was pretty simple: I had freelanced a hasty ambush, feeling it was the tactically prudent choice, but due to poor communications, Grant and Paul had no idea what they were walking into because they didn't know I had set up an ambush. How could they? Likewise, I was unaware that the recce team was heading back to our location. I had initiated the ambush, and I took full responsibility for it. Paul couched his words when he wrote the report and sent it up to higher that afternoon, but he made it clear that we had experienced a friendly-fire incident.

I was deeply ashamed. I had failed utterly. I had let down my unit. One thing you learn in Ranger Battalion is that you can go from hero to zero in the blink of an eye. That was me, down in the zero. I was aware of the pain I had caused Grant and the fact that I had nearly killed God knows how many good men that day. I was ashamed for worrying about what lay in the future for me. I would be kicked out of the Ranger regiment, that was a given. Would I be kicked out of the army entirely? Would I face jail time?

Being a Ranger was at the core of my identity as a young man. I couldn't imagine what I would do without the army. I literally had no idea.

Minutes blurred into hours. As it grew dark, one of the adjacent BCPs on the Pak border came under attack. We had heard previously that these BCPs sometimes got hit pretty hard by Haqqani network fighters crossing the border—in one case, a BCP was nearly overrun. While the other BCP was under fire, the Afghans said we were going to get hit, too. Sure enough, mortar fire started going off somewhere in the mountains next to us.

I quickly jumped into one of our Hiluxes with the recce guys, and we raced up the side of a mountain toward one of the bunkered positions on the BCP perimeter; from our perspective, we needed to be up there to help defend the BCP if we were getting overrun. On the way up the mountain, our Hilux began to backslide on the loose dirt. The driver stopped, tried to reposition the vehicle, and made another go at it. We backslid a second time.

And then we were going over, rolling sideways down the mountain. We crashed to one side, then we were upside down, then on the other side, and finally, the tires slammed back down to the earth and we stopped right side up. Somehow, some way, the truck had done a complete rollover and stopped. Had we kept going, we would have rolled hundreds of feet down to the bottom. Slightly banged up, we got out of the Hilux, and the driver took it upon himself to drive the rest of the way up the road on his own rather than risk another rollover and killing the entire team with him. Paul had to go looking for his NODs, which had flown off his head during the rollover and gone right out the window. A minute later, he found them lying on the ground, still intact and functional.

We ran up the rest of the way to the gun position at the top of the mountain and jumped into the sandbagged positions with the Afghan paramilitaries on duty. Sweating and out of breath, we watched and listened. Nothing. Our BCP was not under attack. We waited for about an hour before heading back to our team house. It was decided that we would each man a separate area of the perimeter until the morning, just in case. We also heard via comms from higher up that a helicopter was inbound to secure Grant's weapon and equipment. That sounded odd to me, as we could bring his gear back with us without any problems. No one sends a helicopter for something so mundane.

I ended up at a guard fortification that night with the recce team's commo guy. He was a good dude. He planned on getting out of the army and going to work on his parents' Christmas tree farm out in the Midwest somewhere. I sat in the cold with a poncho liner wrapped around me, contemplating the day's events. Late into the night, we heard the helicopter arrive. Soon someone was inbound to talk to me. I heard a voice below ask, "Okay, where is Murph?"

It was the recce platoon leader, Lieutenant Hallows. He was a former NCO in the Ranger regiment who had become an officer and served with a scout platoon during the invasion of Iraq with the infantry. I walked down to meet him. Hallows asked me to explain to him what had happened that day, and I did. Several times during my recollection of events, I paused, my voice breaking a little. I caught my breath and continued.

Hallows told me that Grant had received medical treatment at our base and that he was going to be just fine. It was a flesh wound, but they were going to send him home so his wife didn't freak out worrying about her husband. I was relieved to know that he would make a full recovery.

"Who shot Sergeant Grant?" Hallows asked me.

"I did, sir," I replied. "I can't prove it to you, but I know it was me."

I had been thinking over the question all day and arrived at that conclusion. I had fired on the second soldier in the order of movement. The recce team confirmed that Grant was second in the order of movement that afternoon, the team leader walking right behind the point man. After spending a lot of time behind a long gun, you come to understand where your shot is going the moment the trigger breaks and the rifle fires. I had "felt" my bullet pass toward the back of my target, rather than the front or center. The bullet that wounded Grant had grazed his shoulder blades. I had shot Grant, this was the only logical conclusion. Ironically, it was Grant's hunched posture that saved him—otherwise, that bullet would have smashed right through his spinal cord.

Hallows thanked me for giving it to him straight. "I know you feel really bad about what happened today, Murph, but tactically, you were doing the right thing. At the end of the day, you are out there doing the job, while so many others your age are sitting on the couch eating Doritos."

Hallows was calm and reassuring throughout. He did not scold me or belittle me in any way. I learned something from his example that day. Sometimes being a leader wasn't about barking orders at people, it was about providing a calm but strong hand to support your men. I felt horrible about what had transpired that day, but Hallows was telling me that he understood how confusing combat could be and that he knew I'd done my best.

Had it been an older, more experienced Ranger out there that day, maybe things would have turned out differently. Maybe not. Whatever the case, that hypothetical soldier wasn't there that day, I was.

I didn't sleep that night.

CHAPTER 3

Anything That Can Go Wrong, Will Go Wrong

I DREADED THE ENTIRE RIDE BACK FROM THE BCP TO our FOB the next morning. I tried to face my fate like a man, at least. I would have to confront my failure as well as the negative light that I had cast my unit in through what I regarded to be incompetent actions. I mentally prepared myself to be court-martialed and drummed out of the military. Though Lieutenant Hallows appeared to understand what had happened, a decision about my future would be made way above his head.

Back at FOB Salerno, I sat down on my cot. Everything was quiet. The recce platoon sergeant, Randy, asked to speak with me, along with my sniper partner, Joe. We discussed what had happened out there on the Pak border. Randy asked me a no-bullshit question: If I was in the same position today—if I was out on an ambush line, sent out on another mission, and I got the enemy in the sights—would I pull the trigger?

"I would do the exact same thing," I told him honestly. I regarded it as my duty to kill the enemy wherever I found him, notwithstanding the previous day's horrible accident.

"That's what I needed to hear," Randy said.

On our way back to the tents, Joe turned to me and said, "We need to work on you getting better at shooting moving targets."

The three of us couldn't help but laugh. It was some gallows humor. In a firefight, I was expected to kill, not to wound.

The next couple days were kind of a blur. I went for a run with Joe. He told me that in combat, Rangers are expected to take charge and make decisions; any decision is better than no decision. I had made a decision. He said he supported me and supported promoting me to sergeant in the near future. That really meant a lot to me. There were people like Joe, Randy, and Hallows really sticking their necks out for me when the knee-jerk response would have been to throw the book at me. The three of them must have been under a lot of pressure because of me.

Now that we were back at our FOB, we did a full-blown after-action review. A lot of information came out of that AAR. In retrospect, there are so many things I wish I had done differently. The core of the issue was a communications failure, partly due to faulty equipment and partly because we simply did not communicate effectively with one another, either in person or over the radio.

When writing this account, I asked Paul, the assistant recce team leader, for his thoughts. He felt that when our element had split into small elements, we had not thoroughly briefed actions to be taken in case of enemy contact. He also rightly pointed out that I'd had no idea their recce team was heading back to the MSS. If a message was sent, I never received that information. It had taken the recce team about an hour and a half to walk out and recon the objective, but upon spotting an enemy patrol, they'd taken a different, faster route back. Because of this, they were almost on top of the MSS in fifteen minutes or so without realizing how close they were to us. In reality, the enemy patrol must have broken off and headed in another direction, because neither of us saw them after the initial sighting.

There were also issues with comms. When we'd lain in our ambush, Val had not radioed to the recce team that we had set an ambush along the road. Paul recalled that Val had felt enemy contact was imminent and that he didn't have time to set up the message. I recalled that Val had been having difficulties getting the patrol on the radio in the first place, due to the limitations of the small handheld radio. When I'd initiated the ambush, Paul reported, their radioman could not send out any messages because of a faulty microphone on the radio—again, a technical issue had prevented communications between the various elements.

During the AAR process, OGA (CIA) told us that the enemy patrol spotted by the recce team was probably a friendly CIA-sanctioned local group maintaining a presence in the area for them. This would have been nice to know beforehand, to deconflict the battle space.

At this point, I was also learning how the recce team had rightly reacted to contact by turning and firing off 40mm M203 grenades, which had detonated somewhere behind me. Each one of them had fired about thirty rounds of ammunition during the brief firefight. Bullets had landed right in front of my face and slammed into the tree I had taken cover behind. Paul reported a similar situation, with rounds coming down near his feet. How the hell were any of us even alive?

I went to the chow hall, got a full tray of food, sat down and looked at it for forty-five minutes, then threw it in the trash and walked out. I had no appetite. The grumblings on our compound were not lost on me. I heard rumors that I was going to be released for standards (RFSed), meaning I would be kicked out of Ranger regiment. Other rumors had it that I might be kicked out of the army. The regiment, meanwhile, made everyone on our compound go through "retraining," like that was going to fix anything. The Charlie Company Rangers had to go through all kinds of live and blank fire drills to retrain on basic tasks. I was also retrained on basic sniper tasks.

Soon I was informed that an army investigator would be coming down to our FOB to conduct a 15-6 investigation. I believe I was the very last person he interviewed about the friendly-fire incident. The investigator told me that this was an informal 15-6, which meant that I didn't have to sign a sworn statement; the investigation would be kept "off the books," so to speak. He then told me that his investigation had revealed some equipment issues—not having enough radios to go around had led to our communication breakdown—but tactical decisions were made as well. I found it odd that he told me the conclusion of his investigation before he even began to interview me. At any rate, I retold what had happened from my perspective.

Eventually, I confronted my leadership about the rumors. From what they were telling me, Sergeant Van Aalst would have to make a decision about my fate when we got back to Fort Benning, but for now nothing was going to happen except that I was to conduct missions under Joe's supervision and not go on missions without him. In retrospect, my fears of being court-martialed and imprisoned seem pretty silly. Fighter pilots accidentally bomb American positions and kill half a dozen troops and don't get court-martialed.

We were still in Afghanistan, still in combat, so I did what I was expected to do and what I had volunteered for. I laced up my fucking boots and went back out on every mission we got, just like all of the other Rangers. It was a case of Murphy's Law. Anything that can go wrong, will. And you know what really pissed me and the recce team off? We'd all been cheated out of a fucking righteous firefight.

Finally, we redeployed back to the States in early 2005.

The night we arrived back at Fort Benning, we turned in our weapons. I saw Sergeant Grant standing around. I went up to him and told him I was glad he was okay. I put my hand out to shake his. He hesitated, but we shook. I don't blame him for having animosity toward me. I don't blame him for anything that happened that day; I take full responsibility for what went wrong.

Soldiers tell themselves stories, and in turn, they are told stories. We learn heroic narratives starting in early childhood. In the military, we have social narratives, and the social currency in our units is often reputation, which is sometimes earned and sometimes just hype. Every story we are told follows a predictable narrative with a beginning, a middle, and end. There are good guys, bad guys, and dead guys. As soldiers, we are raised on these heroic stories of soldiers parachuting into the middle of the Nazi horde or manning a machine gun against Chinese Communists in the cold mountains of Korea. We watch movies that glorify these tales. As humans, and as soldiers, we love stories.

The one story never told is mine. They never make a movie about the guy who commits friendly fire. I had no mentors to guide me, no sweeping narrative to inform me. I was alone to figure out what to do. I had some support, yes, and I will never forget that, but in the end, I was still disgraced.

Of course, things were not the same for me back at Fort Benning. How could they be? Word got out about me. You may have heard that special operations soldiers fear failure more than death, which is true. But there is one thing that special operations guys fear above all else: being ostracized by their peers. The Ranger regiment is a highly competitive tribal environment. I had broken tribal rules, and socially, it was much easier to push me outside than it was to forgive me, assuming I deserved forgiveness in the first place.

One night soon after arriving back at Fort Benning, I got drunk and could not sleep. What was I supposed to do? How could I rectify this situation? Should I leave the army? Then I wondered, If I am a disgrace, should I kill myself? There is no instruction manual on what to do in this situation. I went to the bathroom and looked in the mirror. I was young and full of piss and vinegar. I was determined but defeated.

It is one of those moments that stick with you forever, because that was the moment I decided that I wasn't going to quit. I decided that I was going to go back into the shit and keep pushing as hard as I could. I woke up in the morning having passed over some kind of threshold. I knew I couldn't control what others thought of me, but I could control myself and what I did.

We had some leave time after our deployment. I went on leave to Prague, the capital of the Czech Republic. There, I spent a lot of time getting drunk. Many times, I would down a few absinthe drinks and just walk around the cobblestone streets at three a.m. in the middle of a snow-storm.

Back at work, Sergeant Van Aalst never mentioned the friendly-fire incident to me. In fact, he continued to give me the cold shoulder, the way he always had. I could walk in to work and say, "Good morning, Sergeant," and he would just walk past me as if I were invisible. That was the kind of guy he was. In time, the anger I felt toward him only grew.

Old friends like Isaiah Burkhart, who served in AT with me, came to sniper platoon. Meanwhile, VA continued to stress people out by playing games. One of his favorites was to wait until 1700, when we were sup-posed to go home, then demand we do a full inventory of weapons and equipment. One evening I brought him the piece of paper with all the serial numbers we had written down. He took the paper from me and, without even looking at it, let it drop to the edge of his desk and went back to whatever he was doing on his computer, saying not a word to me. It was all just Mickey Mouse games in what masqueraded as a professional environment.

One afternoon I was asked to mow the grass in our company area. Upon inspection, I found that our lawn mower needed new spark plugs. I was heading out the door to go buy some new spark plugs when one of the sergeants in sniper section stopped me: "Where do you think you're going, Murphy?" I explained that I'd been told to mow the grass but needed new spark plugs to do it. "No," he said. "No, that is way outside your pay grade."

That was another one of those moments for me. The Ranger regiment trusts me with a loaded rifle to make thousand-meter shots in combat conditions, but it is outside my pay grade to buy a fucking spark plug? That was about the time when I decided I would go to Special Forces selection, or the Green Berets—another army special operations unit, one specializing in unconventional warfare. They had their own selection course, just like the Rangers, but I would have to wait for orders to go to it.

Third Ranger Battalion then went on a two-week training workup at Fort Campbell, Kentucky. We got to work with 160th SOAR again and do some really cool training. The highlight was a training mission in which we hit an abandoned jailhouse. Little Birds landed me and another sniper on one of the rooftops to provide overwatch for the assault teams. The training was a hell of a lot of fun, although I felt like the working relationship with my immediate superiors was only further deteriorating.

When we got back to Fort Benning, one of the team leaders in Alpha Company came up to me and said that I was coming back to Alpha Company and leaving sniper section. I shook my head and said that he must have heard wrong. No, he insisted, my name was up on the whiteboard. Well, this was news to me. Interestingly, my entire chain of command—Joe, Van Aalst, and our company first sergeant—were all away at the time. I asked one of the squad leaders in our section what was up and told him that if I was being fired, I thought I deserved to hear it from someone in my chain of command. He said I would have to talk to Van Aalst about that. He seemed to be enjoying the moment.

I got my meeting with Van Aalst a couple days later. He started off by telling me that he was not going to apologize for my finding out secondhand that I'd been fired. He told me he'd never asked me about the friendly-fire incident because he thought it would upset me. From there he went on to say that things were just not working out for me in sniper platoon, so he had arranged for me to go back to my old company. He thought I was a good Ranger, which was why he'd put in a good word for me at Alpha Company rather than trying to RFS me or something like that. He stated that he didn't consider this a firing—it wasn't like he was telling me to get the fuck out of his office or anything. It sure felt like a firing, but nonetheless, we shook hands like men. Nobody likes being fired, but frankly, I'd had about enough of sniper section, and I think they'd had about enough of me, so it was for the best that I moved on.

That afternoon, after getting shitcanned, I drove over to a bar in Columbus called Memory Lanes. We all called it Menopause Lanes for our own reasons, but at middday the place was empty aside from some seniors watching *The Price Is Right* on the small TV mounted in the corner of the bar. I sat down and drank Red Bull and vodka until I was totally smashed and had to call my roommate to come pick me up because there was no way I could drive myself.

A few days later, I went next door to Alpha Company to meet First Sergeant Sirry and find out what the next steps were. I was transferring back to Alpha Company; I should get my gear together, and he also nicely suggested that I shave my beard now that I was coming back to a rifle company. "Roger that, First Sergeant," I replied. I soon found myself a team leader in 1st Platoon, Weapons Squad. In weapons squad, we had a great crew of guys. Corporal Alex was the other team leader, Staff Sergeant Pav was our squad leader, and we had a solid bunch of privates like Ralph, Jeremy, and others. It was like a breath of fresh air.

A few days after I arrived at the platoon, my squad leader informed us that our platoon sergeant was getting the can. In case you hadn't noticed yet, the regiment fired people like no one's business.

"He's being replaced with Van Aalst," my squad leader told me.

My heart sank.

"You know him, don't you?"

That afternoon, 1st Platoon had a formation to be introduced to their new platoon sergeant. Van Aalst walked in front of us and said, "Hi, Murphy." He was now my platoon sergeant for a second time. I've been asked if this was part of Van Aalst's grand scheme from the beginning—to keep me alongside him so he could watch over me. To this day, I don't really know.

At the end of the day, I was walking down to my barracks room when my roommate, Zach, saw me. "Man, you look like someone just killed your dog, Murphy."

Fuck my life.

Seriously.

To his credit, I must say that things were different with Van Aalst during my second go-round with him. Not completely different but substantially different. He lightened up quite a bit in 1st Platoon. In the meantime, we were gearing up for a deployment to Iraq. While Charlie Company had been in Afghanistan, 1st Platoon (known as the Glory Boys because of a derisive comment made by a Ranger leader many moons ago about our platoon) had been deployed to Mosul, Iraq, and were fixing to head right back.

In order to prepare, we began going out to the range, working our weapons drills, and then went right into our platoon exercise evaluations. Platoon ex-evals used to consist of Rangers choking on mosquitoes at a patrol base in the Georgia wilderness as they were tested on basic infantry tasks, but today the opportunity was used as a pre-deployment train-up that focused on the specific mission set we were about to walk into.

Ex-evals went on for days with little sleep, another way they put you under stress during training. We were out at ranges shooting, conducting immediate action drills, learning how to drive the Stryker armored vehicles that we would have in Iraq, running machine gun ranges, and hitting simulated objectives. Our last training mission was to take down an abandoned middle school right outside the gates of Fort Benning located in Columbus, Georgia, up the street from Taco Bell and Krystal Burger.

We raided the school, and everything was going by the numbers until one of the civilians who was an enemy role player for training purposes decided that he wanted to fight back against one of my privates who was flex-cuffing him. Trying to get into a physical confrontation with a Ranger, especially on a mission, is never a good idea. Our sergeant major had to take that role player aside after the incident and calm him down, as he was nearly in tears.

During the after-action review, we were all exhausted. Some officer was grilling us about who'd searched room 33-Juliet. Each room on an objective receives an alphanumeric code like 1-Alpha, 2-Bravo, and so on. That there even was a 33-Juliet on the mission should tell you how big the objective area was for just one platoon to handle. None of us had a clue what that major was talking about, and half of us were asleep on our feet.

The methodology we used to search objectives was known as sensitive site exploitation, or SSE. For some reason, the media believes that the JSOC-General Stan McChrystal killing machine invented SSE in 2007, but that's a bunch of bullshit. Special operations units were doing it as far back as 2004.

After we finally finished ex-evals, I hopped in my badass 1997 Saturn and drove home. I had been living off-post for a while on my own dime, since my unit would not give me a housing allowance and there was no way I was staying in the barracks. While exiting the highway, I momentarily fell asleep behind the wheel and woke up in the breakdown lane! Oh, shit! Maybe I should have slept a few hours in the parking lot before heading home.

Sergeant Van Aalst had me go with him to Iraq with the advanced party to prepare things prior to the main body (i.e., the rest of our platoon) arriving a week later.

ANYTHING THAT CAN GO WRONG, WILL GO WRONG

I flew to Mosul, Iraq, on my twenty-second birthday. When the ramp of the C-17 lowered and we stepped out, I felt like we were walking on the surface of the sun. It was the middle of the night, but the breeze felt like a hair dryer. How the hell were we going to work, much less fight, in an environment like this?

CHAPTER 4

Ranger Days and Time-sensitive Targets

WE BOARDED SOME MINIVANS AND WERE DRIVEN TO OUR compound. As on FOB Salerno in Afghanistan, we had our own compound within a compound at the airfield in Mosul where the Rangers and Delta Force dudes hung out. My platoon had been to this base six months prior, on their last deployment; they had worked closely with a Delta operator named Ivica Jerak, who was born in Croatia and became a naturalized U.S citizen. Jerak had taught the Rangers the modern method of room clearing called free-flow close-quarter battle. I'm not going to get into the details, but it was a technique that emphasized surprise, speed, and violence of action much more than the antiquated army points-of-domination method that we had always learned. The Glory Boys of 1st Platoon had taken those lessons to heart and were now ready to kick some serious ass in Mosul.

Corporal Alex was with me, and we spent some time talking to the 2nd Battalion about the Strykers we had, convoy operations, and generally, what the lay of the land was like out there. Meanwhile, Sergeant Van Aalst was meeting with senior leaders and fulfilling his own responsibilities as platoon sergeant. One night, I met with Van Aalst in his barracks room, and we walked to the chow hall together—I should probably note that this chow hall had been blown up by a suicide bomber while I was in Afghanistan.

"I have a bad feeling about Tal Afar," Van Aalst told me as we left for chow.

"What's that?" I asked.

"It's a straight muj town not far from here," he explained, making a reference to the mujahedeen of Afghanistan that doesn't necessarily make sense but we used terms interchangeably because we were bouncing between both theaters. While Mosul was sharply contested by what we called Al-Qaeda in Iraq (AQI), the city of Tal Afar was not contested so much as it was simply controlled by the enemy. As I was to learn, the 2003 invasion of Iraq had created a massive vacuum after we deposed the Baath Party and disbanded the Iraqi military. As my new squad leader, Sergeant Ken, once said, the insurgency is understandable. If something happened in the United States and, say, Chinese troops came to help out on American soil, they would be resented. If maybe the Chinese kicked in a few doors, maybe hit the wrong house (as we frequently did), and maybe killed your brother, your cousin, your wife, your kids, who knows—you might wind up an insurgent in the prone position along I-87 with an IED detonator in one hand, waiting for Chinese convoys.

However, these were not Iraqi nationalists; there was no Iraqi Thomas Jefferson or George Washington. The Iraqi insurgency consisted of hard-core criminals, jihadists, and a ton of foreign fighters looking to get their kill on. These dudes were murderers, members of the death cult called Al-Qaeda. It wasn't just that they hated us, they hated their own people. The things the Sunni and Shia did to each other are beyond description. Cutting the heads off of babies is just passé for those animals.

And so it goes. We, the counterinsurgents, see the ultra-violence, the beheadings, the murders, the aftermath of a little kid used as a suicide bomber in a crowded market, and we, too, become radicalized in our own way. The Nazis, the Soviets, and the North Vietnamese Army were at least fighting for some twisted vision of a better future. By comparison, Al-Qaeda was, and is, gutter trash.

"At one point, the guys up at the TOC," Van Aalst continued, referencing the Tactical Operations Center, "actually considered just air-striking an entire city block with JDAMs just to kill one HVT. That is the level of frustration with Tal Afar."

"Are they going to want us to go in there?" I asked.

"It sounds like it," VA replied.

Soon the rest of our platoon arrived to relieve the 2nd Battalion Rangers and begin our own operations, hopefully without missing a beat. Even all these years later, when I think back to that summer in Iraq, dozens of wild images flash through my mind. It was a summer of total insanity.

After doing a drive along with 2nd Ranger Battalion to get a basic familiarity with the area, we were on our own. Mosul was a sprawling, polluted city filled with dilapidated and half-built structures. Thick tangles of black electrical line clogged narrow streets and back alleys. The city was divided by a river, with roughly a third of Mosul on the east side and the other two-thirds on the west. Main roads, called main supply routes (MSRs), were given the names of car brands like Tampa, Nissan, Ford, and the like.

Our first mission was not far outside the FOB. Intel from higher was telling us there was an HVT down the street on route Tampa. We drove out in our Strykers that night and crashed the party, but there was no sign of our target. The next day, the Civil Affairs guys would have to head out and pay the family for the door we blew down. The next night, they sent us back to the same target. Ranger assault teams made entry, and again no sign of the bad guy. Civil Affairs had to buy them another new door. On the third night, we got sent out to hit the target a third time. At this point, it kind of seemed like we had the wrong house and perhaps had lost the element of surprise. Predictably, the high-value target was still not there.

This was a small introduction to the task force's much acclaimed find, fix, finish, exploit, analyze, and disseminate strategy (more like a tactic), or F3EAD. From my point of view, it was just an updated version of the troop leading procedures found in our field manuals rather than the brilliant insight of some swivel-chair general. We were following our methodology of keeping constant pressure on the enemy, but that meant special operations were not being used for specialized missions; we were really just light infantry hitting every target in sight. Not that we were complaining—Rangers love going out on raids.

Over a longer time horizon, I have come to think of F3EAD as a great tactic for kicking the enemy's ass, wearing him down, and disrupting his networks; but as part of an overall counterinsurgency strategy, it was a failure. Somehow, our efforts never married up with other endeavors that had to happen simultaneously, such as infrastructure projects (I also later learned that Congressionally authorized Commander's Emergency Response Program (CERP) funds were being illegally used to pay off the mullahs, but hey, so was the CIA through their own funding channels) and capacity building that should have been run by all of the other U.S. governmental agencies, from State, to Treasury, to the Department of Agriculture. Of course, many of these failures had to do with the pathetic and hopelessly corrupt Iraqi government as well.

In the meantime, every SOF soldier of my generation can tell you stories about so-called block parties or "gang bangs" in which their unit blew down every door on a city block, looking for a high-value target based on the flimsiest of intel. We captured and killed the enemy but did a lot of stupid stuff along the way.

We were all on a reverse sleep schedule, trying to rack out during the day and then be active at night. Not only was it cooler, but we also would take advantage of the darkness for operations, since we had night vision devices and the enemy would be bedded down for the night. Of course, we ended up pulling details during the day anyway, and pretty soon we were doing operations in the middle of the day as well.

The rest of that summer is a series of events that I recall as a frenzy of combat operations, time-sensitive targets, and crisis. It was a summer of gunfire, explosions, helicopter insertions, driving around back alleys, and generally trying not to die.

One daylight mission happened on the west side of Mosul early in that summer but was a bit more humorous than the others. We drove across the cracked pavement in our eight-wheel armored vehicles and stopped outside a neighborhood. I could see the ruins of buildings built on top of the foundations of even older structures, one floor plan overlaid on another, but each with walls and corners pointing in different directions. Mosul was an ancient city; in the Bible, it was called Nineveh. One got the feeling that there were a lot of ghosts there.

I was the tactical commander of one of the Strykers, since I was a weapons squad team leader. While popping up out of the top hatch, I would direct the driver and gunner on what to do. I didn't worry much about gunfire or IEDs but had a phobia about low-hanging piano wire set out between buildings or under overpasses as a booby trap to lop my head off. My squad leader said I had been watching too many World War II movies, but it could happen!

I ordered our driver to stop near the target building, we dropped ramp, and Ranger assault teams flowed out the back and made entry into the building. The 3/75 Rangers would clear the structure in seconds, and then our platoon leader, Lieutenant Fleming, would come over the radio to announce what we were looking at. A tense few seconds passed after the Rangers went through the front door. Would there be a firefight? Would one of our guys get shot? A lot of things could go wrong.

Over my headset, the radio crackled as someone hit the push-to-talk button on their radio.

"Objective secure," Fleming reported. "Six and a half men detained." I blinked.

A moment later, our company commander came over the net from back at our base and asked the question we were all thinking. I can't remember his exact words, but they were something like: What the fuck do you mean, six and a half men?

Fleming's voice came back over the net. "We've detained six fighting-age men and one midget."

On the Strykers, we were all dying laughing.

A few minutes later, our PL announced over the radio that the assaulters had flex-cuffed the detainees and would be leading them out to the vehicles. Meanwhile, he would pack the midget into a rucksack and carry him out.

"LEAVE THE FUCKING MIDGET!" our company commander said over the radio. "We don't need him!"

They say war is hell and all that. I guess for some people it is, but all in all, I thought it was a hell of a lot of fun.

CHAPTER 5

If Enough Data Is Collected, a Board of Inquiry Can Prove Anything

SO IT WENT, EVERY DAY PACKED WITH COMBAT OPERA-
tions. The only time we were really stood down was when a sandstorm
would sweep across Mosul. When a sandstorm blows over you in that part
of the world, it literally blots out the sun. What light does penetrate casts a
red unearthly glow that makes it look like you are on the surface of Mars.
In these conditions, drones and other aircraft can't fly, so it was a rare moment for us to rest.

When we were lucky, we would get an intel brief and have time to hash
out a hasty plan of action. That was rare; most times we got only a grid
overlay on a map and a target name and rolled out the gate. Sometimes we
launched on even less than that.

One operation that we had some time to prepare for was a capture/
kill mission of a terrorist named Zayad. Capture/kill means that our
primary objective was to capture him alive, but failing that, we would
kill him. We'd had our eye on him for a while. Zayad had gotten into the
gangster life, running with terrorists, but now wanted out because of
how many bad guys we had been smoking in his AO. But as they say in
The Godfather, "Just when I thought I was out, they pull me back in." He
couldn't give up the terrorist lifestyle, I guess, and kept popping up as

being involved in nefarious activities. We tracked him to yet another non-descript cinder-block house, this time on the outskirts of Mosul.

We drove our convoy of Strykers down the highway leading west out of Mosul, the road surrounded by a long commercial ribbon of mechanics' shops and other businesses that became more spread out the farther outside the city you got. We made a sharp right turn off the highway and up a dusty dirt road past the shops and into an area that was pretty much open desert with a few structures here and there. The target building was dead ahead. I was guiding the first vehicle in the order of movement.

We could see Zayad, wearing his man-jams and moving briskly from the building as if we were going to let him just walk away. Why he thought he could escape like that, I have no idea. The six Strykers split into two elements, mine going left around the building and the other three going right to surround it. Zayad was still speed-walking away. Under our rules of engagement, we were fully authorized to shoot squirters—they were not surrendering, they were just running away to fight us at a time and place of their choosing.

I'll never forget the look Zayad shot me over his shoulder. He was pissed. I directed Ralph, my .50-cal gunner, to open fire on Zayad. Ralph had a bit of trouble getting the remote weapon system on target. With hindsight, I can see why: Ralph was looking at a small black-and-white screen down inside the Stryker, trying to locate a dude wearing tan clothes in the middle of the desert. I could see him clear as day, but my gunner couldn't. Finally, Ralph let off a burst.

Amazingly, the six or so .50-cal rounds (each about the size of your pointer finger) crept a line of fire up through the sand toward Zayad. Each shot left a little geyser of sand in its wake. One bullet landed just short of Zayad as he ducked; another shot went slightly long and landed behind him. Incredible. That asshole just dodged a burst of .50-cal. Zayad got back up and continued speed-walking, almost like he couldn't be bothered to run. Ralph fired again. I can't tell you exactly what happened after this point, and neither can anyone else, because while I was talking on our internal comms, trying to get my gunner on target, the Strykers had dropped ramp, and every Ranger on the mission had jumped out.

When Ralph fired that second burst, the entire fucking task force opened fire as well. All three assault teams, the two snipers, even staff dudes who really didn't need to be on that mission. Everyone opened up, and this time Zayad went down for the count. The assault teams began assaulting forward to clear the body. I ordered Ralph to cease fire; Sergeant Van Aalst was already giving a similar order.

The boys cleared the corpse, and we pulled the Strykers up to cover down on security around the assaulters. Joe Kapacziewski's squad loaded the corpse in a body bag. After searching the structure, we peeled back and called in an air strike on the now empty building. It was simply to make a point to the locals: Fuck with us and we'll rain down fire on you. Apache gunships swarmed in and began firing their rocket pods at the cinder-block house. Soon a spiral of black smoke was rising into the sky.

When we got back to the FOB, the body was pulled out and laid on top of the body bag in front of the ops center. As I got off the Stryker, one senior leader was already bragging about how he had killed Zayad and how much he'd had to lead him with his rifle sight. What bullshit. Who knows who killed Zayad, there were so many bullets flying through the air.

I walked up and stood at Zayad's feet. I crouched down and looked closely at the embedded shrapnel under the skin on his calf: This wasn't his first rodeo. His skin already had that waxy complexion, flies buzzed around his face, his eyes were locked open and just as dead as he was. I've found that a lot of people like to wax poetic about the dead. I even read a book written by this photojournalist in Bosnia during the war who, in the first scene, describes a dead teenage girl in the forest. He goes on and on about how beautiful she was, postulating about the meaning of life and death.

I never really saw all of that sentimental horse shit in a dead body.

Zayad was living one minute, and we made him dead the next. The disturbing thing was the finality of it, how easy it was just to flip someone's off switch, like flicking off a light. There was nothing special about death at all. Zayad lay in front of me, a dead piece of meat. The only affirmation was that there was nothing magical about life, no sky kingdom waiting for us after we die. Just a pile of black flies crawling around your face. Life is a motherfucker, then you die.

I looked up at a staff officer who was using a digital camera to take pictures of Zayad for the database of dudes we'd killed today. "So what's the verdict on clown shoes?" I asked. "Is he dead or what?" The officer looked horrified.

Standing up, I walked by the OPCEN to drop off some of my gear in our loadout room. One of our company medics came out of the OPCEN and started talking to me about the operation that he had just watched on the predator feedback at the FOB. "Man, I saw him shooting at you guys!"

"What the hell are you talking about? He wasn't shooting at us."

"Yeah, yeah, he was," the medic insisted. "We saw him on the video feed. As he was walking, he had his back turned to you but was reaching around and firing a Glock over his shoulder at you guys."

I was dumbfounded. I had seen the entire incident with my own eyes just minutes before, and now some guy who was sitting back at the FOB was telling me what I actually saw? This was surreal. To this day, there are guys who will claim that Zayad was firing a Glock pistol at us gangster-style over his shoulder as he walked away. This is pure bullshit. There was no reason to make up such a lie, because killing him fell well within our ROE, but some guys wanted to make sure their asses were fully covered in case of a JAG review, and others, I think, legitimately convinced themselves that this fictional story was the truth.

This turned out to be a pivotal moment for me. It was the moment I fully realized how much of what we are told simply isn't true. On any given day, we are told little stories. We are often told outright lies about how the world works and what factually happens. These lies are quickly assimilated by the human mind and, within moments, become indistinguishable from the truth for most people.

My own personal experience makes me wonder how we can believe anything we are told about war.

The MH-60 helicopters set us down in the middle of the desert, their rotor wash visible through our PVS-14 night vision goggles.

My gun team and the assault teams hopped off of the 160th helicopter, ran out into the field, and took a knee. The helicopter lifted off, and we were suddenly left alone in the desert as comms chatter began and we prepared to move out. It was an offset infil, meaning that the birds had landed us maybe ten kilometers away from the village so that the enemy could not hear the rotor blades, which would help give us the element of surprise.

Under the weight of our gear, we stood up and began moving out toward the target area. It was another HVT strike against some Al-Qaeda facilitator, this time in a village south of Mosul. Instead of using the Strykers, 160th had flown us in for what is called a HAF (helicopter assault force) mission. As a gun team leader, I had one private carrying the Mk47 machine gun and two others carrying ammunition to feed it. We shook out into a wedge-shaped formation and walked. Despite it being nighttime, it wasn't much cooler than during the day, especially under eighty pounds of combat gear.

Eventually, we made it to the village and maneuvered through narrow streets and around shanties and cinder-block structures. At one point, my gun team took a knee at a corner of a low wall while we waited for other Ranger elements to get into position. We were concealed inside the dark shadows cast by the wall, against the moonlight. Moments later, we heard someone coughing and gagging, almost as if he were hacking up a hairball.

IR lasers from our rifles darted in front of us, observed through the green tint of our night vision devices. Also hidden in the shadows, in what was basically an open lot turned garbage dump, was a metal bed frame with long slat-metal springs. An Iraqi civilian was sleeping on it. It was normal during the hot summer months for people to sleep on a mattress on a rooftop or in a backyard if they had one. In between coughing, the Iraqi heard the crunch of gravel beneath our assault boots. He said something in Arabic that I didn't understand, but it sounded angry.

He lay back down, coughed some more, then popped his head up to chastise us again. We held our rifles trained on him, but it had become clear that he had absolutely no idea who we were. He must have thought we were some local kids playing around because we were so obscured in the shadows. He was oblivious to the fact that four Rangers had a machine gun and three rifles pointed at him. This was how we liked it. Our best missions were when we got the drop on the enemy so effectively that they never had a chance to fight back and we could drag them out of their beds.

There is an operational art to war, one our platoon had come to understand. Gone were the days of warfare as represented in our manuals or training courses at Fort Benning that envisioned World War II–style urban combat. This was counterterrorism, and we were expected to be like ninjas slowly creeping up on targets unobserved, quietly popping open locks with manual breaching tools, and flowing through the door with the lights off while wearing night vision.

When the order came over the radio, we picked up and stepped off toward our objective. We got our Mk47 into position to provide overwatch on the building, which stood in a large empty lot. The assault team affixed an explosive breaching charge on the door while we stood by to provide supporting fire in case something popped off. Then the familiar words came over the assault net: "I have control. Initiate in five . . . four . . . three . . . two . . ."

BOOM!

The door blasted open in a shower of white and orange sparks. Long before the dust got the chance to settle, all three five-man assault teams were inside; I picked up my machine gun team and headed in behind them. We came into a large atrium with an open staircase that wound around a curved wall up to the second floor. We pounded our way up the steps. Women and children were crying. We found our way up to the roof and pulled security in case any more bad guys showed up to party.

There was bad news—it was another dry hole. The HVT we were after wasn't here. Of course, higher command wouldn't let us leave so easily. We spent the next several hours crisscrossing the entire village I don't know how many times. We climbed over walls, covered each other while we crossed roads, maneuvered between pieces of concertina wire, and found our way around while we went banging on doors. In an unfamiliar sprawling village like that, it is pretty easy to get turned around and confused. Frankly, I was pretty disoriented by the end of the night. Meanwhile, my privates had performed well, but they had managed to drain their CamelBaks of water. Then they'd proceeded to drain my CamelBak, too. Oh well. What are team leaders for?

We never did find the bad guys that night. In the end, we exited the village and moved out to establish a hasty landing zone. I had our Mk47 gunner oriented toward the village up until the MH-60 swooped in and rotor wash blasted over us a second time that night. The gunner cleared his weapon and made it safe, then we hauled ass to the helicopter and caught our ride back to the FOB.

We were all looking forward to mid-rats—midnight rations—at the chow hall and playing some video games, until the next op, anyway.

In Mosul, we worked in tandem with a five-man team from Delta Force, the army's counterterrorism unit. Most Rangers absolutely worship these guys. I have a lot of respect for them, although the hero worship some-times goes a little over the top. The Delta operators and the Rangers were both actioning enemies off of the same target deck, using different tactics.

The funny thing is that while our bosses seemed to expect us to cap-ture high-value targets alive, and got pretty concerned when we had to kill hard-core foreign fighters, the Delta Force team with us was slaying bod-ies like it was going out of style. They were rolling out disguised as locals in low-visibility vehicles and doing vehicle interdictions on terrorists who were driving around town.

The more fainthearted of you might call these assassinations, but we just referred to them as kill/capture missions, with the emphasis on the killing part in this case. Truth be told, there was a real risk of these terror-ist leaders wearing suicide vests, which would make capturing them alive impossible. In one instance, the team's sergeant major smoked a terrorist leader in Mosul called an emir who was wearing an S-vest with the deto-nator concealed in a pocket.

From time to time, our platoon would be on standby to provide sup-port for the Delta team working on our FOB, but this was an exception rather than a rule. They were good dudes doing good work, and while I don't think it is at all wrong for SOF units to support one another, there is an enduring myth that the Ranger regiment is some type of support ele-ment for Delta. This simply is not true. In all the operations I participated in with the 75th, only a couple were in support of Delta Force; the other hundred-something were purely Ranger missions.

Sadly, Ivica Jerak, the operator who had taught my platoon modern room-clearing techniques on the previous deployment, was killed that summer in Iraq during an IED strike down south. The Delta sergeant major on our base gave a heartfelt speech to the task force on behalf of his teammate, telling us how he'd emigrated to America and how strongly he'd cared about American politics. Some said that Ivica had even been interested in pursuing a political career after the military. Unfortunately, it was not the last such memorial that we had during that three-month span in Iraq.

The missions kept coming and coming, the pace relentless. On one mission, we drove outside the city and hit our target building, but the HVT ran. Rangers began chasing him through the tall grass. An F-16 fighter jet blasted about a hundred feet over our heads as a show of force. The Little Bird helicopters providing aerial support for us were running low on fuel, so we pulled our Strykers forward and established a security perimeter to set up a FARP, or forward air refueling point. My team-mate Alex lugged the fuel bladders from the back of his Stryker out into the field and laid them out. A minute later, a Little Bird pilot expertly navigated his helicopter down behind our Strykers and set down. Next, he hopped out and used the fuel bladder to gas up his bird.

This wasn't New Jersey, where attendants pump your gas for you.

And the mission continued.

As time went on, the enemy was adapting. They would come up with countermeasures to stop us from finding them, fixing them in place, and ultimately finishing them. Then we would have to come up with counter-countermeasures, and the game would go on. One creative tactic they used was calling from underneath a cell phone tower, which confused our sensors initially, so we figured out a new way to triangulate on their signal.

This was one of the big reasons why so many terrorists were conducting "rolling meets" inside cars rather than fixed locations, which were easy for a platoon of Rangers to raid. And this was why the Delta operators were doing vehicle interdictions all the time and popping their grapes.

Problem was, the low-visibility vehicles meant that Delta could not go crashing around the streets of Mosul *Mad Max*–style, the way we could with the Strykers. So sometimes we would try to do the VI ourselves. In one case, we were searching for a terrorist driving his car around in Mosul. The frantic updates on his location kept coming in over the net. Imagine

HQ feeding you grids and locations and route names, all while you stare at a map and a GPS beacon on a Panasonic Toughbook computer and try to figure out, first, where the fuck you are and, second, where the enemy is, both locations changing every sixty seconds. When we finally spotted him, he also spotted us, and a high-speed chase through the streets of Mosul began.

Let me tell you something, folks, you have not lived life until your existence has rested with the sweet mercy of a Ranger private driving an eight-wheel twenty-ton armored vehicle at high speeds through twisting urban roads in the Middle East. The engine growled as my driver floored it, sending me lurching forward in the hatch. The goddamn privates were like hound dogs chasing after a fox. We blasted down the streets, cars and people flashing by.

The brown Opel in front of us swerved around a corner. The Stryker barely slowed down, the driver cutting the wheel. I don't know if that kid thought he was going to drift us around the corner or what, but at this point, I was pretty much letting Jesus take the wheel. If JC and his boys wanted me, they could come on down and get me. Amazingly, we cleared the corner and revved down the street, plowing downhill, then churning slightly uphill, the red brake lights of the Opel a few hundred feet in front of us. On the straightaway, we were gaining on him, but the buzzing in my headset was telling me to stand down. They wanted us to break off the chase; our convoy was already getting spread out all over the place.

Until next time, you asshole! The Opel disappeared from view.

On another occasion, there was a lot of traffic on the streets, and the Delta operators felt they would not be able to intercept two terrorists who were having one of their rolling meets. We were driving around town, so they flipped the mission to us: If you can get him, get him. I sensed that the sergeant major of the Delta team was an equal-opportunity kind of guy who liked dead terrorists but wasn't overly concerned with who got credit for what.

Rangers are not about to turn down an opportunity like that. We crossed the bridge and headed over to the east side of Mosul and began searching for the enemy vehicle as headquarters fed us information that they were observing from the ISR feed. My Stryker was second in the order of movement, Alex's, the other team leader in my squad, vehicle was the first.

Then, as we were rounding a corner into a traffic circle, there was a burst of excitement over the radio net. "That's him, that's the car, that's him right there!"

Alex's Stryker slid in right behind the sedan. The .50-cal mounted on the RWS cradle atop the vehicle rotated toward the sedan, the barrel pointed downward to get a proper angle for the shot. Down below, the Ranger manning the gun was using a joystick to point it while looking at a small black-and-white screen. To fire, he then slid his trigger finger underneath the safety guard on the joystick and depressed the plastic trigger. The RWS burped a single shot, and the sedan pulled to the side of the road and stopped. Our Strykers quickly surrounded the sedan and dropped ramp, and assaulters began climbing out.

"Oh, damn, that dude is fucked up," my driver said.

I could see that the rear window was cracked but not much else. When the Rangers popped open the driver's-side door, the grim reality became apparent. The single .50-cal round had gone through the back of the car and pulped the HVT driving. His dome was blasted open, the passenger splattered with gray matter and paralyzed by fear. The Rangers dragged the body out; you could see the top of his skull forming a perfect bowl shape, still attached to the head by a piece of scalp. Better cancel that dude's dinner plans.

The trunk of the car was loaded with AK-47 rifles, ammunition, and grenades. In just a minute or two, the corpse was bagged up and loaded on a Stryker, the passenger was detained in flex cuffs, and our platoon leader tossed a thermite grenade in the dash of the car to torch it. In seconds, the car was a roaring fireball as bullets cooked off in the fire. We closed up the ramp on our Stryker and headed back to the FOB, where I was playing *Neverwinter Nights* on my laptop and really hoping I would beat the game soon. But while I was inside playing computer games, young Rangers, who are generally a rambunctious lot, were getting into trouble. The privates in weapons squad would sneak out in the middle of the night on our compound, wearing balaclavas, and would ball up other privates in our platoon, hog-tying them and taking trophy pictures. What a time to be alive! Those pictures are still floating around the Internet to this day and I dread the moment the ACLU gets ahold of them and says it was detainee abuse, not knowing that it was American soldiers goofing off.

Ah, the winds of fate and fortune. During that summer I watched young men exposed to combat for the first time get hailed as heroes, while others were derided as losers, cowards, and zeroes, as I had been not long before. These facades are all built up and torn down so fast by the wolf pack that is Ranger Battalion that it is hard to keep track of them sometimes. We build our heroes up and then snatch it all away from them in the blink of an eye.

I had one private assigned to me as a .50-cal gunner for a short period of time, as his squad did not want him on their assault team. We made him an M240B gunner in the rear hatch of the Stryker, but he seemed incompetent at that. Other Rangers complained that he kept flagging them with the machine gun—that his IR laser was dancing across their feet all the time—which, understandably, made them nervous. For some odd reason, he was then taken off the M240B and put behind the remote weapon system that controlled the .50-cal on top of the Stryker. I asked my privates who knew the system inside and out to train him. Out on a mission, he was completely unable to orient and aim the .50-cal. It operated with a fucking joystick! An untrained chimp could have operated that system.

I came down out of the hatch, put the soldier's hand on the joystick, then put my hand over his, and pushed the joystick back and forth to show him with certainty how the RWS could be aimed. The second I went back up in the hatch, he was unable to aim the gun again. When we got back to the FOB, I had him kit up in all his gear and practice IMT (individual movement techniques) drills in the gravel.

It may alarm some of the more squeamish among you that I physically corrected a soldier, but war isn't the place for political correctness. We were taking these young men to war, and they needed to be taught the skills to keep themselves and fellow Rangers alive. While under fire, infantrymen will IMT by shooting their weapon from the prone position, jumping up and bounding forward for three to five seconds, then throwing themselves back into the prone to fire their weapon. I had this private practicing the drill without ammunition not so much for training but because he needed to be physically corrected. As my first team leader once told me, and he wasn't wrong: Pain instills memory. However, something was really wrong with this kid. I told my squad leader, Ken, as much: "He is either a retard or deliberately sabotaging himself and the mission because he doesn't want to be here." Ken had previously served in the navy before joining the army, had full-sleeve tattoos, and was one of those larger-than-life characters found only in the infantry. Ken was probably the best sergeant I ever worked with, and Ranger Battalion was lucky to have him. He listened to what I had to say and took the issue higher.

All Rangers are volunteers and can quit at any time, but maybe this kid was afraid to throw in the towel in front of his peers. I told my squad leader that if the kid got killed or got our teammates killed, then the blood would be on our hands because we'd seen it coming.

Ken understood and told me that he would take care of it. To my surprise, the private was inserted back into his old squad and put on an assault team. Days later, we were heading to Tal Afar, the city west of Mosul that Sergeant Van Aalst had been concerned about since we'd first arrived in country. This time, we all knew for sure that we were going into the shit. The enemy controlled the city, and we were heading right into the middle of it on another HVT capture/kill mission.

After boarding our Strykers, we began the hour-or-so drive west to Tal Afar. Driving under night vision with our vehicles completely blacked out had its challenges but it gave us the element of surprise. Not once during our rotation did we hit an IED. That said, it could be difficult to guide the Strykers without having any depth perception and with limited visibility. One time we came up on a checkpoint that wasn't on a map. Suddenly, the Stryker in front of me ground to a halt to avoid the Jersey barriers, but these vehicles don't exactly stop on a dime. Sergeant Van Aalst popped up out of the hatch and shined an IR laser on the ground in front of me, trying to warn me to stop. I ordered my driver to slow down, and then to stop, when I realized the lead vehicle wasn't moving and we were about to hit it. Thankfully, my driver was on it and we avoided a collision.

But now we were heading downhill on the same road. Up ahead, I could see a mound of dirt in the middle of the road.

"Come right," I told the driver.

We stayed on course.

"Come right," I said over the internal comms again.

The Stryker was now barreling downhill at perhaps sixty miles an hour, straight toward the mound of dirt.

"COME RIGHT!" I yelled.

By now it was too late. We hit the pile of dirt going full speed. It acted like a ramp, and that entire Stryker went airborne like a little kid riding a tricycle off a sweet ramp made by his older brother out of a piece of plywood and a cinder block. For a second, it felt like I was floating in midair, because I was. Then we crashed back down to earth, and I whiplashed forward in the hatch. All of the ammunition in the can next to the Mk47 mount beside me had also gone airborne, and now I was draped with 150 rounds of 7.62 machine gun bullets.

"Goddamn, Murph!" my squad leader said over the radio, as everyone in the back had been bounced all over the place.

I was screaming at the driver by this point because it seemed that he had engaged in selective hearing and damn near killed us. Soon we arrived at an American FOB close to Tal Afar where a tanker unit was stationed. I ordered the driver out of the Stryker and "physically corrected" him until my squad leader made me stop. It was probably just as well because I was about ready to kill that kid and drive the Stryker myself that night.

Our leadership element did some coordinations with the tanker unit, as they were going to provide support for our mission by holding down some security positions. Our physician's assistant had already hashed out an entire medevac plan for us, as we all knew what was coming. Meanwhile, we made sure the Strykers were set to go.

Once everything was set to go, the tankers rolled out and locked down a couple corners near their FOB with their Abrams tanks while we rolled out to our objective in the Strykers. Tal Afar was a ghost town. The streets were empty and desolate. It really was too quiet. We slow-rolled the Strykers and stopped several blocks away from the target, where we dropped ramp and let off the assault teams. The assaulters moved in to take down the target while we lay in wait. Meanwhile, a small sniper element was scooting around the black side (the back end) of the target to ensure that no one could run away.

I stood in the hatch watching and waiting through my night vision goggles, knowing that something was about to cook off.

Then came the *crack-crack-crack,* the snap of 5.56 rounds that we had all been waiting for.

"Here we go," I said over my headset.

The Strykers hauled ass down the street and blew around a corner. I came up in front of the target building as a firefight was raging. I didn't know it at the time, but my friend Burkhart with the sniper element had gassed up a couple terrorists trying to squirt off target. Inside the target structure, a hidden room had been missed by assaulters. Another terrorist had popped out as the command element was coming inside, and the physician's assistant shot and killed him. There's something you don't see every day. Speaking of which, as I pulled up my vehicle, I saw another one of our snipers running along the rooftop. He was backlit by a full moon, angling his sniper rifle down and firing into a narrow alleyway.

Then some of the assaulters on the ground tossed a couple grenades into the alley, and the two squirters who had tried to escape were finished. Amazingly, none of the Rangers had been hurt during the firefight. However, one assaulter—the one I had gotten removed as my Stryker gunner after finding him completely untrainable and uncoachable—had frozen up in the heat of combat. He had to be removed and sent to make coffee for the colonel. Sergeant Van Aalst later told us not to judge him and leave the kid alone. He was right. In retrospect, I don't judge him. This shit isn't for everyone.

As the Rangers SSE'ed the target, Sergeant Van Aalst had us reposition the vehicles for exfil. It was a long ride back to Mosul, and we were damn happy to have escaped that firefight with life and limb and get back to the FOB for soup and hot sandwiches.

We were also quite fond of raiding the giant refrigerators in the chow hall for Red Bulls before big missions. Before that one to Tal Afar, our platoon went to chow, and some of the more high-strung squad leaders saw me sending my privates to fill up two plastic bags full of Red Bulls to carry out, and they started losing their shit over it. "WE'RE GOING TO LOSE OUR RED BULL PRIVILEGES!" Dude, seriously, I thought, chill out.

Some people take all this war shit way too seriously, if you ask me. It is combat and all, but that doesn't mean we have to be miserable all the time. Anger is just something deeply embedded in the soul of the Ranger—I mean, it runs deep in our blood. We're used to being fucked with, held to high standards, and having to stand around in the rain all day before our leaders make a uniform adjustment and tell us that we can put on our rain gear after we are soaking wet.

Well, fuck me, the next day there were big signs taped to the refrigerators stipulating how many Red Bulls each soldier was allowed to take. The longer a war goes on, the more pieces of paper with dumb rules appear from the ether.

My interactions with the regular army were also pretty funny. Suffice to say that we come from two very different cultures. It becomes apparent when you get deployed that there are actually two wars being fought by two totally different armies. One culture was sitting around the FOB in air-conditioning all day, wearing shorts and T-shirts, and the other culture was ground pounders who went outside the wire and mixed it up with the enemy. I belonged to the latter culture, with my Ranger teammates, and we were all proud of that fact. Rolling outside the wire every day to put boots to asses requires a certain amount of hubris that I don't think people who weren't there will ever really understand.

The weird thing about FOB life was that you had to carry your weapon with you wherever you went; however, you could not have a round in the chamber. You also could not have a magazine in your rifle when you went to the chow hall. So roll this around in the back of your mind for a moment: It is mandatory that you lug around an unloaded weapon with you wherever you go. The rationale is that this is to prevent accidental discharges, of which that other culture I spoke about had quite a few. So we all carried around useless pieces of metal for show. This was another example of the culture schism between combat troops and everyone else. We were there for war, everyone else was there do something else, and carrying a gun was like some kind of FOB-life fashion accessory.

Coming out of the chow hall one afternoon, one of my privates loaded his magazine into the magazine well of his M4 and slapped it into place. Some first sergeant from a conventional unit saw that and started freaking out, lecturing us on how doing that was how you had an accidental discharge. Now, if you know a single thing about firearms, you know that because of how that rifle is designed, slapping a magazine into a mag well will not cause the weapon to fire; there isn't even a round in the chamber, in this case. During these interactions with "Big Army," we would just say "Roger, Sergeant" until they went away, and then we'd go back to doing whatever we were doing.

There are so many frenzied stories from that deployment, it is hard to recall all of them, as they blend together into a summer of insanity and death. There was another mission to Tal Afar, for instance, and another firefight. Afterward, Sergeant Van Aalst cleared the target structure of civilians, getting the entire family out and making these civilians clear the area. Then, as we drove our Strykers through the city on exfil, an AC-130 gunship orbiting above started hammering the objective building with its big gun. BOOM-BOOM-BOOM-BOOM! The sound reverberated throughout the city as we got the hell out of dodge. It is another one of those memories that you can't ever forget.

But all good things come to an end, and so they did when we got blown up. It started as a mission like many others, with a high-value target and a hastily put together plan for how we were going to capture him.

CHAPTER 6

Luck Can't Hold Out
Against Murph

THE DEPLOYMENT WAS GRINDING ON, AND WHILE OUR luck had been holding out, there was a feeling in the air that it couldn't hold out forever. Every day there were more missions, and it felt like the city was getting hotter. There was more fighting, more contacts, random gunfire. Shit went sideways a couple weeks out from redeployment back to the States.

We were after another emir, or prince, which was what the head terrorist over a city was called. You see, we had a target deck with who knew how many names on it, but as we churned through human souls, the guy who was number 163 on our list eventually became number 1. Our guy was doing rolling meets, so our plan was to trap him while he was going over an overpass by cutting off both ends with our Strykers and then moving in on him.

I knew it was going to be one of those days the second we rolled outside the wire. It was midday, and a thick black column of smoke rose above the city from a fire somewhere in the urban sprawl. I was now the tactical commander for the lead Stryker in our convoy, meaning that I had to get us where we needed to go and get us back home, navigating the streets of the city and not getting us dead in the process. Usually, I was given some grids on a USB drive that I would plug in to a Panasonic Toughbook, which also had this black hockey-puck GPS plugged in to it. I would upload the grid or enter it manually, then see where we were going in relation to our own icon, which moved in near-real time.

In other cases, I was having to improvise on the fly, as we didn't have time for a brief or even handing off a grid location. I would have to enter that information into the computer on the way out of the gate, and more than once I rolled out of the gate without any information whatsoever and just started driving into the city until someone finally told me where the target was. Once we got out there, more often than not, new grids would be coming in for follow-on missions.

This was one of those days where I was just driving us into a general location, looking around for this asshole terrorist. We pretty much drove straight toward the column of smoke over on the east end of the city and pulled up near a flat open area while we waited for the intelligence to be developed so we could, as the officers put it, "prosecute some more targets." Now I could see the source of the smoke—it was a Stryker belonging to one of the conventional units. Flames were belching out the back of the Stryker, with rounds or some type of explosive cooking off inside. Other Strykers were driving around the area like bats out of hell. Whatever unit got hit was clearly in a panic.

One of the Strykers pulled up alongside mine, and a young first lieutenant shouted over to me, exasperated, "Can you pull security on this area for me?" He wanted me to keep guns and eyes on the area to keep it secure from any enemy fighters who might show up.

"I can while I'm here," I told him. "But we could be rolling at any moment. We have our own mission." I felt pretty shitty about that. This guy clearly needed some assistance. About five minutes later, we got the word and were rolling. Our convoy split into two elements, three Strykers in each. The two elements would situate themselves at either end of a bridge, one stretching across the river on the north side of town.

My three Strykers went over to the west side of the bridge and prepared to intercept the HVT when he crossed. On my Stryker was one assault team and Sergeant Van Aalst. The middle Stryker was the medical evacuation vehicle, or MEV, where the medic was. The third Stryker had Kap's assault team and Lieutenant Fleming on board. When we drove down the off-ramp, we would go into a loiter or lager route, which meant we would basically just drive in circles until we got word from higher to intercept our man before he made it across the bridge.

It was midday, and the streets were packed with traffic. If we received word that our target was en route, we would never be able to get back onto the highway or to the bridge in time, due to the congestion on the streets. Sergeant Van Aalst came over the net and instructed me to turn our three-vehicle convoy around and park underneath the overpass. That way, we would just have to make a sharp turn onto the on-ramp, roll right up to the bridge, and be ready to nail this guy.

I did as I was told and maneuvered us under the overpass and stopped. I was cocky to the point that I just sat up on top of the lip of the hatch, totally exposed, while I waited for further instructions. We sat there in that position for perhaps ten minutes; then, all of a sudden, there was an explosion right behind me. The sharp sound of it pounded in my ears, a pressure wave washing over me from behind. A cloud of gray smoke that had the smell of sulfur wafted around me. I looked back but didn't see anything and reached for the Mk47. I was also instructing my RWS gunner to maintain frontal security with the .50-cal.

"Get security up!" one assault team leader yelled at me from inside the Stryker. We were pulling security, but we didn't know what was going on because the explosion was to our six o'clock. I assumed that someone had fired an RPG at the third Stryker in our order of movement. Then I heard a sound I'll never forget. It was the screams of an injured Ranger. Lieutenant Fleming had climbed up and out of the third Stryker's air guard hatch and was howling in pain.

The situation was still confused, but clearly, we had injured Rangers. The MEV dropped ramp, and our two snipers, Michael Kase and Isaiah

Burkhart, got out to help pull security with their long guns. Others were rushing to the Stryker that had gotten hit.

Later, when I talked to the tactical commander, named Matt, of that Stryker, the full story emerged. It wasn't an RPG—some insurgents up on the overpass had hopped out of their car and dropped hand grenades on top of us before speeding off. Matt actually heard the grenades bounce off the roof of his vehicle and ducked inside the hatch. Several detonated on the roof, but one got in the air guard hatch and blew up, severing the hydraulics that controlled the back ramp of the vehicle in the process. Inside, the guys were struggling to manually open the ramp so they could start medical treatment.

There were a number of flesh wounds, but Fleming and Kapacziewski had taken the worst of it. The mission was now a wash—we had to get our guys back to the field hospital on our base, and we needed to get them there now. As quickly as we could, we hauled ass through Mosul, knowing that the numbers could be ticking down for our teammates. RWS gunners were firing warning shots into the ground left and right as we charged down the streets. One gunner fired a long burst into the pavement just in front of an Opel, the rounds sparking off the ground as they made impact.

I was leading the convoy and broke every traffic rule you can imagine. If a street was clogged, I told our driver to just crash right over the median and drive in the opposing lane. If a car was getting in our way, we fired a burst of .50-cal into their tires. My driver saw some of the traffic and remarked that it didn't seem like we were going to make it to our field hospital in time to save our buddies. "We'll make it," Van Aalst said confidently. He was right. We tore into the base and pulled in to the field hospital. The injured were off-loaded into the hospital on stretchers by the medics, nurses, and doctors. We then had to trust that they were in good hands.

We drove back to our compound. Once we parked the Strykers and got out, we all just kind of looked at each other for a moment. I think everyone had a thousand-yard stare that day. We looked haggard. In that summer heat, you would sweat through your uniform two or three times a day, leaving behind long white sweat stains on your fatigues. A couple guys lit up cigarettes, feeling shaken, and who could blame them?

Our platoon was now short an entire assault team. Our colonel decided to plus us up with some fresh Rangers pulled from a five-man Ranger detail that was on standby for combat search and rescue, sticking them in first platoon. Angry words were spoken in the heat of the moment, as many felt it was wrong to just plus up the platoon with warm bodies and send us back out. One sergeant told me that if we'd been in Vietnam, our battalion commander would be dead, because he was the one who would have killed him.

That night we got sent on another mission into Tal Afar.

The missions all run together after a while. Someone shoots at you as you drive down the street; you note it and move on. It was a summer of gunfire, explosive charges, and sweat, all observed under the green tint of night vision. One memory that sticks with me is driving down the street during the day and seeing a huge pothole, more like a crater, filled with black putrid water. Two kids, age five or so, were playing in the water, splashing each other. Try explaining shit like that to people back home.

Another source of consternation came from the Pink Team, a conventional army aviation package consisting of helicopters, crews, and pilots. They were helicopter pilots who helped support our missions, many of them Kiowas. Under our rules of engagement, we were cleared hot to shoot any vehicle that we perceived as a threat to our convoy and fellow Rangers. At the time, suicide vehicle-borne improvised explosive devices (SVBIEDs) were all the rage, and we had little recourse to protect ourselves other than to open fire. What made matters worse was that many Iraqi drivers were reckless anyway. It wasn't uncommon for them to try to charge right through streets we were locking down or to swerve their car between two Strykers in our convoy.

In one case, a driver tried to charge through our security position on a street corner even after we waved him off. Is it an SVBIED? My gunner opened fire and killed the driver. There wasn't a bomb in the car, it was just a dumbass driver who thought he could blast right through our blockade. One of the other guys on the Stryker asked my gunner how it felt to kill a man. "Not good," he replied.

There were a lot of instances when I thought we were completely justified in firing, sometimes warning shots and sometimes shots that killed as things escalated. However, I saw some things I disagreed with. Some guys appeared to take the ROE as an open door to shoot people just for the sake of it. One gunner shot the shit out of a minivan. My Stryker was the next vehicle to drive by the minivan, which was now filled with bullet holes from the .50-cal. The sliding door opened and an old woman emerged, crying and wailing.

From above, the Pink Team saw some of this, too, and would complain about it. It got so bad that at one point a bunch of JSOC officers and sergeants major flew up from Tikrit to address the entire task force and "make sure that we were okay" because we were killing so many people. I don't think any of us had any interest in talking to them; it seemed like a finger drill so the officers could say they came up to check in on us. We were killing people on a daily basis, but it seemed normal, for the most part. Wasn't that what soldiers did in war? Still, there were incidents that did not sit well with me.

Once, my squad leader called the Stryker crews together and tried to make a point about all of the gunfire on every convoy operation. He told us that if we were going around shooting civilians, then who was really the bad guy in that situation? "We are," I said. One of the tactical commanders for another vehicle just shrugged and said, "I don't give a fuck." Though my squad leader seemed upset by this remark, there wasn't much he could do, unable to contradict an ROE that came down from far above any of our heads.

At one point, they wanted me to note every single vehicle we hit, nudged, rammed, and scraped so that the Civil Affairs guys could go and pay the owner to have the car fixed. Well, the streets of Mosul are packed with traffic, and we were driving twenty-ton armored vehicles. I had a clipboard out as we drove to make a note of what vehicles we hit.

"Red Opel," I would say over the radio.

Then two seconds later, "Blue Opel."

Three seconds after that, "Red Opel."

Two seconds later, "White Opel."

It went on like that for maybe fifteen minutes before they told me not to worry about it and to put the clipboard down.

Our sister platoon took their licks as well, unfortunately. They got into a few pretty bad dustups. They would drop their injured Rangers off at the field hospital and then come back to our compound, where we would have Gatorades waiting for them and would all be standing by to receive them. It was kind of a useless gesture, just to remind them that they were not alone, and they did the same for us.

After one firefight in which a couple Rangers got blown up by grenades, we had to clean out the vehicles and get them ready for the next mission, which could be at any moment; the task force killing machine would grind on no matter what. My guys got out the bleach and some brooms. Thick pools of dark congealed blood were in the back of the Stryker. It was the blood and gore of our fellow Rangers injured in combat. I picked up pieces of skin with my hands and threw them in the Dumpster. Body armor was lying around, completely soaked through with blood. We cleaned everything up, and the war continued.

As horrible as it is to see your teammates hurt, the deployment was really a dream come true for any special operations guy who wanted to be in the fight. In the past, Rangers would train for years and years, hoping for one single mission. Now we were doing two or three a night.

One night, we stopped in the middle of a street and dropped ramp. Assault teams began moving into position. Then came the distinctive *snap-snap* that I knew was a suppressed SR-25. It was Kase, shooting two terrorists who had been up on the roof and about to ambush our assault teams. When the assaulters got up on the roof, they found rifles and those football-shaped Russian hand grenades. Snipers saved a lot of lives that night. Ended a couple, too.

Another time I was on radio guard while our sister platoon was out on a mission in Tal Afar. Predictably, they got into a firefight with the enemy. Our company commander, Captain Landers, was sitting in front of his computer working on some paperwork when the air force JTAC stepped in and told Landers that 2nd Platoon had just gotten hit. Landers calmly turned on the ISR feed and began listening to the radio traffic. He asked the JTAC one or two questions, then just watched. To the casual observer, that may have seemed callous, but it wasn't. He trusted his guys and he trusted their planning.

Back at Benning, when he got promoted out of his job and had to move on, he laid a piece of advice on us about leadership: "Make only the decisions that only you can make." Landers didn't have to micromanage his soldiers because he knew they were trained, competent, and prepared. I learned something from his example. He was also a great officer.

We smoked quite a few bad guys that summer, but we captured many more alive. They ended up in one of those "JSOC secret prisons" or so-called black sites that were reported on by the press. These were American-run detention facilities for terrorists we caught. Here, they were interrogated and pressed to give up information about their cohorts. We had to pull guard duty in there once in a while, and we all hated it. The detainees were blindfolded, flex-cuffed, and put into open cells. We detained a lot of innocent bystanders as well; these people were left alone and out-processed in a few days.

In time, I came to learn the methodology of the interrogators, all of whom were contractors, to my knowledge. Basically, they would have the uncooperative detainees put in stress positions in which they were not allowed to sit down or to sleep—that much I saw myself. Then the interrogators would simply lie to them and tell them that they could go free if they dimed out their buddies, which they almost always did. Once or twice, I was pulling guard duty and heard the female interrogator getting a little handsy with an uncooperative terrorist. I'm sure our government would deny that any of this ever happened, but we all knew about it.

Later on, my privates who pulled guard duty without my presence told me that the interpreters encouraged these young Rangers to physically abuse the detainees. I outright ordered these soldiers not to participate in any such activity. Our command was already lecturing us about being mindful of perceptions and how they could lead to a strategic defeat. Abu Ghraib cooked off, and I told these young Rangers that in no shape or form should they get involved, and if someone told them to do it, they should come get me. It never came to that, though.

We were running on fumes by September, everyone tired and stressed out. Kapacziewski and Fleming had been evaced to Walter Reed back in the States and were going to be okay, although they'd taken serious shrapnel to their lower extremities. Whether their army careers were over was up in the air. We were informed that we would be standby for TST (time-sensitive targets) up until the very moment we got on our freedom bird home. We were counting the days.

"You know," I told my squad leader around this time, "my goal at this point is simply not to die each day, for a couple more days, until we get home." He laughed and concurred. I suspect that's what we were all thinking.

I remember the fourth anniversary of 9/11, which we observed as a platoon in Iraq toward the tail end of our deployment. Sergeant Van Aalst had decided we should take a moment to remember. He told us that he felt like what we were doing to fight terrorism was about the best thing any of us could do to protect our families back home. While reflecting on the words of our platoon sergeant and platoon leader, I felt awkward later, when our unit chaplain informed us that we were in fact fighting a religious war. My motivations for being there were not religious in nature.

Then another helicopter assault force mission came at us out of no-where, and it wasn't even in our area of operations! They wanted us to go all the way down to Tikrit, which was weird. But a job is a job. We loaded up on 160th MH-60s and flew south and hit the tarmac at the FOB down there. The target was actually just outside the FOB. However, there were no trucks or anything to transport us to the gate, so we were stuck out on the airfield for an hour or so until they finally sent someone. From there, we just stepped over some concertina wire and walked into town.

The streets were empty at night, and we walked a couple blocks, moving tactically, until we reached the target. We breached, and I had my machine gunner pull security down the street from the front door. We confiscated a bunch of shit off target from the SSE, including entire com-puter towers. Once we pulled off target, we walked back onto the FOB, again stepping over the concertina. There were no guards or checkpoints or anything.

The problem was that our trucks and drivers were gone again—no one had made any coordinations, and these guys had disappeared. Soon it would be dawn, and everyone knew that 160th didn't fly during the day. If we didn't haul ass across the FOB before dawn, we'd be stuck in that dump for a whole day. We took off running in full kit, carrying computers and various cords in our hands as we raced daylight to the finish line. A mile down a dusty dirt road took us to where the 160th birds were wait-ing, and we piled inside.

We thought it would be our last mission, but of course it wasn't. I was cursing a storm as my Toughbook kept shutting down because it was so hot. From the Stryker hatch, I was getting new grids from higher over the radio and trying to input them into the laptop so I could guide us to our follow-on target. Our assaulters were busy inside another target building while I was doing all this.

"FUCKING GODDAMN PIECE OF SHIT!" I yelled.

But you hold on tight and keep going because that is what Rangers do.

The end did come. We packed up our gear and walked toward the bus that would drive us out to the C-17 waiting for us. Sergeant Van Aalst joked with me, lightening the mood. He play-kicked me, and I grabbed his boot by the heel, making him jump up and down on one foot for a few feet. We were happy to be getting out of there.

Then, just as abruptly as we had arrived in Iraq, the bus drove us out to the airfield, where we boarded a waiting C-17 and flew back to the United States. This was deployment life for a lot of guys. Train up, deploy, then turn around and come home, thrown right back in with general pop as if nothing had happened.

The day after I got home, I was at a Laundromat, sitting on a table and reading a book. I had thought I was pretty unaffected by the war, but then some guy came up to me and asked, "Isn't there someplace more appropriate that you could be sitting?" I almost punched him in the face right then.

CHAPTER 7

For Every Action, There Is an Equal and Opposite Criticism

I COLLAPSED TO MY KNEES, PULLED DOWN TOWARD THE earth by the rucksack I wore on my back. I was in my early twenties but felt like I was an old man. The wind blew across the straw-colored grass at Camp Mackall and brushed over my face. My feet were a bloody mess, one of my knees was blown up like a beachball, and I had another open wound on my back where my rucksack frame had cut the shit out of me.

At that moment, I knew that I was mentally and physically done. I hadn't taken any sort of break since my deployment to Iraq, and I was running on fumes. This was the Special Forces Assessment and Selection (SFAS) course. It was December 2005.

I had made it known to my chain of command that I wanted to go to Special Forces selection, and after that crazy deployment to Mosul, I was supposed to be getting on my way.

I was supposed to be given some time to train up before I went to SFAS, but of course, the army had better ideas, and Van Aalst informed me it wouldn't be happening. Right after arriving back to the States from Iraq, I was sent to Walter Reed for two weeks to watch out for the 75th's casualties who were there, to make sure they were being taken care of.

The moment I arrived back at Benning, I was told that I would be participating in airfield seizure exercises before starting SFAS later that month.

We jumped on an airfield in South Carolina. When my parachute opened, I breathed a sigh of relief and looked down. I was expecting the pitch-blackness of night, but instead, there was a raging inferno beneath me! An entire field had been set on fire. It turned out that our colonel did that to simulate pre-assault fires. Thankfully, there was a pretty good crosswind, and I could see that I wouldn't be landing in the fire. Actually, I was being blown out over a parking apron on the airfield, on a collision course with a bunch of F-16 fighter jets laid out on the tarmac.

I was desperately trying to pull a slip and steer my parachute, but those T-10C round parachutes go where they want to go. I held my breath as my feet passed just over a generator and I landed about ten feet in front of the fighter jet. Getting up on a knee with my parachute harness still on, I smiled to myself. They didn't come much closer than that!

Then another Ranger came flying down out of nowhere, scraped up against the wing of the jet, and got his parachute tangled in the sidewinder missile mounted to the side. I ran over and tried to help him; then we put our weapons into operation and moved out to our respective assembly areas. The airfield was a total mess, with dudes landing all over the place. Some guys got seriously hurt—one dude even came down on top of a hangar.

After hitting the assembly area, I linked up with the rest of my platoon, and we commandeered a Ryder truck we found on the airfield and drove the platoon closer to our objective. When we got out, we made contact with the enemy, and I got my machine gunner into action, putting a rapid rate of blank fire on the enemy role players while the assaulters bounded forward.

The day we finished airfield seizures, I got on a plane and flew to the beautiful Fayetteville, North Carolina, where SFAS is run out of Fort Bragg and, more specifically, Camp Mackall. It was raining as I took a taxi onto the base with the two duffel bags of gear I had thrown together in a rush out the door at Benning. I had packed the wrong boots, and before long, my feet had turned into slabs of ground beef on the course.

The Special Forces Assessment and Selection course is four weeks long and consists of both individual and team events. In SFAS, you find a lot of events similar to those in RIP, like land navigation and ruck marching, but the way the course is designed is very different. They are selecting a different type of person for Special Forces. While RIP looks for the perfect private, SFAS looks for a self-motivated individual who can think on the fly and is comfortable working in uncertain environments. I'll give you an example.

The first week we were doing two events a day, a run, a ruck march, an obstacle course, whatever. One day they woke us up in the middle of the night for a third event. As on all the other events, we were to move an undetermined distance for an undetermined time. Guys were already grumbling at this change from the normal schedule. We took off ruck marching into the night. We followed the orange cones, as instructed: They simply led us around the block at Camp Mackall, and we finished in a few hundred meters, near the auditorium. Then the cadre asked us to drop our rucks and remove a single item—our tennis shoes, which should have been in our rucks because that item was on our packing list. Afterward, we were dismissed back to the barracks. It sounds stupid, but I watched six or seven guys quit that night because they were so freaked out by that event and the uncertainty of it. It wasn't the physical activities that did them in, it was not knowing what was going to happen next.

The last week was team week, in which you were put together with other candidates. Every morning you were given a bunch of odd items that you had to transport from point A to point B, usually by lashing them together into some kind of contraption. After moving that thing across Camp Mackall, you got to ruck march another ten klicks, eat an MRE for lunch, and then receive some new items and do it all over again until dusk.

All the while you were wearing your ruck and carrying the additional weight of the items you were given to move, ammo cans, barrels, or whatever the hell else.

It was the sixth or seventh day of team week when I tripped and fell in the field after stepping in a hole. I had hit a wall that I never wanted to admit existed. I was exhausted but struggled to my feet and chased after the other Special Forces candidates. After this, we all thought we were finally finished with SFAS and would be going home for Christmas.

Instead, they woke us up for another ruck march over an undetermined time and undetermined distance. I quickly lost sight of all the other candidates in the dark. I walked with my head down, freezing cold, all through the night. At one point, I stopped and slammed down an MRE I had smuggled out with me. The sun eventually came up and revealed the frost-covered ground. I'd done a lot of ruck marches by this point, and I estimated the distance to be about twenty-five miles. By the end, my joints made me feel like the Tin Man in *The Wizard of Oz*.

I was selected to attend the Special Forces Qualification Course, and if I graduated, I would become a Green Beret. They wanted me to be a Special Forces weapons sergeant and learn Arabic. Go figure. I was excited to have the chance to learn some new skill sets, to work in a small-team environment, and hopefully be granted more responsibility and autonomy in Special Forces than I had in the Rangers.

I flew back to Benning, dropped off my crap, and found out that my unit was on Christmas leave. No one was tracking me at Benning, so I just left and went home to New York, coming back when my unit returned from leave. It was a couple weeks of vacation that I really needed at that point.

Back in those days, guys who went to Special Forces selection from Ranger Battalion were usually treated like shit. Organizations like Ranger Battalion are like organisms that aggressively self-perpetuate and deploy antibodies against any potential threats. Soldiers who were going to Special Forces would be fired from their job, stuck in the mail room, basically shat upon for betraying the unit.

I was very fortunate in that I was allowed to remain as a gun team leader in weapons squad and train with my platoon, which was exactly what I wanted to be doing. Our battalion would remain on Fort Benning and begin training up for their next deployment over the next few months. I had a start date to begin the Special Forces Qualification Course but delayed it a few months so that I could do the entire training cycle with my squad before the guys deployed to Afghanistan. I was in a great squad and in a great platoon.

We really did some fantastic combat training in the run-up to that deployment, but there was also a tough pill to swallow. When you do hard, realistic training, the kind of training that soldiers need to prepare for combat, you will have training injuries. Sooner or later, you are going to have a training death, which seems to happen several times a year in the Ranger regiment. There is an inherent risk in what Rangers do, one that can never be mitigated if our country is truly preparing our young men for war. That said, there are some deaths that are avoidable.

During a battalion physical training event, the four companies in 3/75 were pitted against one another in competition. Out on a field near the officers' housing quarters on Fort Benning (many of you will recall that neighborhood from the Mel Gibson film *We Were Soldiers*), we were tasked with moving heavy equipment like sandbags from one side of the field to the other. The Ranger platoons also had to manually move a light medium tactical vehicle (LMTV), which is a medium-sized army transportation vehicle. There were fast ropes tied off to the bumper so that Rangers could pull the truck while others pushed from behind.

I immediately saw the problem with this, as I'm sure others did, too. A few minutes into the exercise, a kid who had been pulling the rope went down and then went under the tires. The guys pushing from behind had no way of knowing that he had fallen. Medics raced up to work on the young Ranger, but there wasn't much they could do. We all stood on that field that day, the entire battalion, and watched that kid die. Sometimes Rangers die in training, usually from parachute accidents, maybe aircraft crashes, maybe getting shot accidentally, but to be killed during routine physical training is unheard of.

They had us form up, and the entire battalion quietly jogged back to the 3/75 compound in formation. When we got there, Alpha Company broke off, and our first sergeant led us down to the small field in between our barracks. He said we were going to have a moment of silence to pray to God or talk to whoever the hell we talked to at times like this for the soldier who had been run over. We took a knee and had a few moments of silence. Then we went back to work as if nothing had happened.

Some members of my platoon were quietly (and not so quietly) pissed off about what had happened. My platoon leader angrily yelled that he would have been fired if he had ever done something so fucking stupid as to get a kid killed during physical training. I had a conversation with the other team leader in my squad, Alex, later that day, in which he rightly stated that our colonel and battalion headquarters made these decisions and as he put it, "Well, they can't blame this one on some private or some team leader."

One day, we were out at the kill house. It is a specially made structure that simulates interior rooms where soldiers can practice clearing with live ammunition. I led my fire team through, and to my surprise, Sergeant Van Aalst said we'd done the best out of the platoon. I couldn't tell if he was joking at first. To be honest, I was holding a grudge against Van Aalst for a lot of stuff that had happened in sniper section. In reality, he was watching over me and taking care of me in his own way, but I couldn't see through my anger. Looking back, I wish I had.

While we were out there, we got an unexpected visit from Sergeant Kapacziewski. He came limping out to the shoot house with his crutches. His foot was still severely injured from the fragmentation grenade that had detonated in his Stryker, but he was on the path to recovery with all the determination of a hard-core Ranger. Never once did he seem to doubt that he would be coming back to Ranger Battalion and putting boots to asses again.

Kapacziewski told us that due to his prolonged recovery time, he would not be able to deploy to Afghanistan with the platoon, but he would definitely be joining the platoon on the deployment after that. I was shocked. Here was Kap, nearly with tears in his eyes because he wasn't able to deploy with us, basically apologizing to his platoon for not being there. What do you even say about a guy like that? I've never met anyone who had more heart than Kap. America is damn lucky to have soldiers like him.

I had grown quite close to the platoon by now. I had a camaraderie with these guys that I had never found in sniper section, and part of me didn't want to leave. However, when you look at the army over a longer time horizon, all of us are leaving. Platoons do not stay intact for a decade or even for a year. Personnel are always coming and going. Many of those Rangers would get out of the army. Some would go to Delta Force. Some would drop flight packets. One or two would go on to become officers. I and one other guy went to Special Forces.

Sergeant Van Aalst called a platoon formation as I was emptying my locker and packing everything inside my badass mid-nineties Saturn. The Glory Boys gathered around my sweet ride while Van Aalst gave a short speech thanking me for my service and for being the type of dude who always got the job done without bitching and moaning about it. They then presented me with a plaque that thanks me for serving with the Glory Boys and has a few deployment pictures in it. That plaque hangs above my computer as I write this.

When it was my turn to talk, I told the platoon that when I first got there, I would hear them talking about how they were the best platoon in the regiment. I'd dismissed that at the time as a bunch of bullshit. Every platoon in the regiment brags like that. However, having served with the platoon in both combat and training, I'd had a change of heart. "You should tell people that you are the best platoon in the regiment, and know it, because it's the truth," I told them.

With my shit packed in my car, I shook hands with everyone, said my goodbyes, and drove off. The platoon deployed twenty-four hours later, and another twenty-four hours after that, I drove to Fort Bragg, North Carolina, to start the Special Forces Qualification Course that qualifies graduates to become Green Berets.

The Special Forces Qualification Course (or the Q-Course, for short) was ridiculous, fun, challenging, and eye-opening all at the same time. I probably have more stories about that place than Oliver Stone has about Vietnam, but I'll just skip to some of the fun ones from the Weapons Sergeant Course.

The Special Forces Weapons Sergeant Course, also known as the 18-Bravo Course, is an experience that compares to few others in the military. In this course, you learn all manner of killing people, places, and things with a variety of direct and indirect weaponry. Basically, it's a gun nut's wet dream come true. The purpose of the course is to train potential 18Bs in the basics of their job: weapons handling, maintenance, techniques, and employment.

While I carried around a big box full of tools and spare parts wherever I went, legend has it that an 18B needs only one tool to accomplish his job: a big rubber hammer. Weapons sergeants in Special Forces mythology are said to be the dumbasses and/or the angriest guys on the team, which certainly isn't the case, but stereotypes prevail, especially if they include a hint of truth.

We actually got these hammers to take the back trigger plate off the Russian DShK machine gun, but somehow they became the go-to tool for every task and purpose: "Fuck it, dude, just get me the big fucking hammer . . ."

The 18B course is broken down into phases: First you learn how to assemble, disassemble, and conduct functions checks on light weapons. This includes pistols, rifles, submachine guns, shotguns, some sniper rifles, grenade launchers, and machine guns. (I must admit, the MG3 got the best of me, damn Nazi machine gun.)

Next you learn mechanical mortars (60mm and 81mm), before moving on to forward observer tasks and learning how to run a fire direction center. There is also a week of anti-tank and anti-aircraft weapons, which includes familiarization and simulator work. Of course, you get to fire all this stuff out at the range. If you go on YouTube and search for the Special Forces weapons sergeant training video, you will see a really funny satire video, but it is made with real footage from the 18B course. Those guys were my instructors when I went through.

The field training exercise (FTX) was intended to put together all the skills you learned during the 18B course and apply them in a training setting. At some point, the folks running the Q-Course thought it would be even better to combine it with the 18C (engineer) and 18E (communications) students, which was great in theory but led to a bit of drama. (There were also 18D [medics] students, but they were on a longer training track than the rest of us and couldn't be integrated into the FTX.)

While out in the field, we were to simulate an actual combat deployment, conducting base camp operations on an FOB out in the North Carolina wilderness while planning and rehearsing for combat missions that we'd participate in while we were out there.

Our simulated FOB was pretty squared away. We had a mortar pit, a fire direction center, Quonset huts to use as barracks and team rooms, and plenty of Humvees at our disposal. There was a wooden framework as well. The engineer students built that thing over the course of several FTXs. It was a huge lookout tower in the middle of the FOB. I thought it was kind of silly and never went up in it because I was afraid one of the instructors would designate me as a KIA. That tower had sniper bait written all over it.

While we had Humvees, you can see in the picture that we were lacking some of those small luxuries that you take for granted. So, like good SF students, we improvised weapons mounts on the vehicles.

On the first night at the FOB, we got hit by enemy sappers. Pop flares soared over our camp. These were supposed to be simulated mortar fire, but none of us understood that and continued with our business until we were told that we were under attack and needed to hold the line before we got overrun.

The 18B students ran to defensive positions at the concertina wire surrounding the FOB. I ran ammunition and gun oil to machine gunners. Meanwhile, one of our 18B instructors ran around outside our perimeter, yelling, "FUCK YOU, GI—FUCK YOU, GI—FUCK YOU, GI—FUCK YOU, GI—FUCK YOU, GI—FUCK YOU, GI—FUCK YOU, GI—FUCK YOU, GI!" It was some kind of attempt to intimidate us or test our security, I guess.

Eventually, the instructor tripped on the concertina wire and cut himself, so he had to be driven out to the aid station. Before he left, he told me that the reason why our camp was so messed up was because of me, and I had best unfuck it before dawn. This particular instructor had been a Ranger before going to Special Forces, so he expected a little bit more out of me, I suppose. I had never been made patrol leader by the cadre, so I was never actually in charge, but since I was a former Ranger, everything that went wrong was on me. I shrugged and went back to our planning hut.

We were planning to hit a training objective the next day, and our instructors had made the mistake of giving us a grid location for the target.

They also left us alone for the night with our trucks. I quickly organized a recce mission with two 18C students whom I knew, and we rolled outside the wire around midnight to take pictures of the objective, then used them to help plan the mission.

We hit the objective that next morning. Amazingly, we negotiated the maze of woodland trails straight to the target without getting lost. Bread crumbs on a Garmin sure help. Using a GPS system was against the rules, but the first rule of Special Forces is that if you ain't cheating, then you ain't trying. It's right up there with Murphy's Law itself. There was a series of buildings we were to secure, and my assault team quickly took three role players prisoner.

The rest of the assault element showed up as I called in our first phase line. Our war started to deteriorate as we took contact from a machine gunner up in the hills. Organizing an assault line, we crept up through a draw and over a small ridge before bounding forward and "killing" the enemy. From there, we assaulted down to our limit of advance, or LOA. But the real fun was happening inside one of the buildings being cleared by assaulters. An 18E student had taken another enemy prisoner in one of the rooms that his team had cleared.

There are strict guidelines on how to handle detainees. A cadre member told the 18E student to "tag and bag" the prisoner—that is, put a tag on the prisoner with his name on it and bag up any items found on him, so that both the prisoner and his belongings can be sorted through later. The student misunderstood the term, pushed the prisoner into the corner of the room, and "executed" him with Simunition rounds! Thankfully, this was just training, and the role player was only shot with paint rounds.

Back at our FOB, things were not shaking out so well. The 18C cadre up and left: took all of their construction tools and went home. I can't remember exactly what the problem was, but there was a big blowup between the 18B instructors and the 18C instructors about how to run the FTX.

During our after-action review for the mission, one 18B instructor was chewing our ass frontward and back over what a clown show our op had turned into. In the background, you could hear a second instructor riding his ass, egging him with things like "Put 'em in the corner and tag 'em! Do the whole 'vill!" Some of the officers and warrant officers from the Q-Course were there, and I think this may have been the beginning of the end for our 18B cadre.

At the end of the day, the 18B course was memorable. I came to the course having served as a sniper, an anti-tank gunner, and a team leader in weapons squad, but as it turned out, I still had a lot to learn about weapons training and employment. Overall, it was a great experience, even the FTX.

After the AAR, I was conducting an inspection of our assaulters, making sure that everyone's kit was in order, when one of the instructors came into our hut and shut the door. It was the same guy who had tripped over the concertina wire. "What the fuck went wrong out on that objective?" he asked. "You guys looked like a bunch of naked people wearing roller skates locked in a room with the lights turned off. What the fuck?"

You really only get this level of political incorrectness in the military. The same instructor used to call an overweight male student "Sugar Titties," and it only got worse from there. Years later, when I was a student at the hyper-liberal Columbia University, I had an anthropology teacher who was openly Marxist. She said that the U.S. military was a "heterotopia." And you know what? That's exactly what it is, and it is glorious.

The Q-Course includes language training, which I was horrible at; job training, which was weapons, in my case; and small-unit tactics.

The Survival, Escape, Resistance, and Evasion Course (SERE) is fairly notorious at Fort Bragg: During the final exercise, you are in a mock POW camp and put under duress by your captors, who are role players and instructors. They ask us not to reveal too many of the details of the course, so I won't, but I will comment on the liberation of the POW camp, when you are set free after days of sleeplessness, food deprivation, and all sorts of abuse. A lot of guys cried when they ran up the Stars and Stripes. I didn't, but I recall the words of the instructor very well: He told us to salute the flag of the only country that fed us, clothed us, and educated us. That's something that stuck with me, thinking back on the education America gave me both in the public school system and in the military, then later, by paying for my private education in college via the GI Bill. It's hard not to love this country, despite its flaws.

My favorite part of the Q-Course was the final exercise, called Robin Sage. This cumulative exercise infiltrates students into a mock unconventional warfare environment in the fictional country of Pine Land. Students are grouped into twelve-man teams, just like a real Operational Detachment Alpha (ODA), and put into isolation to begin the planning process, which is quite detailed. Day in, day out, planning into the wee hours of the night. They say to never assume, but a military operations order essentially consists of assumptions built upon assumptions, with a lot of blind faith placed upon intelligence information, which is as minimal as it is questionable. But that is true of real life. After 9/11, the ODAs that inserted into Afghanistan walked into a fluid and uncertain environment.

Interestingly, the lead instructor of my Robin Sage team was a master sergeant whom I knew. We had shot together in the All Army shooting competition on Fort Benning when I was a sniper in Ranger Battalion. I was fortunate to have him take me under his wing a bit and help show me the ropes. I had been attending the Q-Course with his son, whom I recognized by his last name on the day I started the course.

In the planning bays, we did what we could to maintain our sanity while drawing up what seemed like a hundred map overlays. In the mornings, I would run the team through battle drills for physical training as well as a refresher for us to hash out our SOPs. One night, one of our team members asked another to borrow an M16 magazine. When he went to retrieve it out of the soldier's web gear, a folded piece of paper came spinning out and landed on the floor. The guy who borrowed the magazine unfolded the note and started laughing. It was a super-detailed hand-drawn cartoon of a male stick figure boning a girl stick figure from behind. There were even veins on the cock.

This was just another one of those weird army moments.

The rest of us were lying in our bunks, cracking up. What the fuck, man? Who was this guy, Patrick Bateman?

But hanging out in the planning bay wasn't for me, so I convinced our team leader (a captain) to take me along on the pilot team. The pilot team is a small forward element that hits the ground first and makes an assessment before the rest of the team arrives. We infiltrated "Pine Land" in a small prop plane, flashed the correct signals to the sixteen-year-old resistance role player who had met us at the airport, and we were off.

That night we met with the underground, sitting in a private residence while role players drank red wine and chastised us for not doing anything to help them, telling us that we were just a bunch of worthless Americans. We had to begin convincing them otherwise. We traveled the underground railroad, staying in another role player's basement, conducting meetings, hashing out tactics, plotting against the enemy, and all that jazz.

After a few days, the rest of the ODA infilled, and we had to try linking up with them in the field. I went into the field and met one of the guerrillas who would walk us into his base. He was fishing on a lake. We exchanged some code words, and we were off. That night, we linked up with the rest of our ODA and were escorted into the G-base. The G-chief gave us some more lectures about how much we sucked. He asked when we were ready to begin training, and I said right away! Let's get this show on the road and kick some Communist ass.

That night was to be our initiation into the tribal culture of the guerrilla group we were trying to work with. Robin Sage is based heavily upon Special Forces unconventional warfare doctrine and also carries the institutional memory of the Green Berets who came before us, notably, the brave men who served alongside the Monteynards in Vietnam; American Special Forces had, and continue to have, a special relationship with the Monteynards. During Vietnam, Special Forces soldiers worked hand in hand with this Vietnamese minority group. Friends of mine, like Green Beret officer Jim Morris, even helped many of them immigrate to the United States after the war. Some of the old-timers were still role players out at Robin Sage when I went through. Those old-school dudes will tell you stories about having to eat rotten turtle meat while wearing loincloths. The role players also made us get initiated by drinking their ceremonial grog.

For those of you thinking about becoming a member of U.S. Special Forces, allow me to impart some practical advice. When it is time to drink the ceremonial grog, do not be the last guy on line, because all of your teammates will simply pretend to be drinking this vinegar concoction, or whatever the hell it really is, and leave you out there flapping, forcing you to man up lest you offend the sensibilities of your hosts. I took one for the team and downed nearly the whole thing by myself.

"Wow, Brother Jack is a man!" one of the female Gs exclaimed. Fuck my life. I staggered off into the wood line and projectile-vomited about five feet into the woods.

Our team leader was a good guy, but I found myself clashing with him, as he was a very straitlaced, by-the-book kind of guy, which is about what you expect from a West Point graduate. I wasn't, and so I volunteered for every mission that we got, just to keep myself out of the G-base and away from all the reindeer games. There were recon missions, sabotage missions, ambushes, secret missions meeting with contacts at church and having handwritten notes passed off to you. I loved the training and had a great time.

On one mission, I learned that I still had a lot of work to do on getting myself out of the Ranger mind-set and into the Special Forces mentality. We had to ambush a truck filled with ammunition that we wanted to recover for our own use. I botched the patrol, the enemy was alerted, and we got into a big firefight (with blank fire). Now the enemy checkpoint was wiped out, which would alert the truck drivers when they arrived. We're fucked! I thought.

Not so, a young soldier on our team informed me. He was an 18X-Ray. These were young people who joined the army and went straight into Special Forces training rather than doing their first stint in the infantry, like I did. Though they were often inexperienced, they hadn't been institutionalized yet, so they came up with outside-the-box solutions more readily. This guy said we should just toss the dead "bodies" in the woods and impersonate the guards ourselves, then take control of the truck when it came through the checkpoint. Well, that's what we did, and it worked perfectly.

Later, I helped set up a drop zone in the middle of the night: A small plane flew overhead and dropped a bundle out of the back ramp, which parachuted down to us and landed in the woods. We did a direct action raid on a small farm where some bad guys were laid up. I did a recon on a dam that we would later "blow up" with explosives. Robin Sage was a hell of a lot of fun. Our final target was to rescue a resistance member and destroy a railroad junction in preparation for a full-scale American-led invasion of Pine Land. This was exactly what the American, British, and French commandos who served in the Jedburgh teams did in Nazi-occupied France prior to D-Day. I had a small three-man element, me and two G's. We infiltrated the target area on the river, going in on a small boat, planting explosives, and then linking up with the rest of the team, who had conducted the hostage rescue mission.

The last day of Robin Sage just happened to be July 4, and what do you know, we had a ton of pop flares, blank ammunition, and other pyro left over from training—in other words, a recipe for disaster. Our instructors threw a party at a house on the river that night. There was a 60mm mortar system set up on the dock, and we were dropping pop flares down the mortar tube. Civilian role players came over and were blasting away with the M249 SAW on full auto with blank ammunition. Residents were cruising by in their riverboats and jet skis, freaking the fuck out over this.

At one point, our team's captain came up to me and said, "Jack, does any of this look right to you?" I paused, hesitant to criticize the party that had been thrown for us. "No, not really, sir." A pop flare went all the way across the river and set some guy's front lawn on fire. A couple students took a boat across with an instructor and stomped the fire out before it could get out of control. We each had a couple beers, got our final counseling from our instructors, and racked out. Robin Sage was over.

A few days later, I was sleeping on my couch when my phone began ringing. I ignored it. Then it rang again, and someone started texting me. Then it rang again. Goddammit, I'm trying to sleep here, I thought. I opened the phone and saw that one of my good friends was trying to get ahold of me. We had been the two weapons sergeants on our Robin Sage ODA. On the phone, he told me that some kind of investigation was going on in regard to our Sage team and that all the other guys were at work, waiting for me.

Son of a bitch. I drove in to work. I believe it was a Saturday because Fort Bragg was basically empty. When I arrived at student company, my entire Robin Sage team was sitting in the wooden gazebo out front. As it turned out, we were under investigation because of our Fourth of July party. Remember that lawn we accidentally set on fire? Apparently, the property was owned by some bigwig Democrat in North Carolina who had complained to Fort Bragg about our shenanigans.

When the investigating officer arrived, he took all of our sworn statements about the party and informed us that we would not be graduating the Q-Course, pending a decision on the matter from the Special Warfare Center. Graduation was in two days, and my family from New York had already shown up at the house I rented with a couple army buddies. I had to inform them that I might not be graduating after all. I think they were all so accustomed to my bullshit by this point that it barely fazed them.

On the day of the ceremony, we learned that we would in fact be graduating. We donned our Green Berets. One of the SWC officers even came out and spoke with my team directly to inform us that these types of wild-ass parties were unacceptable, but now it was time for us to go out and do great things for the U.S. Army. Unfortunately, our three instructors were relieved of duty and lost their jobs, which was too bad, because they were really great guys who had a lot of knowledge to impart to students.

I packed up my stuff in my Toyota pickup and drove off. I was heading to 5th Special Forces Group at Fort Campbell, Kentucky.

CHAPTER 8

The Wedding Crashers

I ARRIVED AT 5TH SPECIAL FORCES GROUP IN 2007. I GOT assigned to 4th Battalion. After 9/11, Donald Rumsfeld had issued a directive that Special Forces was to rapidly expand. The Pentagon, Special Forces Command, and General Parker at the Special Warfare Center complied with this policy decision but in the process ended up violating what are known as the Special Operations Forces Truths, which are as follows:

- <u>Humans</u> are more important than <u>Hardware</u>.

- <u>Quality</u> is better than <u>Quantity</u>.

- Special Operations Forces cannot be mass-produced.

- Competent Special Operations Forces cannot be created after emergencies occur.

- Most Special Operations require non-SOF assistance.

As I had begun to see in the Q-Course, then more so as a member of Special Forces, we were violating all of these so-called truths and continue to do so to this day. We mass-produce young soldiers for these units while turning a blind eye to the massive retention issues. No one wants to ask why hardly anyone stays in these units.

I tried to get out of the 4th Battalion assignment because it was a brand-new battalion that we had to stand up from scratch, so we would not be deploying anytime soon. I was unsuccessful in this endeavor. When I showed up, the ODA teams were filling up with sergeants, but we had no equipment and few officers. We didn't have team rooms and hung out in 5th Group's isolation facility. Our first battalion commander got into trouble and was allowed to quietly retire. He allegedly had classified information on his personal computer and his wife dimed him out to Army investigators during the course of a messy divorce. These types of incidents are rarely reported in the press but they happen just about every day.

I had expected to be the youngest, most inexperienced Green Beret on an ODA filled with salty old sergeants. It turned out that I was one of the more experienced guys and was immediately made the senior weapons sergeant on my team. It was kind of a frustrating mess. In time, weapons and gear floated in, and we began training on Fort Campbell. We all tried to make the best of it.

One advantage of standing up a new battalion is that there is no shortage of training to attend. Personally, I enjoyed combat training and liked learning new things and mastering new skills. It was head and shoulders above garrison life, which was mostly about getting down on your kneepads for the officer class and endless online training modules that are done simply to "check the block" on some spreadsheet that shows you are "T" for trained in some useless administrative task.

I went to the Military Free Fall Course, which, of all the classes I attended in the army, was the most fun. We also got to do off-road driving at AM General, urban driving at Gryphon Group, which is a training program run by a private company in Flordia, live-tissue medical training, shooting courses at Mid-South, which is a privately run marksmanship school, the Glock armorer's course, the SOF armorer's course, and more.

More than once during this period of time, I packed two bags, taking one to a course and leaving the other at my apartment in Clarksville. I would return home from one course, drop my bag, pick up the one I had left behind, and go right back out the door to the next course.

It wasn't all fun and games, though. At the SOF armorer's course in Indiana I went out for dinner with my junior weapons sergeant. I probably had seven glasses of Johnnie Walker Black Label; I don't remember what my junior was drinking. A third student drove us back to our hotel, and my junior decided that it was time for me to go to bed. I said, "Yeah, sure, but I need to brush my teeth." I got up and headed to the sink. My junior was not having it; he had decided that I needed to go to bed right goddamn now! He tackled me from behind, and we both went flying into a corner, wrecking a lamp and a trash can. As we fought each other, he decided to bite down on my shoulder with his teeth. "Ow, you goddamn asshole, what the fuck is wrong with you!" Convinced that I would now go to bed, my junior finally knocked it off and went to his room.

Normally, I would have just shrugged something like that off, but get this: We were done with the course and heading back to Clarksville the next day. My girlfriend was flying in to meet me, and guess who now had a huge bite mark on his shoulder? You could see individual teeth marks, for Christ's sake! Yeah, good fucking luck explaining that to your girlfriend: *Oh, yeah, honey, that was my battle buddy. He had a few too many, tackled me into the corner of a hotel room, and bit me.* I wouldn't believe that shit if someone told me. But by the grace of God, she never noticed the bite mark. This is where being Irish pays off, as it must have blended in with the freckles on my shoulder.

Back at the home station, we got team rooms, and our gear was filtering in, but most important, we got a deployment schedule. We had some great guys on my ODA, but overall, I found 5th Group to be insanely bureaucratic and very conventional in how they did things. The nickname "5th Ranger Battalion" often gets applied to 5th Special Forces Group. It was a sharp contrast from Ranger Battalion, where we had our own compound and did things our own way; 5th Group seemed shackled by Mother Army. Officers and senior NCOs treated it like a conventional unit despite its being organized and equipped for unconventional warfare. This resulted in suboptimal performance, to say the least.

We were also bombarded with asinine online training modules. The modern army has gone completely corporate. Strong leadership has been replaced by statistical analysis and measuring metrics. The sole purpose of soldiers is to provide warm bodies so that officers can claim they command a unit. Their task from day to day is not preparing for war but filling trackers. Soldiers need to be "green" on their tasks at all times. That isn't to say that they need to be technically and tactically proficient; no one cares about that, no one measures that. What is most important is that they have an up-to-date medical profile, their sexual harassment training, their quarterly information security training, their online SERE refresher (where they run around in a bullshit video game, rubbing sticks together to make a fire), and a hundred other completely worthless requirements that do nothing other than help some careerist officer cover his ass. It is a soulless, counterproductive, and cynical approach to leadership that places "qualifications" ahead of readiness.

Dr. Leonard Wong at the U.S. Army War College did a study that found that our soldiers are tasked with so much mandatory training army-wide that leaders don't have any time to train soldiers on their actual jobs. Furthermore, the army tells us to conduct more mandatory training than there are training days on the calendar. But it gets better, because officers are reporting to higher-ups that yes, they are in fact conducting all mandatory training to standard. This is impossible. Every officer in the U.S. Army is sending up false reports. What the army has done is conditioned entire generations of soldiers to feel that it is okay to compromise their integrity, not once but twice. The first compromise is the criminally negligent act of not preparing their men for combat. The second is lying about it.

Let me explain how this works on a team level. Your team sergeant comes into the team room and lectures you all on how you need to have your trackers up to date and be in the green on all assigned admin tasks. He is saying this because his bosses are holding his feet to the fire. So instead of training, troops are busy sitting behind a computer, mindlessly clicking through an online test module from the bullshit army safety center. No one gives a fuck, and no one gives a fuck that no one gives a fuck. It is a military culture of not taking pride in your work. You finish your online training, print out a certificate, hand it to your chain of command, they update the tracker, and your team is "trained" up on the whiteboard.

I understand that running a team is about more than what you see in the recruitment commercials. There are logistics and administrative tasks that need to be handled. Guys need to go to the dentist, soldiers need to understand the Geneva Conventions, but at some point, this shit has gotten completely out of control. I really can't begin to explain how dehumanizing and demoralizing the cynical corporate culture is. More so when, on a daily basis, you hear about our troops being killed fighting our war overseas. Some of us joined the army and took this war seriously. We wanted to win. I never gave a fuck about having a "career" and would have been happy to just be a senior weapons sergeant forever. I mean, when you look at your senior NCOs and see that they are emasculated secretaries for some colonel, you have to ask why the hell would you want to get promoted in the first place?

As an ODA, we were now going into our pre-deployment workup in 2007. We did a HALO/HAHO train-up in Las Vegas and then a few weeks of pre-mission training (PMT) at Fort Knox. HALO and HAHO are both forms of military free-fall parachuting. High-altitude low-opening is when you jump from an airplane at high altitude, up to thirty thousand feet, and deploy your parachute around four thousand feet. In a high-altitude high-opening jump, you deploy your parachute immediately after exiting the aircraft and glide under canopy for long distances, perhaps even across an international border. These are clandestine infiltration techniques designed to insert Special Forces teams into denied areas.

The parachute riggers were good to go, but most of the group support personnel were about as lethargic as you could possibly imagine, supporting no one but themselves. They seemed to expect a bribe of a bottle of whiskey just to get them out of their chairs. Talk about frustrating. At the end of the day, it is the ODA itself that pulls together, works as a team, and ultimately bends if not breaks the rules in order to complete its mission, out of necessity.

A new team sergeant who came to our team before our HALO train-up asked that I refer to him as Michael Bluth, the name of the main character in *Arrested Development,* which he got me watching on DVD while we were in Iraq. He told us that no one can be trusted outside our team room doors. He wasn't mistaken.

Finally, our deployment date rolled around. Guess where we were heading? My old stomping grounds: Tal Afar.

ODA 5414 deployed to Iraq in the winter of 2009. It was our first operational deployment. We hit the ground at FOB Sykes and conducted a relief in place with the ODA that was on the way out. The outgoing 18B (weapons sergeant) walked me through the situation, taking me to the arms room, the CONEX containers full of ammo, and then introduced me to the Tal Afar SWAT team.

The Iraqi SWAT team members were living in some old Saddam-era bunkers on the FOB, alternating between two shifts, each consisting of a platoon-sized element. One platoon would be at home while the other was in the bunkers, training and waiting for missions. These guys had been selected and trained by U.S. Special Forces, and frankly, I was just the latest cock on the block to take them under my wing. Inside the bunker, we met the SWAT team leaders, smoked cigarettes, and played get-to-know-you. Iraqis will ask you what your birthday is and be impressed when you tell them the month and day. They usually only know what year they were born, such are the medical records in that part of the world. I met Salim, the SWAT commander, and his right-hand men, Qasim, Faisal, and Shahab. They turned out to be great partners and friends. Unfortunately, the other platoon turned out to be subpar.

My ODA's compound consisted of a series of CHUs, or containerized housing units, set on cinder blocks in long rows; two CHUs could be welded together, and this was the case for our arms room, our loadout room, the operations center (OPCEN), and a couple other structures. The mechanics had a large tent where they could work on vehicles, and we had a small fleet of Humvees and MRAPs and some civilian cars and trucks for driving around the base and to the chow hall. We also had a firepit, around which many a party was had.

On our initial ride through Tal Afar that deployment, I recognized many sights, even though it was my first time being there in daylight. The city was transformed. Four years prior, you could not set foot in Tal Afar without getting into a firefight; now we could walk around the market without body armor and just a pistol on our hip. Finally, a positive counterinsurgency story!

Sure, five years later, the American presence would no longer exist, and the entire city would be taken over by ISIS and its population enslaved by jihadists, but that's another story. Let's bask in our successes for a few moments, shall we?

While we drove down the streets on that initial ride-along, I was up in the gun turret behind the .50-cal. I silently observed several collapsed houses where the roof and individual floors had pancaked on top of one another, concrete left crumbling under the hot Iraqi sun. These were the houses we had called in AC-130 strikes on four years ago. There was no reconstruction for Iraq, and this became even more evident when we began making trips in Mosul.

The enemy situation had changed drastically. By this time AQI had been brought to their knees. The special operations task force had pushed their shit in, but that's something you won't hear much about in the press. The task force I'd been a part of had in fact helped quell the insurgency, and now there was a great opportunity to consolidate gains, build infrastructure, and enable good governance in Iraq. Sadly, none of this was to happen. Before we left, our commanders had told us that our mission success would be based on how few combat operations we'd done, because now we were to transition authority over to the Iraqis, especially with a new Status of Forces Agreement (SOFA) being signed. This opinion changed when we hit the ground, and our chain of command began pushing us to submit CONOP (concept of the operation) plans for combat missions.

Everyone knew that Obama would have us withdraw from the country. In the end, the administration uprooted the entire infrastructure that had been built in-country, including vast intelligence networks, something that had never been done before. I and many others quickly deduced that this was a bad idea. Yes, the Iraqis needed to step up, and none of us wanted to be their colonial masters, but the reality is that the country wasn't ready. The government did not function and was rife with corruption. However, orders were orders, and during this time, the army put in a diligent effort to make it look like things were good in Iraq.

Commanders on the ground were being actively encouraged to send up false reports to higher, making the situation on the ground look much rosier than it was. A policy decision had been made from up high, and now the foot soldiers in this war had to make reality fit into the bubble that our politicians had created back stateside.

When I mentioned to my team leader that if we left, Iraq would become a terrorist state like Afghanistan in 2001, my captain said, "Well, that is just stating the obvious."

We all knew.

While AQI had been all but put out of business, another enemy was beginning to rear its head. They called themselves the Islamic State of Iraq (ISI) and were based out of Syria, where we couldn't touch them. The group consisted of former Baath Party members like Al-Douri and Saddam Hussein's daughter, visions of the old regime dancing in front of their eyes like sugarplum fairies. Their primary tactic was to attack only coalition forces in Iraq, rather than alienating the locals, like AQI, which was basically a glorified death cult. The enemy was learning.

So, we came up with a training schedule for the SWAT team, getting them out on the range shooting, running through the shoot house, doing medical classes, and all of that good army training, while we put together targeting packets. Soon the intel that the previous team had developed on a terrorist in Mosul named Abu Gahni began to come together.

If you want to catch a terrorist, you have to locate him first, and the one place where you know he will be is at his own wedding.

By 2009, insurgents and terrorists in Iraq had gotten fairly wily. The enemy had learned from their engagements with U.S. special operations forces, and they were taking increasingly sophisticated measures to try to trip us up and avoid our raids. So, when we found out that a big-name terrorist was getting married, and where the marriage would be held, a lot of uncertainty was taken out of the equation. This moron *had* to be at his own damn wedding.

Once we had solid intel on the date and location of the wedding, we rolled into Mosul that afternoon in our Humvees, heading toward the target house. One difference between my time with the Ranger regiment and my new job was that, as a Special Forces team, we were always partnered with our Iraqi counterparts, in this case a SWAT team from Tal Afar. With a platoon-sized element of Iraqis, our ODA snaked the vehicles through the flooded back alleys of Mosul.

The city had taken a beating since I was there four years before. Mosul had looked like Beirut back in the eighties, with a number of collapsed buildings and structures covered in bullet pockmarks. Mosul had always been one of the most violent cities in Iraq, and now the enemy was building bigger IEDs to defeat the armor packages that coalition forces had put on our vehicles to protect us from the previous IEDs. Like I said, the enemy was learning and adapting.

We navigated our way through the labyrinth of back roads on the north side of the city. The streets were partially flooded with brown water; rocks and pebbles gathered in clusters on the roadsides. Kids looked at us with a mix of curiosity and shock as we slow-rolled past them, searching for the target building.

As silently as possible, we pulled up in front of the objective building and unassed the vehicles. We quietly opened doors and crept down the street in broad daylight.

I was an assault team leader, taking four Iraqi SWAT troops through the front door. We quickly pushed through the open front gate into the inner courtyard. It was all over in a flash, fairly anticlimatic, which is the way it should be. If the enemy has time to react to your raid, then you've lost the element of surprise and, with it, the advantage. Special Forces soldiers like to engage the enemy at a place and time of their choosing, rather than letting the enemy dictate the terms of the fight.

We flooded the compound with assaulters, clearing rooms, sending men scurrying up ladders to the roof, locking down every doorway and potential avenue of escape. The fighting-age men had guns trained on them and were flex-cuffed in short order.

Abu Gahni, the terrorist we were after, was in the courtyard with the other men. The wedding ceremony was complete, and at this point the men would have begun drinking. The dowry (a lethargic goat that sat panting in the courtyard for the duration of our stay on the objective) would have been killed and a meal cooked. Instead, Abu Gahni was put on the ground; a Glock 19 pistol was found tucked into the waistband of his suit.

In the back room, the women were holding court separately. A lone Iraqi SWAT team member stood sentry in the doorway but wasn't interacting with the women in any way. The SWAT guys were scared to death of women, it seemed, but I suppose that was better than the opposite—we never had to deal with them acting inappropriately toward women on target.

The bride broke out in tears as we secured the home, and the Iraqi women began screaming at us. As we soon found out, the bride was only sixteen years old. We left the women alone and didn't put our hands on any of them—we prefer not to, and it is additionally offensive to the culture, so we avoid it.

But it gets better. We'd crashed the wedding at the eleventh hour. Had we delayed any longer—had we gotten lost down one of the side streets, for example—the terrorist would have consummated the marriage. We crashed the wedding just in time to save a teenage girl's virginity from this terrorist asshole. This was how our ODA got the name "The Wedding Crashers."

While one of our ODA members questioned the terrorist, the bad guy said to him through an interpreter that if we knew who he was, then we knew what he had done—killing people and setting off IEDs for cash and for his terrorist cause. "Just put a bullet in my head now," he begged. No dice. Under the recently signed Status of Forces Agreement, he would be sent directly to an Iraqi prison. After flex-cuffing the terrorist, we decided to haul in his old man as well. His father was involved in his son's criminal enterprise on some level, though we weren't sure exactly how.

I grabbed the father under his arm, helped him up, and led him through the gate and out into the street, where our vehicles were waiting. Our source sat in one of the Humvees, wearing a scarf around his face. When I led the old man in front of the source, he silently nodded. This was the guy. The old man just laughed; he looked back at me and chuckled. I stood him next to a wall while we prepared to load all of the detainees on our vehicles. Abu Gahni's father was totally nonchalant about the whole affair, as if it were all a joke. I couldn't figure him out.

Back at our base, FOB Sykes in Tal Afar, I sat down in the bunker where our Iraqi SWAT team was quartered. We were just sitting around, smoking cigarettes and generally shooting the shit. One of them mentioned to me that the "old man," the terrorist's father, had killed his cousin, who had been a police officer. This piqued my interest, and I asked him what he was talking about.

Back in 2005, Tal Afar had been a straight-up terrorist sanctuary. Recall my previous experiences in Tal Afar, when I was in Ranger Battalion. Back during the bad old days of Tal Afar, which in 2009 was fairly peaceful, the father had been issuing fatwahs on people and was known as an accomplished insurgent sniper. One guy told me that the old man could take the cherry off of a cigarette from a thousand meters away. Surely an exaggeration, but it showed how afraid of him they were. Abu Gahni's father had murdered a lot of people, including policemen, and the citizens of Tal Afar had no sympathy for this guy.

I walked into the back of the bunker where the old man was sitting on the floor under guard by the ISWAT team members. He was looking around and smiling at everyone with not a care in the world. I asked him some questions through our interpreter about his past activities. I told him that I had heard he was a pretty good sniper. He just laughed and threw up his handcuffed hands. "No, no, mister, you got it all wrong." He was like a serial killer. A psychopath.

We used to visit the prison in Tal Afar every so often to see what was up. The terrorist we'd captured in Mosul was always there, even months later, still wearing his wedding suit. The Iraqi warden kept him hand-cuffed to the bars of his cell in the standing position so he could never sit down. Don't blame Americans for this sort of mistreatment—we were completely hands-off due to that Status of Forces Agreement I mentioned previously. We would have imprisoned him humanely, but what the Iraqis did to each other was their business. As American soldiers, we could ex-press disagreement to our host nation counterparts, but we had no power to do anything about it.

Sadly, the prison warden was himself killed by an Al-Qaeda suicide bomber who showed up at his front door one night during this same six-month deployment. Took the warden's entire family in the blast, everyone except a second cousin. The cousin felt that the attack had been directed against his family by Shias because they were Sunni. To get revenge, he went into the market with an AK-47 and started gunning down Shias in cold blood until the Iraqi military showed up and wasted him.

This is the insanity that is Iraq.

Now, how about the terrorist's father, the old man? He had murdered too many innocent people in Tal Afar to be allowed to live. I never saw him again after we dropped him off at the prison that first time. I later heard through the grapevine that the Iraqis disappeared him out in the desert somewhere.

In 2009, the situation on the ground in Iraq was getting increasingly convoluted. The amount of bureaucracy you had to go through to get anything done was off the charts. Giving the Iraqis medical training in a classroom on our base required a memo from a colonel; the conventional American troops did not like interacting with my ISWAT team; every col-onel in the country had a big idea about how they were going to win the war. One unfortunate statement from our high headquarters was that we needed to get them all the information they needed to win the war. How the hell was a Special Forces staff office going to win a war? We needed their support, but from their perspective, we (the maneuver element) had to support them (the staff element) in their effort to achieve total victory in Iraq. Man, this shit was getting weird.

As Colonel Hunter Gathers said in *The Venture Bros.*, our homecoming queen—the army, in this case—"got fat on red tape and bureaucratic Big Macs." Hunter Gathers would say we joined with "high ideals and pie-eyed dreams of saving the world from baddies. But what did we get? Hot bureaucracy poured in our laps."

Even veteran Special Forces NCOs were saying that it was the most difficult operational environment they had ever seen. The difficulty was twofold: By this stage in the war, the United States military had a heavy hand in Iraq, while, simultaneously, the Iraqi government was attempting to exert some semblance of authority. What this meant for soldiers who did the day-to-day grunt work was that they had to navigate an increasing level of bureaucracy from both the U.S. and the Iraqi government.

Seriously, needing a memo signed by a colonel to train your own soldiers? It was getting ridiculous. This was the situation that led the long-range surveillance company (LRSC) unit stationed on our FOB to approach our ODA and ask for some assistance. At this time in Iraq, it was required that Iraqi soldiers "action" objectives. In other words, U.S. soldiers were no longer permitted to kick in doors and shoot terrorists unless they were already coming under fire. For this reason, they asked my ODA for some support during their upcoming area reconnaissance mission.

I was happy to volunteer, as I had established a good rapport with our ISWAT unit and felt that we weren't seeing enough action on our own missions. It was decided that I and one other SF soldier from our team, along with five ISWAT members, would accompany LRSC on their five-day mission out in the desert. We hit the road in about a dozen Humvees.

This was a little different from how most of us traditionally think of LRS units, but as I've said before, everyone has had to adapt as the

GWOT has changed forms, me included. Area recon with our CF brothers isn't really a Special Forces mission, but as it turned out, this mission was well worth our time.

I had forgotten how wild young infantry dudes were, but I really enjoyed working with them. One aspect I missed as a Special Forces weapons sergeant was working with and leading privates in a fire team. It was the best job I ever had, before or since. These kids were also lucky to have a strong platoon sergeant to hold them back a little.

While the platoon leader was off conducting leadership engagements in the small villages that we traveled to, I took the opportunity to walk around and meet the locals. It turned out to be a great opportunity for me to introduce my Iraqi SWAT team members to the villagers. You see, these villages are spread out like an archipelago through the desert—known locally as the *jeezera*, which actually means "island"—and serve as ancient smuggling routes for those crossing the Syrian border.

Many of the villagers knew nothing of the Iraqi military, and what they did know probably wasn't good. Giving them some face time with ISWAT guys who could help repel terrorists and criminals was definitely a good thing.

The big find on this mission started with a young PFC identifying a massive cache while we were making a recce of one of the many wadis that crisscrossed the desert. I was probably a little reckless when I jumped into the pit with an LRSC sergeant and started digging up the weapons. My ISWAT guys stood a safe distance back, making little explosive motions with their hands to try to warn me. We ended up digging out dozens of AK-47s, PKMs, three mortar tubes, Egyptian grenades, a couple SVD sniper rifles, and detonation cord smuggled from India. I wished that I had brought more demo—all I had was my drop-kicked Claymore mine, which wasn't adequate for the job. We ended up calling in EOD to demo the entire cache.

It went up as a bright flash of light in the night.

———

The night I got back from the LRS mission, I walked back onto our compound and began stowing my gear. I was the resident gun and gear geek on our team. I had all the cool stuff and spent a ridiculous amount of my own money on high-end stuff I wanted, like the Kifaru rucksack I took out into the desert with me. Money well spent, as far as I was concerned. I still have it today.

Piece by piece, I doffed my gear and stuck it in the cubbyhole in our loadout room. My plate carrier had a basic load of 5.56 ammunition for my M4, shotgun shells for the twelve-gauge I carried for ballistic breaching, five flashbangs, two frag grenades, a CamelBak bladder, flex cuffs, a thermite grenade, a pen flare, and some other odds and ends. On my pistol belt were: my Safariland holster for an issued M9 Beretta pistol, a med kit, four spare mags, a spare M4 mag, and a small Escape & Evade kit pouch on the back of the belt. On my person, I had taken to stashing some other items, including a razor blade and a handcuff key. All the normal gear without the rucksack weighed ninety pounds or so.

Liberated of all that kit, I walked into our OPCEN to check in and let the guys know that I was back. Our warrant officer and several other team members were sitting around shaking their heads. The rest of our team had made a run to Mosul for a key leader engagement, in army speak, which was a meeting with an Iraqi general. On the way back, they'd radioed that they had hit a pothole and blown out a tire. "A pothole! Are you fucking kidding me! We drive that route all the time, how the hell did those idiots hit a pothole!"

About half an hour later, our warrant officer had gone to his CHU to go to sleep. The second his head hit the pillow, he had a realization. "Pothole" was an operational code word that our headquarters element had come up with to say over the radio if a specific event occurred. "Pothole" was the code for an IED! We all thought they had hit a literal pothole, a hole in the road. Our teammates had gotten blown up.

Thankfully, no one was seriously injured. Our teammates got their Humvee rolling again after a tire change and soon arrived back at our base. My junior 18B looked drunk. He wasn't; it was due to the blast overpressure from the explosion, which had knocked him unconscious for a few seconds. Our medics kept a close eye on him to make sure he didn't have a serious concussion. My junior, ever the smartass, put a Band-Aid on his helmet where a piece of shrapnel had hit him after that. We also wisely changed our code word for an IED strike to something less confusing.

Every deployment is a little different; no two are exactly the same. This one was longer than my deployments with Ranger Battalion. We were in Tal Afar for six months, though we probably should have stayed a full year. Special Forces missions require long-term engagements and building relationships with the locals. By the time we were getting the hang of things, we were redeploying back home.

As a Special Forces soldier, you come to have a very odd relationship with your own chain of command out of necessity. Your loyalties are with the mission and with your teammates. You need space and wide left and right limits to accomplish your mission, but your chain of command does little for you aside from imposing unnecessary bureaucracy. I could go on and on about this subject, but in short, higher headquarters would demand more and more "products" from the ODAs. The burden of creating these products becomes so heavy that you end up finger-drilling them because you are overtasked between your real-life important tasks and the bullshit that you are forced to do by an increasingly email-driven organization.

I'll give you an example. One of the responsibilities I had was to send up "FID pics" every week. They wanted pictures of me training the Iraqis every day (in the proper uniform, of course) to prove that I was doing my job. I was the senior trainer and advisor to a hundred-man SWAT team, and every day that we were not conducting combat operations, we were training. But since I apparently couldn't be trusted to do my job, I had to send these pictures. I sent the same ones every week—some random pictures I'd found on the shared drive from a previous ODA training the SWAT guys. The fact that no one ever caught on to this is proof that no one even looked at the damn things. The ODAs produce more products than higher can ever process. The whole exercise just turned into tick marks on a ledger that goes on to a PowerPoint slide for a staff officer to look at for .05 seconds.

In one particularly egregious example, an ODA (not any of us) deployed to Iraq and sent a concept of the operation (CONOP) to higher in which the enemy was described as "sand niggers." This report went all the way up to CENTCOM before anyone noticed the use of racial slurs. CENTCOM, located in Tampa, Florida, is the highest regional command that encompasses the Middle East. Yes, the use of racial slurs was disturbing, but what I found more unsettling was the fact that no one actually read the fucking reports that were getting sent up the chain of command. The reports were just busywork, and everyone treated them as such.

In the past, the model of unconventional warfare was that ODAs would deploy to austere environments and operate in a decentralized manner. This is unlikely to ever happen due to the army's culture of zero defects and risk aversion, along with the evolution of modern telecommunications technology, which allows high-ranking officers to reach all the way down the chain of command to micromanage the smallest ground elements in combat. Meanwhile, deployed Special Forces sergeants like me end up working as company commanders or battalion commanders, which replaces the jobs of captains, majors, and colonels. Suffice to say this does not sit well with our military orthodoxy. Special Forces is a great idea and one that is completely antithetical to army culture.

I always loved reading books written by my predecessors, and one of my favorites is *War Story* by Special Forces captain Jim Morris. You can replace Vietnam for Iraq and replace the word "Communist" with "terrorist," and our two experiences in Special Forces, separated by fifty years, are nearly identical. The big change is how technology has allowed higher to micromanage the man on the ground.

But I don't mean to be overly negative here. I was a Special Forces weapons sergeant, and I had a hundred indigenous troops to train and work by, with, and through to defeat the enemy. I also had some great teammates helping me with this effort, such as my junior weapons sergeant and, later, our senior communications sergeant, James Hupp. It was a terrific experience for me to be able to draft the entire training plan and execute it, and I am grateful to our team sergeant for allowing me to do so. Instead of micromanaging me, Bluth afforded me the opportunity to make mistakes, knowing that I would learn from them.

With Tal Afar more or less pacified, operations did not come at us hot and heavy, like they did during my last trip to Iraq, and that was probably for the best. We were not a forty-man Ranger platoon, we were a small team, and we took forty-some Iraqi troops on our operations, all of whom we had to run through rehearsals, then spot-check and supervise throughout the mission. Salim, the SWAT commander, was the old man who had served in the Iran–Iraq war, in what we call Desert Storm, and then once again in the 2003 war, all with the "previous regime," as he referred to Saddam's government. I worked closely with Salim and came to respect his advice and judgment. To this day, I extend to Salim the same respect I would to my own father. If Iraq had been run by men like him, that country never would have fallen to the likes of ISIS.

One operation turned out to be quite frustrating for all parties concerned. When we first arrived at FOB Sykes, the outgoing ODA warned us about a target that the special operations task force (that I was previously a part of) kept wanting them to raid a house in Tal Afar over and over. The team would go there, but there were not any bad guys in that home. The ODA kept checking it out, because if they didn't, the task force would send in Rangers to blow down the door and make a big mess in Tal Afar where there didn't need to be one. Every so often, the task force would get a wild hair up their ass about this issue, so we would go into town and have some tea with this family to demonstrate that there were not any bad guys there, then head back to the base.

We continued this tradition. The task force would loudly proclaim that there was a high-value target in the house, and we would roll up the street and have chai with them. The family who lived there had been past victims of terrorism, and many of their men were police officers; as unlikely as it was that they had anything to do with terrorism, the task force kept insisting. Eventually, I found out what was happening: In Tal Afar, they speak a dialect called Turkmani, and the task force had only one Turkmani interpreter, who kept telling them that a voice intercepted by Signals Intelligence (SIGINT) sounded like the voice of a high-level terrorist she had previously heard.

This was another startling example of how the brass accepted the flimsiest intelligence over the word of twelve barrel-chested freedom fighters on the ground. I could see why the task force left a bad taste in a lot of people's mouths: They had a bias toward action, one that wasted resources and was counterproductive over a longer time horizon. They wanted short-term measurable results counted in terms of high-value targets' captured or killed. In some ways, it was reminiscent of officers in Vietnam who wanted specific body counts, thinking that would win the war.

Another boondoggle was called, no shit, Operation Blind Hope (the name was later changed to Black Star). There was a big push from the American side to get the Iraqis to run their own large-scale unilateral combat operations in order to demonstrate that the U.S. presence was no longer needed in Iraq. This took on the form of Blind Hope. The problem was that the Iraqi military approach to operations was either running checkpoints on the road or raiding entire villages in large-scale military operations like the Keystone Cops.

Once they raided a village (one to which they had no ethnic or tribal links, of course), they would pull all the villagers out of their homes and line them up. A "source" wearing a balaclava would then walk down the line, pointing to people: "Guilty, guilty, guilty!" Holy shit, I didn't want to be involved in some half-assed ethnic cleansing, and when our SWAT team was getting pulled into Blind Hope, I strongly resisted it. This was not the type of example we wanted to set for our partner force. Our captain supported my decision and expressed my concerns to higher, which I'm sure didn't endear him to his superior officers.

However, it was the mission that just wouldn't end. It would get shut down, then started up, then shut down again. It dogged us throughout the deployment. At one point, I was to take a Humvee loaded with a few of our ODA members and tons of weapons out into the desert to supervise our SWAT team while they raided a village. I didn't like it but knew that if I were out there, at least I could try to protect our partner force from some of the stupidity. We were also taking a female dog handler and her K9 from a conventional unit, as someone had requested K9 support for this mission. She didn't look pleased when I candidly told her that this was a bullshit mission that would probably get us killed. I began mission planning for what amounted to urban warfare in a town out on Iraq's western border, but then the mission got scrapped again.

On another occasion, I was out at the gate helping the SWAT team rotate back home when the ODA from Mosul came rolling through. They thought I was there to help them find their way and prepare for Operation Blind Hope, but I had no idea it was back on. So much for coordination. We hung out together on our compound for a bit, and then the mission got stood down again.

Despite my protests, the mission did go down, with our SWAT team participating. When they returned, the Iraqis told me what a disaster it had been. The Iraqi officers got them lost driving on paved roads; one colonel even broke down crying. They had zero logistical support, no food, no water, no gasoline. The Iraqi general in charge of the entire operation took leave and went home on the day the mission kicked off, seemingly in order to defer responsibility for its failure. That's just a typical day in the Iraqi military.

Oh, but that's not all, folks. Someone got the bright idea that we should run Operation Blind Hope II! This time a bunch of Iraqi staff officers rolled onto our compound from Mosul to brief me on their plan of action. An Iraqi colonel explained to me that the first operation had been a mess because the enemy saw them coming from a mile away. He got out a piece of paper and a pen to explain how the second mission would work. This time they would drive their convoy down the road toward one village, then, at the last minute, change direction and hit a different village!

"That last mission was like a *Tom and Jerry* cartoon," he told me. "But this time we will surprise them! I learned how to do this in the war college." I think it was at this point that I realized our war in Iraq was unsalvageable and that this country was totally fucked beyond all repair.

Little did I know that there would be not only an Operation Blind Hope II—I mean Black Star II—but also an Operation Black Star III. The war in Iraq was such a damn circus.

CHAPTER 9

The Firepit

IN BETWEEN MISSIONS, WE HAD LOTS OF TIME FOR COM-
bat training and physical training, and I read about twenty books during
that six-month deployment. I brought an Xbox with me but quickly got
bored with it, and then it displayed the Red Ring of Death that says your
Xbox doesn't work anymore, so I threw it in the firepit. Speaking of the
firepit, things got a little out of hand some nights. I don't want to alarm
anyone here, but Special Forces guys do find ways to procure alcohol
while deployed overseas.

It was maybe the second or third day when one of our interpreters, a
Kurd nicknamed Creepy Steve (whom we joked looked like Gollum from
The Lord of the Rings) came and said he was busy with work and couldn't
make it out to the front gate to "pick up the stuff."

You have to understand that being in the army means you're part of a
massive bureaucratic institution and you're a cog in the wheel. You can
walk around an army base all day with a clipboard, pretending to write
stuff down, and no one will say a word to you about it. In the case of being
told to go pick up what I assumed to be illicit contraband, I just nodded
and said, "No problem," as if I knew what was going on.

Steve said I should drive out to the gate to meet some local. Outside
the gate, a middle-age man in a black leather jacket was waiting. He motioned me over. I parked the car and got out, a Glock 19 resting on my
hip, because seriously—was I about to pick up a couple keys of heroin or

something? The older guy had a thick jet-black Saddam 'stache, and his sixteen-year-old son stood nearby in a red and blue tracksuit. The dealer popped open the trunk of his car and displayed his wares.

I was looking at cases of beer, bottles of vodka, and numerous plastic bottles of a mysterious whiskey named Mr. Chavez. I didn't have any dinars or Yankee currency on me, but it turned out that it was prearranged, everything already taken care of. We slid the contraband into my car, shook hands, and the handoff was complete. I had unintentionally stumbled into the Special Forces clandestine ratline of cheap Kurdish whiskey.

Our parties out at the firepit were the stuff of legend. The boys would procure wooden pallets and stack them sometimes six feet high. The flames would leap high into the night sky, to the point where passersby would see the fire licking up above the Hesco barriers that surrounded our compound. One night the guys were setting off pop flares, so I had them enact the base defense plan that I had developed, driving a Mine Resistant Ambush Protected (MRAP) vehicle and parking it behind our gate in case the military police tried to get onto our compound.

The American base commander was always telling us that we needed to take down the American flag that flew over our compound because we were transitioning control of the country to the Iraqi forces. Our Iraqi SWAT team had no issues with us flying Old Glory above our compound—the concern came from hand-wringing Americans. Often, while deep in our cups at the firepit, several of us would run to our flagpole and run the flag back up to its rightful place. The next day the base commander would get angry and complain again, and the process would repeat itself.

There was a revolving cast of characters around the firepit, including contractors and some girls from conventional units whom the guys invited. They all had gnarly nicknames like "Choppa" and "Scarface." Who was banging out whom could at times become a major point of consternation. Personally, I couldn't have cared less. There was nothing on that lonely FOB worth chasing after.

On one occasion, some of the younger guys on our team got ahold of an elastic slingshot and started firing off water balloons at people. Michael Bluth, our team sergeant, was well into his cups by the time he saw this. He began pulling our team members aside and yelling at them in slurred speech: "YOU ARE JEOPARDIZING MY FAMILY!" Of course, there is a flip side of that story. If you ever meet Mr. Bluth and ask him about me, you may hear a story about how he found me wandering our compound in the middle of the night without any pants on, complaining that I had lost my shoes. I can neither confirm nor deny such allegations.

Launching water balloons at one another was the tamest thing we were up to. On another occasion, we were doing joint operations with a SEAL platoon. Our medic got pretty trashed and decided to do combatives with the SEALs—just the one medic versus all comers. I was watching in case things got out of hand, but the SEALs were restrained, despite my teammate provoking them. The next day our medic looked as if he had been in a fight with a grizzly bear, as they had been doing the combatives on hard gravel.

The best story was when James Hupp thought he was being fired from the team. Some water pipes had broken in his house back in Clarksville, and he wanted to go home for a few days to help his wife get things straightened out. Everyone on the ODA was fine with this; we could spare James for a week. However, our headquarters said that if he went, he would be fired from the ODA, forcing him to choose between his family and his team. James chose his family.

So one night out at the firepit, a plot unfurled. Though our captain had supported James from the beginning, he had the misfortune of being the only officer within striking distance. James grabbed up a grenade simulator normally used in training and decided to give our captain a good scare. We stalked between the CHUs in the dead of night and slipped out to our team leader's hooch. James looked down at the grenade simulator in his hand and said, "Fuck it, I'm fired anyway." He activated the simulator and tossed it under the captain's CHU.

We took off running at high speed as the simulator detonated with a loud boom that echoed across the base. Our captain would not talk about that night for a long time because he was so pissed.

Jeez, I could probably write an entire chapter about the firepit, but some stories are just too ticklish to tell.

That said, it wasn't all just fun and games. We had some real work to do. We trained the hell out of our ISWAT guys. Every day was a range, a run wearing combat equipment, a class on map reading, machine gun drills, and more. I set up stress shoots, making the guys run around and fire from behind barricades at targets. I had them clear our shoot house over and over and over again. There was time to get creative with things, and I did a whole week of countersniper training. I taught them how to react to sniper fire, tossing smoke grenades and running in a zigzag motion. I staged mock assassination scenes and taught them how to figure out where the shot came from. One of our communications sergeants even taught them how to track footprints.

At the end of it all, I went to a granary down the street and coordinated with the engineer and director who worked there to stage a big training exercise. The ISWAT guys set up decoys for the "sniper" to shoot at by building a model head on a stick with a helmet on it. Other teams went through the granary, clearing the complex floor by floor. It was a great event to be able to organize, and I was proud of what this particular SWAT platoon had accomplished.

But they can't all be winners. Our other ISWAT platoon was dismal. All I could figure was that over time, all the good dudes had filtered over to Salim's platoon, while all the lazy (and corrupt) ones stayed. I had constant problems with these guys stealing gasoline and batteries from us and generally being unwilling to do their job. I would watch them clear a room in training in the most half-assed manner; then I would yell at them, and suddenly, they would remember how to do their job. It was like being in charge of a bunch of small children.

I recall the first mission we took that platoon out on. They had previously done a unilateral mission into Mosul with their company commander. They told me that they were rescuing kidnapped girls being held by gangsters in the city. I didn't believe a fucking word of it. Everything this commander did was to personally enrich and benefit himself. He didn't give a shit about running actual operations.

When we took that platoon into Mosul, it was a clusterfuck. The Iraqis left their breaching equipment on the Humvees because it was too heavy and they didn't want to carry it, so our senior Charlie, Mike, exploded on them. They ran back to get the prybars and sledgehammers, poor babies. Finally, we made entry into the building, and it was like that M. C. Escher sketch where there are stairways leading in all directions. It was as if totally different people with different ideas had built on top of previous structures. The floor plan was a maze. We cleared a few rooms, and I spotted one door that no one had gone through yet. We got it open, and I stormed up the stairs with our senior medic and some ISWAT guys. We went up. And up. And up. It was a spiral staircase, with each step being about two feet high. We kept going and going until we came out on what turned out to be the third floor.

Now we were looking down on an open area in the middle of the building. An open corridor crisscrossed on the second floor, which had not been cleared yet, and deeper down, you could see the ground floor, where the Iraqis were running around. It took a while, but eventually, we got the whole building cleared, although the HVT we were after was not there.

The worst thing, though, was the kid we found locked in a closet. Mental health care is basically nonexistent; it is hard to imagine someone who is more fucked in life than a disabled Iraqi person. For example, midgets are treated as "crazy" people who get slapped around and beaten just for fun. On this objective, we found a teenage boy who was seriously disabled. He was reaching through the grating in the door, trying to swat at people and get their attention. Our medic felt bad for him and gave the kid an apple he had been carrying with him. The kid ate the entire apple, core, stem, and all.

Experiences like this make it hard for me to sit and listen to affluent New Yorkers whining about how hard they have it in America and how evil and racist our country is. America is an amazing country existing in a golden age, while our citizens do little but wring their hands and complain. The distance between their lives in New York City and the lives of people in Iraq isn't just a chasm, it is as far away as Earth is from Mars. It is almost like the human race is evolving into two or three separate species—those who live in the twenty-first century, those who live in the eleventh century in the Middle East, and those who live in the first century in places like Afghanistan.

When we got back from that mission, the ISWAT platoon seemed to lose their minds. I caught one guy rummaging around my arms room and another one picking through a closet for food and drink. I came damn close to beating the shit out of both of them. Some remedial training was in order. Every time that platoon screwed up, I would take them on a random training event at a random hour, day or night. From there, they would have to kit up and move out. It was just like SFAS. We would move for an undetermined time and an undetermined distance. Their sad expressions were spectacular. When one of them would quit, I'd tell him not to bother coming back to work.

There were fun times out at FOB Sykes as well. We had quite a cast of characters around us. We had a couple interpreters who were from a minority group called the Yazidi, from the city of Sinjar. There was a myth that these people were Satan worshippers, a misconception that I believe originated with the seventeenth-century mystic Madame Blavatsky, who supposedly tooled around the more austere parts of the world and then pitched those experiences to European bourgeoisie for profit in the form of "spiritualism." In fact, the Yazidi people practice an ancient religion that predates Islam and Christianity, one that worships a peacock god. They have their own unique traditions and customs.

For instance, our interpreter Gomez told me the story of how his father married his mother via kidnapping. When a Yazidi man wants to marry a Yazidi woman, both families must agree to the union. If the woman's family doesn't think the man is good enough, they will refuse. However, there is a loophole in the system. If the couple is quite in love, the man will tell the woman that they're going to her cousin's, or something like that, but instead, he will spirit her away to a safe house and hide out, essentially forcing the woman's family to the negotiation table with his family.

Gomez's brother, nicknamed McLovin, also worked on the FOB, cleaning up the compound for us. He was learning English very quickly from being around Americans. Our warrant officer took it upon himself to teach McLovin some American colloquialisms, so if you asked him a question, he might answer, "Does a hobbyhorse have a wooden dick?" One day McLovin was taking out the trash and throwing it in the Dumpster when an American first sergeant from the military police unit next door saw him, an Iraqi alone and unescorted, on the base. He went up to McLovin and asked who the hell he was.

McLovin replied, "Who am I? I'M THE GRAND SHEIK OF POUNDING VAG!"

Our ODA pulled together and functioned well enough with a mission in front of us, but there was a tremendous amount of friction between the top three guys on our team: the captain, the team sergeant, and the warrant officer. For a lowly weapons sergeant like me, this was like being trapped between Mommy and Daddy going through a divorce. Daddy slaps Mommy in the face at the dinner table, and you are left sitting there thinking, What the fuck is wrong with these people? I was told later that our team leader and team sergeant felt that our warrant officer was pushing the team to do things that were illegal, and unethical. One incident involved a bag of money found on a target; some of it went missing. Who was right and who was wrong wasn't something I could state as a fact, but these kinds of conflicts happen on ODAs all the time. I believe our team leader and team sergeant did their best to protect me and the rest of the team from any sort of inappropriate behavior.

Somewhere around halfway through the deployment, we were tasked to work with a SEAL platoon who came up to liaise with us from an FOB farther south. They had an HVT they were tracing in Mosul, and they had an Iraqi partner force, but the problem was that those Iraqis could not operate in Mosul. At this point, who could? The ODAs in Mosul were stymied by corrupt Iraqi politicians. Even the much vaunted JSOC task force was getting shut down. None of these elements could operate without an Iraqi partner force, so if the government of Iraq prevented them from doing ops, the Americans were not doing ops, either. The reality was that corrupt Iraqi politicians didn't like any of us running around and rolling up their cronies, who were often Mafia types, if not outright terrorists.

Since all these other elements were being stood down, we started to get assets pushed to our ODA. In this case, 160th Special Operations Aviation Regiment would be flying us to our target in Mosul. The SEALs showed up, and we began mission planning. The SEALs have a different unit culture, being a maritime commando unit within a branch of service where everything is big, gray, and floats. They were loud and over the top, but these superficial differences aside, they were good dudes, and we found that we worked well together. Luckily, the weak ISWAT platoon was rotating out and the new one was coming in. Once they arrived, I would have to scramble to prepare them for the mission.

That was when I got a phone call from the gate. They were not letting Salim and his ISWAT platoon on the base; they required that I come and escort them. I was furious. It wasn't the first time that Mother Army had wasted our time with all this dick dancing. While my team's mission was to prepare the Iraqis to take control of their destiny so that America could leave, the conventional U.S. Army saw the mission as simply not to die in Iraq. Because of this, they wanted me to confiscate all of the ISWAT guys' guns whenever they came onto the base; they wanted us to constantly supervise them every time they took a piss. While we were trying to make them independent, the U.S. Army wanted us to handhold them lest some Iraqi get a wild hair up his ass and try to kill someone. Talk about conflicting missions.

I tore down to the main gate as the 160th MH-60s came blasting overhead to land on our FOB's airfield. I stopped my truck, got out, and proceeded to scream at the gate guard. In retrospect, it was a silly thing to do; that Sergeant was just some dude doing what he was ordered to. He didn't set policy at the base. But I was angry and had a mission to accomplish.

Eventually, I got the ISWAT guys through the gate and out to the airfield. James Hupp and I were chalk leaders, taking the patrol to our target, which was located smack dab in the middle of one of the most dangerous markets in Mosul. After going through some rehearsals, we boarded the helicopters and took off. As we approached the city, lights swirled below us. James and I sat on the edge of the helicopter with our legs dangling in the breeze. We circled the objective once, then the pilot set us down in a large open area. We got off the bird, jacked a round into our M4 rifles, and scanned for targets.

The only noise was the buzz of the occasional fluorescent lightbulb that cast the streets in a yellow pitch. Mounds of dirt and garbage were everywhere, and the smell reflected that. There were four or five helicopters full of ISWAT, ODA, and SEAL team members dropped off on the LZ in total. I led us down the road, but I got a bit turned around on those confusing Iraqi streets. The AC-130 in orbit above us illuminated the target building and got us back on track.

We crept up to the objective and made entry. The SEALs and ISWAT members quickly captured their high-value target. As it turned out, they caught him in the act, balls defiladed in his old lady, as it was described to me later. (FYI, the defilade is a portion of low ground where troops take cover.)

I took some ISWAT guys around back and secured the door, then went in and cleared a kitchen area. When you enter and clear a room, there are certain priorities of work, depending on a unit's standard operating procedures. A priority could be to eliminate enemies, search dead bodies, mark casualties, or search for documents. One ISWAT member's first priority of work was to raid the refrigerator looking for goodies. I went ballistic for the second time that night, screaming at him to get his shit together. He went into the next room where the SEALs were and sat down on the couch to relax. I believe our senior 18C yelled at him before I even had the chance. Suffice to say my blood pressure was a bit high at this point. With the objective cleared and the HVT captured, we prepared to exfil off the target.

Soon, we moved toward our exfil LZ, walking through some more empty lots and stepping over mounds of trash. About this time, the talking penis started spouting off. That would be the minaret screeching a three a.m. call to prayer over the PA system. Hupp and I got our guys organized into our chalk: the two of us, a couple SEALs, and about ten ISWAT members. Just as the birds were about to come in, the ISWAT guy who'd raided the fridge took off his helmet. When I started telling him to put it back on right goddamn now, he complained. Our interpreter Gomez corrected him and made sure he got his helmet back on.

The Black Hawks came in, but our bird overshot our location, so we had to get up and run to it. Hupp and I headed into the storm of dust kicked up by the rotor blades, which browned out everything. When we got to the side of the helicopter, we stood facing each other to create a choke point and count everyone. One by one, everyone slipped between us and piled into the helicopter. We got full accountability, and then Hupp and I sat down and snapped into the fuselage before giving the crew chief a thumbs-up.

A minute later, we were airborne and heading back to FOB Sykes for hot sandwiches.

On another operation, we hit what had been a terrorist safe house. Intel was leading us to a secret room inside. I pulled some rebar out of the way so we could crawl around back. Our intel guy knew exactly where he was going. There was a hole in the back wall that had been filled up with cinder blocks. We removed them, then had to take off our body armor to slip inside. It was a barren room with no doorways, just a metal bed frame and a single lightbulb. We were cold on their trail. Just another stop on the terrorist underground railroad that had funneled foreign fighters into Iraq to kill coalition soldiers.

Rolling outside the wire to conduct so-called key leader engagements with important Iraqi nationals happened often. These meetings would be extremely frustrating, as the Iraqi military and police officers really didn't want to have them: They might end up with tasks to complete. If they had tasks, they would have to do work, and if they did work, they might be held accountable for that work. One officer's attempts to delay our meeting were like something out of an old Steve Martin movie. He took a phone call every minute; on the thirty-second mark, his secretary would come in, salute, take some mysterious order, and head back outside. We ended up turning on the IED jammer on our Humvees so that his cell phone wouldn't work.

On occasion we did aerial recon by helicopter. Sometimes we assisted the Civil Affairs unit with us who had projects under way to build schoolhouses and such. We were staged for an operation up at the castle in central Tal Afar one afternoon when, suddenly, a new mission came down on us and we had to decide which to do and which to let go. One was to recover an enemy cache inside Tal Afar. I lobbied to go by myself with a few ISWAT members. Michael Bluth, our team sergeant, wanted me to take another ODA member but agreed. We rolled out with two Humvees into town and moved to where the cache was supposedly located.

At one location, we turned up a plastic water bottle with some rusty AK-47 rounds. At the next, a "source" prodded the ground with a metal rod until he found something: We dug up what turned out to be an RPG-round crate. I had the Iraqis open it with a string from a distance, just in case it was booby-trapped. It turned out there was nothing inside. Another waste of time. Of course, you don't know what you don't know. These fake caches were how we were able to pay sources for intel against actual terrorists. Special Forces doesn't get any money to pay sources, so we had to get creative and find other things we could pay them for, like a random dude turning in munitions.

Special Forces has a really archaic and backward approach to intelligence gathering, which lulls us into paralysis, since we can't do anything, because then they will know that we know that they know that we know they know . . . and on and on. If you want to do real intel gathering, pray for military reform, or just join the CIA—if anything, they're notorious for overpaying their sources. Special Forces wants to play in the world of intelligence gathering, and our bosses convince their men that they are better than CIA case officers, but in actuality, Special Forces is at the bottom of the barrel when it comes to intelligence collection. They gather some decent tactical intelligence, but that is about it.

On the way back to our FOB, the Iraqis suddenly pulled over to the side of the road while still inside Tal Afar. ISWAT guys jumped out of the vehicle and ran into a store. What the hell is going on? I thought. Is one of these guys stopping for a quickie with his old lady before we go to the base? Don't laugh—it happens. I jumped out and walked into the shop. It turned out to be a candy shop. The boys were rapping with the store owner while stocking up on candy, ice cream, and some local type of baklava, which was offered to me as well and tasted amazing.

The boys were like that. When I would take them to our chow hall on the base, they would ask me for "scream," which I came to understand as them asking for ice cream. Uncle Sam was happy to provide.

The longer this deployment went on, the more hard-core things got, due to the aforementioned political situation and the impending SOFA. This was supposed to be a slow deployment for us, but the JSOC task force and the ODAs in Mosul were shut down entirely, unable to run any missions at all. This left ODA 5414 in Tal Afar with our ISWAT members as the only maneuver element that could still run operations in the area. All the intel and resources that would have gone to Delta Force and other units in Mosul were suddenly pushed to us. We were in business, doing joint ops with Delta or unilateral operations hitting targets the task force had a hard-on for.

Suddenly, our ODA became the go-to action element for northern Iraq. We did a second joint operation with the SEALs, flying into Mosul again. On another mission, 160th flew us into Mosul and landed us right in the middle of the street: James Hupp and I sat in the door, and I watched in amazement while the pilot maneuvered the MH-60 helicopter in between the power lines. The cables whipped back and forth under the rotor wash as the pilot guided his aircraft with the precision of a surgeon, slowly lowering us down to ground level, or so I thought.

Here is another useful nugget of knowledge—just some practical information for all you wannabe commandos out there. When you are

wearing the PVS-14 night optical device, you don't have any depth perception. So when you are on a helicopter wearing night vision, say, in the
middle of Mosul, and you look down, it may appear that the helicopter
has landed when in fact it hasn't. I heaved myself off the helicopter, thinking we had landed, but instead was airborne for a hot second before slamming into the pavement with my ninety-odd pounds of gear.

Hupp jumped, too, but being the stud that he was, he managed to
land on two feet and took off running toward the objective. I was lying on
the ground, trying to pick myself up as the helicopter landed behind me.
Kouri, one of our interpreters, ran off the helicopter and kicked the barrel
of my M4 as he ran by. The buttstock of the rifle slammed into my jaw.

I've said many times that these things are never enough to kill you,
just enough to hurt you really bad. I got up, pretended that I wasn't all
skinned up from my swan dive into the pavement, and ran after Hupp,
who was barreling down on the objective building. I passed Kouri and
arrived at the objective a few seconds behind James. Once the ISWAT
guys arrived, we made the breach and cleared the building. Nobody
home. Dry hole.

James was our senior 18E, Special Forces communications sergeant. I
found that we worked quite well together, as he had previously served in
the 82nd Airborne and was a Ranger School graduate. We spoke the same
language, and when he helped me train ISWAT, we were on the same
sheet of music. On another HVT strike in Mosul, we cleared our target
building and then flexed to hit the building next door. While our teammates cleared the ground floor I took James and a few ISWAT guys onto
the roof of the adjacent house to make sure that was locked down.

I tried the door that would have led us into the home, but it was
locked. I gave the door a couple kicks, but frankly, that just hurt my
foot a little. The door didn't budge. Then James stepped in and started
kicking the door. I figured he was wasting his time and said so, but as
he kept stomping the door, the metal bent bit by bit around the locking

With my mom at the Ranger Memorial at Fort Benning, Georgia, the day I graduated the Ranger Indoctrination Program (RIP).

When I got leave while in the Army I often used it to go places like Costa Rica, the Czech Republic, Mauritius, Mexico, or Belize (*seen here*).

Rangers take their training seriously, as seen here during an exercise we did at Fort Campbell when I was a sniper.

Inside a castle near the Pakistan border with an Air Force JTAC. Sergeant Admundson was tragically killed during the patrol to get there.

Myself, Joe, an Air Force JTAC, and Staff Sergeant "Grant."

Doing some call for fire training with Cobra helicopter gunships between missions.

Coming back from a combat operation in Afghanistan where I helped provide sniper support.

(*Above*) A picture of our recce patrol at the border control point. Paul is wearing the brown pakol and I am wearing the gray one, both of us standing.

(*Right*) At the mission support site for the recon to locate the guy who planned the Tillman ambush.

This picture was taken just minutes before the friendly fire incident, a hasty near-ambush that almost killed many of us.

Moments prior to taking off to provide aerial sniper support for Ranger assault teams raiding a compound in Khowst, Afghanistan.

With weapons squad, 1st Platoon, "The Glory Boys" of Alpha Company, 3rd Ranger Battalion. Note the black eye on the private on the far right, from a bar brawl the night prior. We had a lot of fun back then.

13

(*Left*) On my second deployment I was a weapons squad team leader in Mosul, Iraq, in 2005. One of my main jobs was to be in charge of a Stryker armored vehicle and make sure we got to where the bad guys were bedding down.

(*Below*) After graduating from the Special Forces Qualification Course, I was assigned to ODA 5414. We were a military free-fall team, as seen here during a train-up in Nevada.

14

15

In 2009, ODA 5414 was deployed to my old stomping ground, Tal Afar, Iraq. This is a picture I took of the 3,000-year-old castle at the center of the city.

(*Right*) A shot of me inside the castle.

(*Below*) A picture taken in 2018 by one of the ISWAT members I trained. This is where the castle above once stood before ISIS destroyed it.

16

17

18

Jon and I in the market in Tal Afar.

(*Above*) We trained our ISWAT members every day we didn't have a combat operation. This was a road march on our base.

(*Left*) ISWAT member Saddiq and I out on a recon patrol in the desert southwest of Tal Afar.

Jon and I with ISWAT members, including my friend Shahab on the far right.

Meeting with the village elders in a remote area of northwestern Iraq.

Jon and I during a visit to a schoolhouse during the same patrol. It was a great opportunity to introduce ISWAT to these youngsters as police officers who were here to help.

Our Senior Communications Sergeant, James Hupp. I'll always remember him as seen here, handing out candy to kids in Iraq. His suicide years later is something I still can't make sense of.

This picture was taken at about two in the afternoon. Sandstorms make it look like you are on the surface of Mars.

26

Trying to be a bit more nondescript in the Kurdish city of Dohuk.

One of my favorite pictures from my time in the military. I was outside the wire with one other American and our ISWAT team when they abruptly pulled over. I followed them inside a store and found them going to town inside a candy shop.

A picture I took during a recon done by helicopter, showing typical terrain in the desert around Tal Afar.

Before leaving, I handed out training certificates to the ISWAT team before shaking their hands and thanking them.

ODA 5415 team photo. "Michael Bluth," our team sergeant, is on the far left.

After leaving the Army in 2010, I began finding my own missions, like this training exercise in Switzerland that I participated in.

In 2014, I was smuggled into northern Syria by the PKK while working as a journalist. I've since quit smoking.

While in Syria, I met this all-female sniper unit, which was a part of the Kurdish YPJ militia.

Visiting a medical recovery center for Kurdish veterans of the Syrian conflict in 2014, I look a bit parched while my girlfriend, Benni (*second from right*), looks none the worse for wear.

Myself at the Kurdish base at Derik in Northern Syria, with a YPG soldier and a ubiquitous picture of their movement's founder, Abdullah Ocalan.

While stranded in Syria, I met a Christian checkpoint guard who called himself Rambo. He said, "Take picture of me, put on Facebook, show the whole world." So I did.

My next adventure was reporting from Iraq in 2015, when I went into a battle with the Peshmerga outside Kirkuk. This picture was taken as the Pesh razed the village behind me.

In 2016, Benni and I were invited to Damascus.

On my second trip to Syria, I was able to interview President Assad in the middle of the civil war.

Inside the courtyard of a home in Damascus.

Becoming a father changed my life forever, as well as for the better.

Benni and I
getting married.
As they say,
the couple that
gets blown up
together, stays
together.

mechanism. Finally, with one last front kick, the door blasted inward. Damn, son. I was glad that James was on our team.

Our slow deployment had turned into a Rip It energy drink–fueled frenzy of Kalashnikovs, helicopters, gun trucks, and after-parties at the firepit. One night, our warrant officer got a little too deep into his cups, I suppose, and tried to manhandle one of the guys on the team, and actually bit him from what I was told. James Hupp didn't like that and knocked our warrant officer unconscious with one punch. The guy ended up walking around the chow hall wearing sunglasses to cover his black eye. It was just one of those moments that only happens in the army.

There was a friendly competition between my team and the dive team from our company to see which of us could secure the most extravagant "pimp cup" off an objective. Pimps are known to have a type of trophy cup, sometimes for drinking from but other times purely ornamental with lots of bling. We wanted our own. The Pimp Cup Challenge was on.

When we were tasked to ball up a couple Baath Party douchebags who had been making IEDs, I knew it was my time to strike. The mission was to be a Trojan horse operation that embedded a few ODA members and ISWAT troops with a conventional army unit. As evidence emerged about an IED cell in Mosul, it turned out that the conventional army unit in that area was well acquainted with them. It was the family of a colonel who had served under Saddam. The American soldiers would check in on him once in a while and drink some chai.

It was decided that we would roll out with the regular army troops so that the enemy thought it was just business as usual: They'd have a few cups of chai and then get on with their day of building improvised road-side bombs to kill coalition troops—or so they would think. We drove into Mosul and liaised with the conventional unit at their FOB and did some mission planning.

When we were ready to roll, I was inside one of the unit's MRAP vehicles with a handful of ISWAT guys. One of my main men, Shahab, was with me, as was Omar, one of our Iraqi intel dudes. We stopped near the target building, and the conventional troops got out and knocked on the door to see who was home. Once it was confirmed that everyone was there, my warrant officer waved me forward. I charged inside right behind half a dozen ISWAT members and quickly detained all of the male family members.

While searching the house, I found a contender for the Pimp Cup Challenge and stashed it inside my dump pouch. The challenge would be mine—or so I thought. We ended up losing to the dive team, who found a pimp cup worth writing home about on one of their missions. They found a cup covered in silver and gold, a really baller-ass cup to be proud of. Sadly, this wasn't one of those deals like in *Indiana Jones,* where the plain-looking cup was the winner because Christ was a carpenter.

Back at the FOB in Mosul, we took biometrics of the detainees with a new device called a Cogent and then tested their hands for chemical residue associated with explosive materials. The father and his two sons both popped positive. From there they were handed off to the Iraqi police to face whatever justice their courts decided to dish out. Half of the time, the police just released terrorists because the judge was from the same tribe or was their second cousin's uncle or what the fuck ever else. This is why we were just spinning our wheels in Iraq a lot of the time. Even if they went to prison, they would eventually get released, but more radicalized from having a terrorist powwow with their jihadi homies in the joint.

Another opportunity arose that we were all quite doubtful about, if not outright terrified, but things worked out better than any of us could have expected. It was a joint operation with the Iraqi air force. Yes, they have an air force, but I thought that if Iraqis flew helicopters like they drove cars, we were in some real trouble. The opportunity to train with them also became an opportunity to combine two or three missions into one.

While doing the countersniper training at the granary, I had been ambushed by a news crew from Al Iraqiya, wanting to know what we were up to. They had been tipped off, most likely by the managers at the facility, eager to demonstrate their worth to their bosses. I quickly grabbed Salim and had him talk to the press. It wasn't my job to parade around in front of the cameras. Special Forces guys work by, with, and through our host-nation counterparts.

With a couple Huey helicopters en route to our FOB, we devised a day of training for ISWAT in which the news crew we met at the granary would be invited. They could record the Iraqi SWAT team members training and report it on television, which would be a great PR win for ISWAT and Iraqi security forces as a whole. The next day, we would utilize the Iraqi helicopters to run a live operation in the desert south of us known as the Jazeera.

When we went out to the airfield, I felt a little nervous as the two Hueys showed up. One was flown by an Iraqi pilot, the other by an American pilot. The aircrews were Iraqi. The helicopters landed, and the pilots got out to meet with us and plan the next couple days. The Iraqi pilot had a nice potbelly under his tan flight suit and a thick Saddam 'stache. As we talked, he held the American pilot's hand, which is a local custom, a display of affection. The American pilot smiled and tried to play along.

I think one reason why Americans are so bad at counterinsurgency is that we are afraid to walk a mile in the enemy's flip-flops. We just are not comfortable getting that close to foreign cultures. We want to hang out on our FOBs, eat American food, lift weights, watch satellite television, and basically bring America with us wherever we go. In a counterinsurgency, you live alongside the insurgents, and in the process, you become a little more like them while they become a little more like you, defeating the conflict over a long period of time. I think this type of unconventional warfare scares the shit out of most people, including many American special operations troops.

Over the years, I've been immersed in some very curious foreign cultural idiosyncrasies, having listened to anti-Semitic sermons from Arabs, heard Masonic conspiracy theories in Africa, been told that the CIA is behind Iraqi terrorism in Kurdistan, and even sat in a room politely listening to a traitor on our ISWAT team who I knew was secretly feeding information to our enemies. I would just grin, nod, and play it off cool. Some people just can't handle this type of shit. This is why America isn't going to be any better at counterinsurgency in fifty years than we are now. It is because of our national style. We prefer high-tech smart bombs, laser beams, and SOF teams carrying carbines with all kinds of high-tech bullshit strapped to the sides. Our adversaries in Iran, Russia, and China are light-years ahead of us when it comes to the unconventional stuff.

The ISWAT guys then received a familiarization of the Hueys from the Iraqi flight crew and learned basic loading and unloading procedures. Meanwhile, I talked with the Iraqi pilot. It turned out he had been flying since the Iran–Iraq war in the 1980s. He told me that he liked to fly solo because when you were reliant only on yourself, you really had to fly to your full potential. He would also worry more about the lives of his flight crew if they were on board.

I understood what he was laying down. I had been ruck-marching all over our FOB, leading some of my teammates to speculate that I was preparing to go to Delta Force selection. This would have been the next step for me, but I had grown disillusioned with the army and its capacity to fight and win wars. The Delta recruiters would come around and show us these cool-guy videos, but every unit had a cool-guy video. I had served in two army special operations units and no longer believed that things would be different if I went to a third. Delta wasn't doing much that we weren't doing. Everyone was hitting targets, it was just that their gear was a little cooler than ours. No, I had something different in mind.

After some ground training, I rode in one of the Hueys with the ISWAT members and a cameraman from Al Iraqiya. We hit an empty building on our FOB just like it was a real operation. That night, the footage was already on television. For what seemed like over an hour, film of Tal Afar ISWAT flying around in the helicopter played with patriotic Arabic music in the background. The news crew played by the rules: You got to see the back of my helmet on TV but never my face. It felt like a good moment at the time: the Iraqi air force supporting Iraqi SWAT with Iraqi television showing the populace that they had someone out there fighting for them.

The next day was a live mission without the news crew around. We took off and flew out in the middle of the desert. I snapped a couple of pictures with my digital camera as the Hueys flew side by side with PKM machine guns sticking out of the sides, manned by the aircrew. It looked like a scene out of *Apocalypse Now* aside from the desert speeding below us. We landed in the desert and got out. It was a pretty routine mission, rightly so, since it was our first time working with Iraqi air assets. We ran a checkpoint along the road or, rather, ISWAT did. After being out there for a couple hours, James radioed that we were ready for extraction, and I tossed a red smoke grenade. The birds showed up about fifteen minutes later, and it was back to the FOB for hot sandwiches and ice cream.

All good things come to an end, and our six-month rotation in Iraq was coming to that end. It wasn't easy for me. Soldiers are taught never to leave a man behind, while Green Berets are trained to work themselves out of a job, train the locals to do the task at hand so that Americans don't have to be deployed to those countries forever. The two doctrines resulted in psychological schism for me, the Ranger and the Special Forces soldier at odds. We were leaving a lot of good guys behind, and I knew damn well that the government of Iraq was not going to take care of ISWAT.

As things spun down, I began to say my goodbyes. Shahab got emotional about it, crying and hugging me. We were bros now. That's the bond between soldiers that transcends nationality. You either understand that or you don't.

I tried to set my emotions aside and accept the reality of it. Our ODA had come to Iraq to do a job, move the ball a little further toward the end goal, and I thought we'd succeeded in that endeavor. That's what I told myself, anyway, but it didn't make things any easier. The shame I felt over leaving them is real and long-lasting.

Our last night in Iraq, we had a huge party out at the firepit with another ODA that had joined us. They were stationed way out in the hinterlands and had been brought back into our FOB to fly out with us. I had been liaising with the ODA that had come to replace us and was now staying in the guest CHUs. I woke up in the morning and opened my door. It looked like a Vietnam-era firebase outside, with trash strewn everywhere, something on fire out on the gravel, and Green Berets passed out cold. Goddamn, those guys really burned it down after I went to bed.

Our pallets were built, and a forklift came to move them over to the airfield. Our rucksacks were laid out, bulging from the seams, with our body armor, gun bags, and helmets beside them. We had downloaded all of our 5.56 magazines, leaving the ammo in our loadout room. This was really happening—we were headed home. But one of our ODA team members was missing. Where the hell was he? In the revelry last night, everyone had lost track of him.

About an hour went by, and we had to head out to the airfield to catch our freedom bird home. Michael Bluth, our team sergeant, started getting in everyone's ass, asking where the hell our teammate was. "What the fuck is going on? This is your fault, Murphy!" I was pretty sure the dude hadn't been kidnapped by Al-Qaeda, but nonetheless, this was getting troubling.

The minute hand on the watch (or digital counter on my Suunto Vector, rather) was ticking. Our team sergeant was becoming increasingly agitated, as we were supposed to be walking up the ramp of a C-17 right then to get the hell out of Iraq. Finally, a sedan pulled into our compound and drove across the gravel toward us. Our teammate was hanging out of the passenger window with his arms in the air. As he approached, he cried out, "I don't care what the fuck you do to me, it was worth it!"

At least one Green Beret had found love at the firepit that night. They ended up getting married.

All these years later, I have a lot of mixed emotions about the war in Iraq. We got into that conflict under some very fishy auspices, and the American public is right to be upset about that. We soldiers had a different perspective. What was done, was done, and we were there to clean up the mess. We had our hearts in the right place and wanted to create a better situation for the people of Iraq, but sadly, that was not to be.

The brass demanded unrealistic false reports about positive progress in Iraq, so that's what they got. One fake report card about the stability and competence of Iraqi security services was run up the flagpole. The real report card was issued a few years later, when ISIS came to town. The rest is history, a history of dead bodies, slavery, murder, and ash.

PART II

CHAPTER 10

Anything You Do Can Get You Killed, Including Doing Nothing

I DIDN'T SEE ANY FUTURE FOR ME IN THE ARMY.

We stood tall on the parade field out behind our buildings at Fort Campbell, Kentucky. The field is lined with small trees, each planted to symbolize a member of 5th Special Forces Group who had been killed in action. Today, the reason for our formation was less solemn: We were receiving deployment awards. I was being awarded the Bronze Star for my work in training ISWAT. Like most Green Berets, I felt that it was an unnecessary award for doing my job; however, it was a nice gesture from my ODA's leadership to submit my name for recognition.

A burly command sergeant major came down the line of young Green Berets from Alpha Company 4th Battalion and shook our hands as an officer pinned the awards on our fatigues. One by one, he asked what we had planned for the future. Just about every guy said he was getting out of the army. The sergeant major tried to talk us out of it by telling us how great the army had been to him.

I felt that my best days in the army were already behind me. I had gotten to do the cool jobs, being a team leader in Ranger Battalion and a weapons sergeant in Special Forces. I had gotten to go to all the cool schools as well. From here on out, it was going to be training billets, admin slots, and worst of all, becoming a senior NCO who ran around yelling at young soldiers because they weren't wearing the right type of belt or boots. In the army, you either die a hero, or you live long enough to see yourself become a banal midlevel civil servant enforcing army boot-lace standards. It is an unappealing future of bureaucracy and backward thinking that doesn't exactly attract the best and the brightest that this country has to offer. It seemed to me that I had been trained and selected to do a job, and then the very unit to which I was assigned had done its damnedest to make sure we didn't do that job.

I outprocessed from the army, got my DD 214, packed up my Toyota Tacoma pickup truck, and drove home to New York, about twenty-seven hours of straight driving. I spent the next month doing the stereotypical thing to do when you get out of the military: I lived in my mom's base-ment and played video games. I was also working out every day and continuing to figure out how college would work, trying to use my GI Bill to go to school in London, since I wanted to study abroad. Larger in my mind, though, was my plan to travel to Burma and Sudan and deal myself back into the action on my own terms.

All that changed when I found out that my girlfriend was pregnant.

The idea that I was going to be a father was thrilling and terrifying at the same time. It was to change my life forever, and for the better. School in London didn't work out, so I moved back to the town I grew up in, Tar-rytown, New York, and started at Mercy College in Dobbs Ferry.

In a flash, my daughter was born, and I carried this little pink person home and laid her down in her crib. My life was changed forever.

I was still trying to figure out how to live a regular-person life. My mind was a frenzy of ideas and activities. I decided to write a novel—I mean, why not? I saw a lot of authors attempting to write military fiction who had no idea what they were talking about. I had the background, so why not take a stab at it? I ended up starting a small blog to try to generate interest. In time, I was contacted by a much larger blog at military.com; they brought me on to write for them. I self-published the first novel and dived right into the second. I was a full-time student, novelist, blog writer, father, and now husband. I had no idea how to balance these different roles.

Around this time, I submitted college applications to go to Columbia University and New York University. I got in to both schools and decided to go to Columbia, moving us down to student housing for families on 112th Street in Manhattan. I was an ambitious guy, perhaps overly so.

At Mercy College, I'd had a great professor for a class in European history named Dr. Leahy, who may have been the best professor I had in college overall. When I transferred to Columbia, I found some great professors, but more than a few who were mailing it in and didn't seem to really care about their classes. Overall, I was kind of disappointed with what I experienced at Columbia, but looking back on it, I can also see that I learned a lot.

On the first day of school one semester at Columbia, I walked up Broadway toward campus with a backpack full of books slung over my shoulder. When I arrived at the main entrance, I found it absolutely packed with paparazzi. Trying to struggle through the throng of photographers, I paused as a van pulled up and the sliding door opened. Bright flashes from the cameras popped off left and right. Was Lady Gaga paying our campus a visit?

A young woman hopped out of the van and lugged a mattress out, then began carrying it onto campus. As I came to learn, the so-called Mattress Girl's name was Emma Sulkowicz. She claimed that she had been raped by a student named Paul Nungesser. She had decided to carry the mattress that she was allegedly raped on everywhere on campus as a piece of performance art that the college gave her course credit for.

The problem was that her story didn't hold up. Nungesser was cleared of any wrongdoing by the university. Sulkowicz went on to make a porn movie with an actor in which her alleged rape was reenacted. There is a very real problem with sexual assault and rape on college campuses, and I find it baffling that universities are allowed to try to handle these things as internal matters rather than reporting violent crimes directly to the police. In the case of Sulkowicz, I'm convinced she needed professional help, and instead, the college feminist scene encouraged her to make a public spectacle of herself.

In the end, I was an old student who started college at age twenty-seven and finished at thirty-one. I've talked to other veterans who reveled in their ability to lord it over younger students and act as a mentor, sharing their life experiences. I was not one of those people. While I found a lot of the younger students to be great young men and women, I had nothing in common with them. I learned a lot from them, however.

At a school like Columbia, you will get assigned about a hundred pages' worth of white papers to read each week in each of the five classes you are enrolled in. On top of that, you have to write papers, study for tests, and complete projects. For a literature class you will be expected to finish a five-to-seven-hundred-page novel in one week. The expectations are simply unrealistic, and I had brought my soldier mentality into the classroom: I took notes on everything, studied for hours, and ground through paper after paper. While I was trying to complete the task 100 percent and then some, the younger students showed me what to study and when. Basically, I learned from them how to game the system and pass classes without killing myself.

I often heard of other students pulling all-nighters, camped out in the student lounge to study. I never did that once in college, and my diploma looks just the same as theirs.

I started off intending to major in history but changed to political science after I took a class in West African history. When I pitched a project proposal to the teaching assistant that I would do a cross-comparison of historical trans-Saharan trade routes with modern-day drug and human trafficking routes in North Africa, I was looked at like a crazy man. "Where would you even find sources for that?" I was asked.

Then, on a test, I mentioned how certain interracial people in Africa were referred to as "half-breeds" by European colonists, a perceived slight that the professor decided to point out in front of the class. According to him, I couldn't just use racial slurs and think that putting the term in scare quotes made it okay. I thought this was very odd, considering that on his own syllabus, he mentioned how certain Africans were used and referred to as "mules," which also appeared in the aforementioned scare quotes. That professor was a fucking clown, and I was about done with the history department after that.

One thing you have to understand about colleges is that they masquerade as an ivory tower. A school will put itself up on a pedestal and act as if it is a forum of enlightened thought where people of diverse backgrounds come together and discuss the quandaries that plague our times before coming up with logical compromises and solutions. Of course, this is merely window dressing camouflaging the reality that, in class, the conclusions are all predetermined and the professor will guide you (applying force and coercion as needed) to those conclusions.

Yeah, you have your frustrating moments. In a class on comparative politics, we were asked to give some examples of a failed state. I raised my hand and said, "Mexico." The professor was flabbergasted and claimed he had never heard anyone argue that Mexico is a failed state. I was shocked in return. How could a professor in the political science department of a major university not even be aware of an argument openly debated in books, on television, and in professional literature? Mexico is a country where lawless organizations seem to have more power than the government, where the institutions of government are corrupted, and where there are more murders per year than people died in the Syrian civil war.

I got a B on my paper on Chinese intelligence. The teacher's assistant who graded the paper did not understand how open-source intelligence collected from hundreds of thousands of sources could be used as strategic intelligence. Honestly, when it came to that misunderstanding, he was just a microcosm of America's entire defense intelligence apparatus.

But there are some great professors in the mix if you go looking for them. I had a professor in my African politics class who was amazing. She was the only teacher I had at Columbia who would assign us readings and then openly defy them and make her students question the conclusions in the papers. Almost like, you know, critical thinking or something! Most professors just assigned readings in a very lowbrow, pedantic way in order to fill up their syllabus—or, as one history professor joked, it must look like a "COLUMBIA SYLLABUS."

That means the school valued quantity over quality when it came to readings. I got the impression that some of the professors hadn't read all of the stuff they assigned. If I'd been assigning nothing but drivel, I wouldn't have read it, either. One other thing on this topic: I love the students who pop in the first day of class, ask the professor to add yet more readings to the syllabus so that they sound smart, then drop the class and are never seen or heard from again. In the army, this is referred to as a buddy fucker.

Some other good classes I took included Special Operations and Low-Intensity Conflict and Understanding Intelligence Operations. These were graduate classes that I was able to sneak into, something I did as often as possible. By the fifth poli-sci undergrad class, you are sick of hearing about Hobbes and the state of nature. Now, this is the other thing about college: No matter how stupid it gets, you have to keep an open mind and be open to learning new things. I did learn quite a bit from political theory classes.

I approached my classes on SOF and intelligence from the perspective of a student rather than some self-styled "expert." I learned a ton in those classes. I started out knowing a lot about weapons, but the more knowledge I gained, the more I realized how much more was out there that I didn't know.

This was how I approached college: There is a lot out there that you don't know. Being an infantryman or a Green Beret doesn't make you an expert on geopolitical matters. I found the professor who taught these classes to be one of the more reasonable and sound-minded thinkers on special operations and intelligence.

Going from the U.S. military to Columbia University, I experienced all of the culture shock that you might expect. I sat next to the door on the first day of one of my history classes. While the professor was lecturing, one of the students got up halfway through the class and headed for the door, one of those metal fire doors that you typically find in schools. So this man-child gripped the knob and pulled.

But the door didn't open.

He pulled again. The door wasn't locked, it was just a little heavier than a conventional wooden door. He pulled a third time, but the door didn't open. The professor continued to talk, but this sorry excuse for a male was clanking the doorknob every time he turned it and quickly attracting the attention of the entire class. One of the girls in class motioned to him that you really have to pull on the door to get it open. This cat continued yanking on the door for another full minute but couldn't get it to budge. The door wasn't locked or jammed, he was just pulling on it like a Nancy. Finally, in one of the lamest acts I've ever seen in my life, this excuse for a man conceded defeat and took a seat. Just like that, he up and quit.

I was awed by this walking fetus that had somehow passed itself off as an adult. After he had disgraced himself and his family name, all I could do was hang my head in the collective shame of American men everywhere. What had we become?

I went to college, but I was never really in college. I just took classes there; I didn't hang out with those people.

I do want to take this opportunity to clear the air a bit. In recent years, much has been made in the media of so-called social justice warriors on college campuses. I didn't encounter much of that nonsense, probably because I was in the political science department, where professors weren't interested in hearing personal opinions because the classes were about studying facts. I could probably tell funny stories about college all day, but it wasn't quite the neocommunist cesspool that the media would have you believe.

I sometimes hear people talk about campus life who have never been on campus. I listen to them whine about left-wing politics that our young people are exposed to, along with a litany of other grievances that old white people have about higher education. This is the point when I look at them and remind them that, at any given time, Columbia has something like 350 veterans enrolled and working toward college degrees. The next time you feel the need to get your whine on, ask what you've done for veterans lately. At least Columbia is educating them and positioning them for success in life.

The vets are put into the School of General Studies, then overseen by Dean Peter Awn, who held the position for twenty years. He was always exceedingly polite and friendly, a man of short stature who I remember as always being well dressed, walking around and engaging general studies students in conversation. I was fortunate in that I never had to pay his office a visit and throw myself at his mercy, but I knew other veterans at Columbia who did, and Dean Awn came through for them in a big way. Just keep all of this in mind the next time you hear some crazy right-winger going on a rant about Columbia.

While at Columbia, I continued writing for military.com, where I met a former SEAL named Brandon Webb. He was much more entrepreneurial than I was, and he was frustrated with what was going on at military.com. The problem was that hardly anyone working there had ever been in the military. They didn't understand the content or the audience. Brandon made me a proposal: Why didn't we strike out on our own and make a news and information website about the special operations community?

The first name he came up with for the new website was SpecialOperationsHQ.com, which sounded pretty iffy to me. The next day he called me back and said he had a better idea—we could call it SOFREP, for Special Operations Forces Report. Brilliant! I agreed and came on board as the site's managing editor. We launched the website in January 2012.

Since I was then a rather sober thirty-year-old married man, I spent more time at Lehman Social Sciences Library working rather than doing the normal college extracurricular activities. Down in the basement, among the stacks, I was pulling double or triple duty on school projects, my third novel, and a new nonfiction book about the tragedy that had recently unfolded in Benghazi.

SOFREP had been growing exponentially, and we were very excited about it, but we had already taken a blow. Glen Doherty, a former SEAL and our first naval special warfare editor at SOFREP, had been working as a CIA contractor in Libya. He was killed when their compound came under attack in Benghazi. I had met Glen at a book signing in Manhattan, and he'd seemed like one of those all-around likable and fun guys to be around. He was Brandon's best friend, and I know the loss hit Brandon hard.

I had begun poking around, trying to uncover the real story of what happened that night in Benghazi, and I was making some real progress. I connected with some sources and was filled in on important details. Then Brandon got the firsthand account of how the firefight unfolded on the ground. Now this was getting interesting, as we had the most complete account of what had happened that night, aside from internal classified after-action reviews. We published an ebook called *Benghazi: The Definitive Report*, which went on to become a *New York Times* best seller.

This was a baptism by fire for me. I was just learning how the media worked, and now I had our book publisher lining up interviews left and right, plus others who reached out to me directly. I would walk out of a political philosophy class at the Barnard campus, the all-women's school that is a part of Columbia University, and immediately get on my cell for a radio interview, then I'd field a second interview fifteen minutes later. I'd jump into a literature class, then rush onto the subway to midtown and go on Fox News. After that, I'd get back on the subway heading home, reading and underlining white papers I had printed out for a class the next day. It went on like this for a couple of months. On one occasion, I did an hour-and-a-half interview in an old empty telephone booth in Lewisohn Hall.

These were moments of activity and excitement, when new opportunities were presenting themselves and anything seemed possible, much like my early years in the army. However, what I realize in retrospect was that I was having serious issues adjusting to civilian life. I told myself I was fine, that I was the same guy who had first joined the military, that I was unchanged. In fact, I had gotten addicted to the adrenaline and the adventure.

I did this by burying myself in more work than anyone could realistically expect to accomplish. I was a husband, a father, a student, a novelist, a fledgling journalist. I was running all over New York City, sometimes all over the country. I was at the Shooting, Hunting, and Outdoor Trade, or SHOT, show in Las Vegas, I was in L.A. meeting with film producers, I was in Africa testing open-source intelligence-gathering methodologies for an interesting group of people. I had escaped eight years in army special operations with hardly a scratch on me. There was no reason to believe that there was anything I couldn't do. Nothing could stop me, or so I thought.

My marriage fell apart the same year I graduated from Columbia. Something had to give, and it was me. I was having fainting spells, checking out for microseconds here and there. I couldn't figure out why at the time. One afternoon, I collapsed in the middle of 114th Street in Manhattan. I picked myself up, ignoring my bloodied hand and knee, then went to class. Of course, the fainting was related to stress.

I didn't get it at the time, but what I was doing was subconsciously recreating the high-stress environment that I'd been used to in the military. By trying to do everything and deceiving myself that I was some kind of unstoppable Übermensch, I was psychologically placing myself back in that do-or-die mentality. I was addicted to the adrenaline, and it was coming back to bite me in the ass.

It was a dark period of my life. I pulled through and began to get my life together, largely thanks to my friend Jim West. We had been introduced by a fan of my novels who worked with him on a construction site and thought we should meet. Jim was a retired Special Forces warrant officer who worked as a safety supervisor for the world's largest construction company. I could tell right off the bat that he was a pretty hard-core dude.

The second time we met, at a diner down on Fourteenth Street, he showed me his paperwork from his military career. I pulled out his award for service in the Gulf War. That didn't make sense, because Jim had been in 7th Special Forces Group, which was not a part of Operation Desert Storm. Jim laughed when I told him that, because actually, there had been one 7th Group guy there, and he had quite a story about how that came about. Jim had heard that there was a war going down and went and knocked on the door of a general he knew at Fort Bragg, pleading to be deployed to the Gulf. He got his wish. Over time, Jim West became someone I could trust, and I frequently sought advice from him. To this day, he is one of the most important people in my life.

I was learning that I could see things that others couldn't, developing a critical eye and an inquisitive personality. This was a learned skill set, one that would help me as a writer but would also serve me well in some challenging situations that were yet to come.

CHAPTER 11

Covering Conflict:
Switzerland to Syria

I STUMBLED INTO JOURNALISM WITH NO FORMAL TRAIN-
ing or mentors and with little guidance. I had to learn by watching what
others were doing, emulating the parts that made sense, and casting aside
the dogma that I felt no obligation to adhere to.

Over time, I came to understand how the media interacts with the U.S.
military. Unlike in years past, only 0.5 percent of our population decides
to serve in the military, so the public ends up seeing their soldiers as part
of some strange, closed-off subculture—which is not entirely inaccurate.
The press, on the other hand, finds itself groveling for access at DOD
press briefings, and favorite journalists at big-name outlets receive controlled leaks to help the Pentagon craft the public narrative. I often laugh
at the stuff I read in the paper, as journalists lap up everything they are
told by DOD public affairs officers. There are some great journalists out
there who know how to deliver the meat and potatoes and keep Americans informed about what their military is up to. There are far more who
couldn't find their ass with both hands in the dark.

One of my first stories was on the massacre of Maguindanao, in which a
convoy of journalists was caught between feuding families in the Philippines; a contact had leaked video footage of the mass grave filmed by

local police after the attack. In another story, I began researching George Washington Bacon III, who died fighting as a mercenary in Angola back in the 1970s. Prior to that, George had served in MACV-SOG in Vietnam and as a CIA paramilitary in Laos. Eventually, I was able to get in touch with a close friend of his who worked with him in Special Forces and at the agency.

In other cases, I wrote articles that were more informational in nature, adding context and explaining little-known aspects of the security world such as the maritime security industry, the geopolitical considerations of the arctic, how the Special Forces Military Free Fall Course had evolved over the years, or how technology was impacting the way our spies operated overseas. I became passionate about recording the "lost" chapters of special operations history. I met with and interviewed those who participated in Blue Light, America's first counterterrorism unit; Detachment A in Berlin and Detachment K in Korea; and the Ranger Reconnaissance Detachment.

At SOFREP, I published never-before-seen pictures of Pablo Escobar after he was killed in Colombia. I broke news stories about the killing of Osama bin Laden in Pakistan, special operators killed in Mali, record-breaking sniper shots in the Congo and Iraq, and exclusive interviews with people like Eeben Barlow, the chairman of a private military company fighting in Nigeria.

We had put together a good team, but I knew that in order to really stand out as a news outlet, we needed to not just produce unique articles but also get boots on the ground. The trial run was in Switzerland, of all places.

My friend Quentin met me at the terminal in Zurich, holding a sign that said WELCOME TACTICAL OPERATOR, knowing how much I hate that term. Once upon a time, only members of Delta Force or SEAL Team Six were operators, but today everyone is an operator and pretending to be something they are not.

Quentin brought me to a friend's house, where I stayed for a couple days, waiting for a training exercise to begin; I wouldn't just be reporting on the event, I would be participating as a guest. Quentin left me an SIG 550 rifle on the coffee table to familiarize myself with and set up the way I wanted, with a sling and so on. This was just the normal state of affairs in Switzerland, where, in the almost exclusively reservist military system, the troops take their rifles home with them.

Our training would be held within a system called Asso Sion, essentially an infantry association that was run privately by Swiss noncommissioned officers but had the ability to tap into military resources. The Asso put on an event once a year to give the reservists—actually called the militia in Swiss terminology—extra training on infantry and unconventional warfare tasks. The day before training, Quentin and I got on the public transportation system in full battle rattle with rucksacks, web gear, rifles, and fatigues. No one batted an eye. We then met a young officer named Diallo and some other Asso members at a hotel bar near Lusanne for beers. When we walked in, the manager of the hotel greeted us and opened up the coat closet for us to store our rucks and SIG rifles. He locked the door, and we walked off to the bar for drinks. I decided that I rather enjoyed Swiss life.

We slept out at the range that night and woke up before dawn to begin preparing for the exercise under the direction of Sergeant Major Francois. I found him polite and professional. Once he stepped in, everything started running by the numbers, and although it is a cliché that the military is a type of machine, the Swiss have a predisposition toward running theirs like a well-engineered watch. One militia member commented to me that the Swiss-made SIG rifles were like AK-47s manufactured by Rolex.

After our gear was set up, we were trucked up the northern part of the country, which took only a few hours. We were inserted into the countryside to conduct a foot movement to a Swiss training base and assault their urban warfare complex. This was a far cry from my previous military experience: We were moving overland through the postcard-worthy Swiss outdoors.

At one point, we were walking up a hill, and our formation of twenty-five or so Swiss (plus one American) passed by an old lady. She stopped one of the Swiss soldiers to tell him how handsome he was. When we took a tactical pause inside a farmer's barn, the farmer walked inside, started his tractor, and took off to go about his work, paying us no mind. The Swiss militia basically uses their entire country for training, and the population pretty much supports this endeavor. The militia isn't supposed to be running around firing blanks at one another in populated areas, but a few Swiss troops will smile and relate a few amusing stories from past training.

As we came up on the training site, we put together a hasty operations order and then moved forward with the assault as the sun was setting. We moved from house to house, shooting it out with the opposing force's role players. At one point, I made it down into the cinder-block basement to shoot it out with the role players, but they had already been "killed" by a simulated frag grenade. We then reset and hit the objective a second time, infiltrating from another angle and using foliage as cover to creep closer to the primary target.

It was a great training event, although I did note a few small areas for improvement. The Swiss have a small and highly motivated force, but they have not had the benefit of combat experience. Switzerland follows a policy of neutrality and does not participate in any actions abroad aside from a small peacekeeping force in Kosovo. Even participating in joint training exercises could be seen as a breach of neutrality, but they base many lessons on formal and informal relationships with the French military, with whom they do train with on occasion.

With the after-action review completed, it was time for the cookout. The Swiss do it right. I had a sausage, some bread, and one beer before exhaustion totally set in. Stretching out on the basement floor of our training building, I wrapped myself in a poncho liner and was immediately out like a light until Quentin woke me in the early-morning hours. We now had a designated casualty whom we had to load on a litter and carry eight kilometers or so through muddy tank trails to our extraction point.

The trip to Switzerland made for a great article, but it was just a dry run for something a little riskier. In 2011, Gaddafi had been deposed, and from there the Arab Spring had moved over to Syria. Pro-democracy rallies may have started it, but before long, I was seeing videos on YouTube showing fighters in Syria. A contact of mine was saying they were just "Syrian hillbillies," with their huge beards, but I knew that was bullshit. While the media was in a frenzy about Islamic radicals, I knew the real players behind the scenes were Baath Party members, notably the same cats I had been fighting back in 2009: the Islamic State of Iraq, ISIS, which had been based out of Syria. That ISIS was packed with Baath Party members came out much later, in leaked documents.

To understand how I got to Syria in November 2014, we have to start the story with the tail end of my time at Columbia University, when I got an e-mail from a guy named George Marshall Lerner, who wanted to interview me for some kind of war-and-peace podcast supposedly put on by Oxford University. So, sure, why not? I met George at a café just down the street from Columbia, where he interviewed me for about an hour about counterinsurgency tactics. George struck me as an intelligent young guy, if a little timid and socially inept.

A week or two later, I get a message from a friend who worked at a bar named Mulligan's, in Hoboken, New Jersey. He says this weird dude in a seven-thousand-dollar suit was sitting at the bar asking questions about me. After we went back and forth for a bit, I showed him a picture of George, and my friend confirmed that it was him. What the hell? George must have heard me mention Mulligan's on our podcast and gone there to check up on me. What a weirdo.

Now fast-forward to after the Switzerland trip, when the Syrian civil war was breaking out in earnest. George started emailing me again, sending me pictures and telling me stories about how he'd joined up with the Kurdistan Workers' Party—called Partiya Karkerên Kurdistanê or PKK— and YPG in Syria, where they were fighting ISIS. It was a strange story. A nerdy awkward rich kid joined up with Kurdish guerrillas? But it was true. Now the next question: Could he get me in? This was a major conflict that needed to be covered by SOFREP, ideally from an on-the-ground perspective. With my military background, I knew I could lend a perspective that people just would not find on CNN, Fox News, or MSNBC.

This was still early on in the war. There were no U.S. military forces in Syria and few foreign journalists. The entire country was in a death spiral that reached new lows every day. In the meantime, George got arrested by the Peshmerga when he tried to cross the border back into Kurdistan. At the time, he told me it was because he had been with the YPG; later, he told me it was because he'd been trafficking in arms. Who knows what the truth is. But he got out, and the plan to travel to Syria was back on.

Coming along with me was my girlfriend, Benedetta Argentieri, an Italian journalist whom I had met in a class on intelligence studies. After I'd separated from my wife and begun working on the divorce paperwork, Benedetta and I had begun dating. Also along for the ride was a female photojournalist who was fluent in Arabic; I'll call her Amanda. First I would fly to Dubai and meet George, then we'd head to Sulaymaniyah, in Kurdistan, where we would link up with the women.

Dubai was like a giant mall. I soon realized that it wasn't even an Arab country. There are Filipinos, Indians, and Sri Lankans living there as migrant workers, but they are more like indentured servants. After a day or two, I met George in the lobby of my hotel. Keep in mind that I maintain a low profile when I travel abroad: no tactical gear, no rowdy behavior, keep it low-key. Most people think I'm just some overgrown frat boy backpacking around the world. George walked in wearing his full PKK regalia: OD pants and jacket, bushy black mustache, and Communist pins on his lapel. He told me later that he'd become a Leninist.

We sat down and began having a conversation, and it was clear that something was pretty off with George. He was extremely shy, scatterbrained, anxious, and just plain weird. The mistake I made was chalking a lot of it up to PTSD, trying to be sympathetic (against my better judgement!) for once.

The next day, we met up in the international terminal to catch our flight. I found myself sitting across from a trio of Afghans. The Afghans often travel to Dubai to deposit their gold, which may have been paid to them by the CIA or another intelligence service. They sat and stared at me, picking at their feet and looking wide-eyed. I choked back any "Didn't I kill your uncle?" jokes.

We boarded the small airplane and took off; George was stressed out the entire time about one damn thing or the other. In a lot of ways, he came off like a lost child rather than the hard-core Communist insurgent he was desperately portraying himself as. The plane came in blacked out, landing at night in Sulaymaniyah. We went through more security than I've ever seen at an airport before coming out in the parking lot. There was my girlfriend, Benni, waiting for me. There was George's PKK contact, waiting for all of us. He was an international arms trafficker but generally a nice guy. I will call this gent by his nickname, Caravan. He took us to our hotel, where we got some kind of discount for PKK party members, and racked out for a few hours. Then George got up and paced around the hotel, knocking on my door, asking questions.

The next day, Caravan came and picked us up and brought us to his safe house and office. He had all kinds of fun stories about how and where they sourced weapons. Apparently, some of their resources abroad were drying up, so they were emptying their stockpiles cached in the mountains around Qandil. He painted a dire picture of what was happening in Syria. There had long been a Kurdish population in northern Syria. Under the regime, they had been second-class citizens who could not hold a passport, get a job, vote, or have basic civil rights. However, Assad had let the PKK operate there, one of those odd quid pro quos that often happen in international politics. At the same time, he had opened up Syria for jihadists to travel through to fight American troops in Iraq. (I would know.)

With the central authority of the Syrian state faltering as the war ramped up, the Kurds saw their opportunity. Town by town, they wrestled away northern Syria, which they called Rojava, from ISIS. Now they were at a stalemate in Kobanî, fighting off wave after wave after wave of ISIS jihadists, who were also receiving state sponsorship from nearby Turkey. Syria was, and is, a complex mess of tribal conflicts, constantly shifting alliances, foreign-sponsored proxy forces, and armies all mixed together in a sort of twenty-first-century form of full auto capitalism in which militias double as criminal rackets, and alliances come together like LLCs from one battle to the next, depending on the realpolitik of the day. Is this how medieval wars were fought in Europe? Give me a good American war any day, because this shit was bonkers.

After we waited around for a few days for Caravan to set all the pieces in motion, a driver met us outside our hotel in a pickup truck. At that moment, I was fed into an underground ratline, a clandestine logistics network for moving people, guns, and even ideas.

The night before we were to leave, I sat outside a hookah bar with Benni, George, and Amanda. The topic of conversation, unsurprisingly, turned to the recent history of war in Iraq. When Benni asked about his motivations for serving with the YPG militia in Syria, George refused to answer. He then launched into the most surreal justification for war profiteering that I'd ever heard—probably George at his most candid.

According to George, war will always happen, and those who are smart and placed correctly can and should exploit the situation for maximum profit. He gave an example of some shady banker at the World Bank who jumped into bed with nefarious characters and terrorists in Afghanistan to make his fortune. For George, war was just a reality, and the human costs didn't really matter, so you might as well cash in. No matter who wins, it just leads to another war, so who cares?

I had to restrain my disgust and calmly remind myself that George was just a twenty-three-year-old kid. I believe strongly that killing can serve a legitimate social function and that sometimes it must be done in order to preserve your country and culture. However, the use of war simply to enrich yourself at the cost of human lives flushed down the toilet is repugnant, unethical, and immoral. I had led young men in combat. They were not toy soldiers. They were not disposable pawns in some asshole's self-rationalized and selfish grand scheme of things. Not for me they weren't.

The driver showed up early the next morning. He was to drive me north, from Suly up into the mountains of northern Kurdistan. It was about a five-hour ride by truck, my bags tossed in the back. As we drove, the driver made calls and received updates about checkpoints up ahead. However, he didn't usually make this trip and got a little turned around in the mountains. Down in one of the gullies was a large flatbed truck, Kurdish resistance fighters filling the back with supplies destined for the front lines in Rojava.

Eventually, our driver asked a couple kids playing with sticks for directions. Although I don't speak Kurdish, I think the conversation went a little like this:

"Hey, kid!"

"Yeah?"

"Where is the secret base?"

"Oh, you went right past it. Turn back and make your first right."

"Okay, thanks!"

Backtracking, the driver went down a muddy slope and crossed a creek. Of course, the pickup truck stalled out before we got to the other side. A little jury-rigging and we were back on the road, where we soon linked up with another contact. Transferring to the other vehicle, I said goodbye to my driver.

The new driver drove about five minutes away before stopping his vehicle. We got out to walk the rest of the way. What followed was like something straight out of the Robin Sage exercise I'd done as a part of my Special Forces training. By now it was dark, and I stumbled a few times down the muddy hill. After crossing a creek, I was suddenly inside a hidden encampment.

The hut appeared almost out of nowhere, as it was camouflaged with the surrounding terrain. A burlap flap was swept out of the way of the entrance, and I stepped inside with my backpack slung over one shoulder. Inside were about two dozen Kurdish resistance fighters sitting around a table. Only a long naked bulb and a space heater illuminated the interior.

The Kurds all stood and welcomed me inside, shaking my hand one by one. They were mostly women. I was offered food and chai tea. Soon I would meet the person we refer to as the "G Chief" in Special Forces training. This is the head honcho who runs the entire guerrilla camp. A woman had been running this way station for resistance fighters for twenty-some-odd years. In a little notebook, she kept track of everyone who passed through her camp, including me. She was killed a few months later, when the Turks launched an air strike against the camp.

The hut was constructed with old rice bags that had been filled with dirt. The roof consisted of tree limbs holding up a roof made of cardboard with plastic sheeting over it. The whole hut was then wrapped in brown burlap and covered with dead foliage to help keep it concealed from the Turks, who occasionally flew overhead and bombed the resistance fighters.

After food and chai, I went down to my quarters for the night. It was a similar hut with bedding inside, which I shared with a fighter who was recently off the front lines. He was being recalled to work in the mountains as a trainer for other fighters. Together we spent a few minutes watching a martial arts film that had been dubbed into Turkish on his old laptop computer. When the computer died, we decided it was time for one more cigarette and then bedtime.

I was now bunking with people in what the United States government considered a terrorist organization. This was nothing like my service in uniform with the military. I was off the reservation, going where I wanted to go and doing what I wanted to do. Living by your wits and surviving in an environment like that is a unique experience. I pulled the blankets over me and set my head down on a pillow made of wadded up T-shirts. Sweet dreams.

CHAPTER 12

Flapping in the Breeze

I WOKE UP EARLY IN THE MORNING AND PUSHED THE heavy blankets off me, trying to use the cold to wake myself up a bit. The Kurdish fighter I had met the night before had already left, but his AK-47 was propped in the corner of the room. I began the daily ritual that the camp's PKK members had repeated probably every day for the past ten or twenty years.

Hobbling a bit, I made my way uphill to the latrine. It was a basin set into a cement foundation under a leaky roof. Because I'm taller than most Kurds, I had to hunch over while relieving myself, or my forehead would be pushing up the cardboard and plastic sheets that served as a ceiling. Next, I headed down to the hut that served as a common area and chow hall. I sat down next to a PKK fighter who greeted me warmly. He told me his name was Haider, which means "lion." It is a common war name for the Kurdish fighters. He was a radio operator and repairman who described himself as a "freedom soldier." Soon a few more PKK soldiers stepped into the mess hall, and we shook hands. They struck me as pretty badass dudes. They were rugged, with giant bushy mustaches. The skill set of PKK soldiers is very interesting. They are trained to conduct guerrilla warfare or, as we would call it, unconventional warfare. However, they are also trained to cook, indoctrinated with political ideology, and, as this PKK member showed me when he fixed our satellite television, know about electronics.

***

In a sense, they struck me as more well-rounded soldiers than American troops, who receive highly specific military occupational specialties (MOS). That said, I'm glad that American troops don't receive political training, as that just isn't our way. U.S. soldiers serve the national interests of their country and are a reflection of American culture. PKK members consider themselves part of a revolution fighting for democratic confederalism, which is also deeply steeped in Kurdish nationalism. Democratic confederalism is a interesting political philosophy that blends the direct democracy practiced in Switzerland with socialist economic policies, along with other political theories from anarchist Murray Bookchin, all of it synthesized by the writing of Abdullah Öcalan.

George was increasingly erratic, not to mention disrespectful to the Kurds. In English, he would actively insult and belittle them, talking about how stupid they all were. He was desperate to portray himself as the most hard-core Communist (most PKK members are not really Communist anymore and follow ideologies such as communalism and democratic confederalism, but that's beside the point). He wanted to show himself as the true guerrilla who fought harder than everyone else. This was a problem with George but also with other foreigners who joined up with the Kurds. They came to Kurdistan with extremely limited knowledge and never took the time to really learn about the people or gain any real empathy for them. Instead, they showed up beating their chest and trying to compensate for their insecurities. They took some selfies holding guns near a war zone, uploaded them onto social media, got bored, and returned to their home countries.

George managed to start a fight with Benni by acting like an asshole, making condescending comments that betrayed his youth and immaturity. Benni started screaming at George, telling him to behave like a professional. He stared at the ground like the shy, timid boy he was. The Kurdish female fighters loved that Benni had put him in his place.

As I prepared to make the trip from Kurdistan to Syria, a young woman sat down with me to write out my visa for my entry to Rojava, on a small piece of notebook paper with a ballpoint pen. I was also given a war name—Jakdaw—meaning "rifle." Like the other PKK members, she asked if I was going to Rojava to fight. I kept having to clarify that I was just a writer. I was taking a highly unusual route into Rojava: I was on the underground railroad.

The visa was to be flown across the border via pigeon, or so I was told at the time. It would not surprise me, as the PKK is still at heart a mountain guerrillas' organization that relies on old-school methods and techniques.

That night we were driven out to the border crossing. On the side of the road, we picked up a Canadian named Peter Douglass, which had been prearranged with the driver. He was a sixty-six-year-old Canadian who had lived in Germany for ten years and worked an assortment of odd jobs. He was adamant about wanting to fight ISIS, figuring that he had another ten years or so before he had a stroke or developed dementia, so he had to go get his licks in before it was too late. George, ever the charming personality, promptly started a fight with Peter.

Also in the car were four teenagers who had been turned into refugees when ISIS took over Kobanî. Without any future in Kurdistan, they had decided to fight with the YPG to take back their hometown. The driver played patriotic Kurdish music from the tape deck during the entire ride, which kept the young men amped up. They chanted, "Kobanî! Kobanî!" They really wanted to go and mix it up. The Syrian civil war was, and is, a meat grinder, with battle after battle depleting a generation of Middle Eastern young people. I'm sure most of the young men I met back then are dead by now.

After driving down some dusty roads, we finally made it to the river crossing. As we approached, the headlights illuminated a small inflatable raft already crossing the Tigris. We were near the tri-border region between several actual states and nonstates: Kurdistan, Rojava (formerly

Syria), and Turkey. We unloaded, and I was on the first lift across the river. Tossing my rucksack inside the raft, I sat on the side as we pushed off into the cold waters. I knew never to wear my ruck during maritime operations. If you fall over the side, your ruck might drag you straight to the bottom. I told Benni to take hers off for that reason.

The small electric engine purred, and we churned our way across the river to a new country, one with new possibilities and a very uncertain future. On the other side of the river, we stepped off onto a rocky outcropping and were immediately greeted by about a dozen Kurdish teenagers. One of them asked where I was from.

"America," I replied.

"Oh, you are American ninja!"

He then showed off some of his ninja katas, and I started laughing. These Kurds had a reason for being in good spirits. They were coming off the front lines and getting some time off. They began loading onto the boat that we had just gotten off of, to head back to Kurdish Iraq. The boat took them across, then made another trip back to us. This time the heavy shit was being off-loaded: DShK barrels for the 12.7mm Russian machine guns. Ammunition. Hand grenades. This was their logistical resupply for the fight against ISIS.

A couple pickup trucks met us at the shore, and we threw our bags in the back with the war material and were driven up the hill to the YPG headquarters, situated on a mountaintop overlooking the town of Derik. When we drove onto the base, I saw CONEX containers and a fleet of white trucks with some kind of logo on the doors. I soon found out that the base had been a Chinese oil company until the war kicked off. In Rojava, oil just bubbles up out of the ground in some places, naturally staining everything black and crumbling the asphalt. There were inoperable pump-jacks on the base and, as I came to find out, spread out across the countryside.

While we waited to be shown to our quarters for the night, we sat inside an office chain-smoking with an older YPG member. Peter Douglass told us all a bit about his background living in Berlin and Canada; he seemed like an interesting guy. The girls were then taken to bed down with the YPJ female militia members, while the rest of us were trucked off to bunk with the YPG. We had the pleasure of a hot shower that night. The next morning, we were waiting for George's contact to show up. I noticed that every time I tried to have a conversation with Benni, George would come strolling up and hover over us. He wanted to control the flow of information and the decision-making process.

Later that morning, Havrem showed up. This was George's war buddy who would escort us around Rojava. He was twenty-four or twenty-five and spoke with a British accent. He wore baggy Kurdish pants and a fatigue jacket, all in the U.S. Marine Corps MARPAT camouflage pattern that the YPG favored. Havrem and George sat down to have a powwow; George left the room several times in tears as he learned about all the Kurds who had died since he'd left Syria. He was in a perpetual state of shock while we were in Syria, as if the entire country was supposed to wait for him in vapor lock. But war is war, and things change rapidly.

Benni and Amanda were also getting upset. George was an emotional train wreck, and we really didn't have any kind of a plan. From the moment Benni and Amanda had stepped through the door the night before, the YPJ women's militia had begun coming up with their own plan for us. This was our introduction to the complexities of Kurdish intra-politics. When you travel to this part of the world, you sometimes have to "pick a side" and travel with them. Kurds see you as a favored guest and want you to be on their side. This makes it difficult to be a journalist, obligated to cover more than one side of a story. From here on out, we were contending with two plans, that of Havrem and that of the YPJ, who insisted on sending escorts with us.

We left the base at Derik with a minivan and a pickup truck filled with YPJ women and went down to another base just outside of the town. At that point, I had everyone sit down and try to get on the same sheet of music. We hashed out the gist of a plan. From there, we spent the next several days traveling all over Rojava: We visited a YPG training base, a hospital in Qamishli, a recovery home for YPG fighters, and more offices, for more cups of chai, than I could count.

While in Rojava, I had a constant feeling of dread. There was something hanging in the air. The areas we were traveling in had once belonged to the government of Syria. You could see a statue of Hafez al-Assad in a town square, see Syrian policemen still manning a checkpoint. Then ISIS came to town, and you could see bullet holes in buildings everywhere from the battle to clear them out. The Kurds had fought for every inch of Rojava in order to push out the forces of evil and establish a secular democracy. We drove past a YPG base where a giant car bomb had gone off. ISIS liked to use vehicle-borne IEDs to kick off raids.

Rojava was the birth of a new nation, the Kurds trying to create a state while fighting a war. You could see culture changing before your eyes. The mullahs were out of power. Kurds who had been second-class citizens were now empowered. Women wore fatigues, played volleyball, and carried Kalashnikovs. It was the type of radical feminism that I could understand. But the eerie feeling of death lurking just around the corner was a feeling that I couldn't shake while I was there. I've never felt that aura anywhere before or since.

Havrem took us to visit the front lines. The Kurds would bring in excavators and pile up dirt mounds to create defensive fortifications. A bunch of middle-age men were standing guard; Grandpa's Army got these types of jobs when there was no active fighting. We looked through binoculars at ISIS positions about a kilometer away. Havrem strolled around the base, pointing out things that should be fixed.

It was a cool day under a bright blue sky, but in that part of the world, when the sun is on you, it feels three feet away; when it dips beneath the horizon, the night becomes freezing cold. Stepping up on top of the sand berm, I could make out ISIS jihadists milling about in the distance. It was an old-fashioned tactical standoff, neither side going on the offensive despite being about a kilometer away. Not today, not until someone thought they would have the upper hand.

Havrem talked a good talk. He proclaimed himself a general. He told tales of commando operations in Turkey, undercover missions in Germany, and fierce fighting in Syria and at Sinjar, Iraq, all for the party, for the PKK. Havrem would carry on in-depth conversations about Abdullah Öcalan, communalism, democratic confederalism, feminism, and other aspects of Kurdish ideology. Problem was, he was full of shit.

In the meantime, at least we were getting to visit front-line forces, YPG bases, people at government buildings, and hospitals for injured soldiers, and generally learn the lay of the land.

When we arrived at an apartment complex in Til Kocher, things really began to go sideways. The apartments sat right on the Syrian side of the Iraq/Syria border, which once was a hub for commerce between the two countries; there were staging areas for big-rig trucks and warehouses. The apartments themselves were once luxury suites but were now occupied by a female YPJ sniper unit in one building and foreign volunteers in the other building, which Havrem more or less claimed for himself. Situated between the apartments and warehouses was a water tower that had been shot to hell during the battle to reclaim the area from ISIS. Little piles of shell casings, black scorch marks, and craters from mortar fire were everywhere.

I met two of the YPJ snipers in an alcove that led into the apartment building. I could tell they were different from the way they carried themselves. This was their home base, where they hung out until they received word to deploy to the front lines and provide sniper support. Some of these young women had quite a few kills under their belt. George wasted no time in freaking them out by crying in front of them and then insisting that one of the guns in their armory belonged to him.

The YPJ members who had been with us headed back to Derik, as our "tour" was complete. I stayed in the second building in a room with foreign volunteers, including a kid from Germany, a guy from Holland who claimed to have served in the French Foreign Legion, and an American of Mexican descent. Everybody has a story, and these guys were no exception. The Mexican American dude told me he was a former marine whose life at home had been turned upside down; a woman was involved. He'd crossed into Syria from Turkey and been nearly kidnapped by ISIS during the process. He kept telling me his life story over and over. Eventually, I figured out that he had come to Syria to die and was telling everyone about himself so that he would be remembered. Part of me understood him, but another part of me realized that I had left that devil-may-care attitude behind with my military service. I was a different man. I had responsibilities in life; I had something to live for rather than just something to fight for.

The leader of the YPJ snipers was a Kurdish woman who had lived in Germany up until the war kicked off. Some of them were very young. One told me she was sixteen, then quickly changed her answer to give me a more politically correct answer (eighteen). When they showed me their scrapbooks and diaries there were pictures of them wearing PKK uniforms up in the mountains of Qandil.

The YPJ and YPG militias had been created specifically for Syria because the PKK was on America's list of foreign terrorist organizations. Many of the militia members were actually Syrian Kurds and Arabs who had little or nothing to do with the PKK, and while this became truer as the war went on, initially, the militias were largely composed of PKK cadre members who had been seconded into the YPG and YPJ. Most of those PKK cadre members were Syrian Kurds to begin with, sent back home in order to ensure that the Kurdish guerrillas had legitimacy with the local population. After all, northern Syria had been the main headquarters for the PKK until President Assad's father kicked them out in 1999. It was interesting to see the convoluted but logical marriage of politics and war. Making sense of it all felt like a fusion of my work as a soldier and my studies as a political science major.

Amanda and Benni stayed with the female sniper unit. The Kurdish girls figured out that Benni and I were an item and began giggling to each other, calling me "blue eyes." They were very nice and offered us chai in between singing songs about Kurdish nationalism, conversations about Apo, their nickname for Abdullah Öcalan, and reading books by philosophers like Friedrich Nietzsche.

That night, George found out that his friend was in a building across the way from us. Supposedly, it was some kind of Kurdish prison and torture center. I declined the opportunity to visit for professional as well as personal reasons. I wasn't going to condone or appear to condone what I'd been told was happening there. George did visit and came back in a daze. He talked about how his friend had become a sadist who now tortured prisoners. Every damn thing that we experienced out there was some sort of hysterical crisis for George. What did he expect from a war zone? His behavior became more unhinged each day, something we had to manage.

I slept on a rollout bed in a room with George, Havrem, and the three foreign volunteers. I kept a knife on me just in case; I'd survived too much gnarly shit to take it like a sucker one night in my sleep. Thankfully, it turned out to be unnecessary. The foreign fighters were nothing but polite the entire time.

In the morning, it was the normal ritual of chai and flatbread for breakfast and generally struggling against the cold to wake up. Off in the distance, toward the warehouses, I could hear gunshots. Sounded like some large-caliber target practice. I grabbed my camera and climbed over collapsed walls and through a staging area for trucks crossing the border. I made

it to the warehouses, where a group was firing the locally made Zagreb
.50-caliber sniper rifle at a spray-painted mark they had made on the side of
a warehouse at a range of fifty meters or so. What the practical purpose of
shooting a large-caliber rifle at fifty meters was, I could not begin to fathom.

At this point, I went up to people and started shaking hands. They
were all camo'ed up, most of them Kurds, but a few were big dudes who
just grunted when I said hello. They were white guys who couldn't speak
the local language but somehow thought I wouldn't know they were foreigners. Then the Kurd who was apparently in charge asked if he could
talk to me off to the side. He had shoulder-length hair combed back and
a mole on his right cheek. First he asked me not to take any pictures of
them; then he told me that none of them could talk to me because they
were on some kind of big secret mission. Finally, he asked me to leave.

This is the kind of amateurish shit that happens in a war zone without
adult supervision, and I understood it well enough not to even be of-
fended. These guys were running around playing mercenary and tactical
dress-up. When I got back to the apartments, I told George what I had
just seen. He said they were wasting ammunition and ran over to the
warehouses to give them a good scolding. The group had left before he
got there, so he missed his opportunity.

Havrem arranged a vehicle to take us to another YPJ base, where they
would be able to help us for the rest of our trip. We said our goodbyes to
the foreign fighters and YPJ snipers, threw our bags in the pickup, and off
we went. We were driven about a kilometer down the road to the base and
dropped off just inside the gate. Some YPJ fighters were playing soccer on
the base, and when I approached them to announce that we had arrived,
they just looked at us sideways. None of them had known we were coming.

At that point, I realized that Havrem had just dumped the four of us.
The YPJ girls would not let us walk back to the apartments because they
felt it was dangerous, so they called their commander to come talk to us.
She arrived a few hours later, as the sun was beginning to set. She was an

Arab woman in her forties and seemed very self-confident and professional, but George kept telling her he was a PKK cadre member on a mission for the party's high command; she was basically laughing in his face,
but he was too stupid to see that. Benni and Amanda did a much better
job of convincing her to help us. Eventually, she agreed to simply drive us
back to the apartments. When we arrived, Havrem looked shocked. He
and George immediately got into a shouting match.

Some will ask why I put up with George as long as I did, which is a
valid question. By this point, I was ready to shoot him myself and do us
all a favor. The reality is that I was traveling in a war-torn foreign country
with two young women. I did not know the culture, terrain, or language.
Unfortunately, George was my link in Syria. If I burned him, I'd be out
there flapping, with George undermining my every move. For now, I had
to put on a nice face and manage as best I could.

I got the impression that Havrem wanted to get rid of George and, by
extension, us. The sniper unit was surprised that we were back, but happy
to see us. We were a distraction from the violence they dealt with on a
day-to-day basis. During dinner, I tried to have a chat with George about
PTSD and how it really got its hooks into some guys. He wasn't listening
to a word I said. I don't think George had PTSD in retrospect; I think he is
just an asshole and that is his natural state of being. After dinner I became
aware that George had disappeared. No one had seen him. I walked around
both buildings asking if anyone had seen George, becoming increasingly
concerned. We had been dumped once today, we were losing rapport, and
we were at risk of being stranded in a Syrian war zone. I grabbed my head-
lamp and headed outside, looking around the entire compound for George.
I expected to find his body, figuring he had finally decided to kill himself.

It was about this point that I realized how badly I had fucked up. As
I shined my flashlight around the debris and methodically scanned the
compound, I thought about how I had rolled the dice with George and
taken too big a risk on an unstable kid who had in turn grossly overplayed

his hand. Now we were in Syria, and how the fuck we were going to get out was highly questionable.

After I'd searched for an hour or so, George suddenly reappeared at the apartment building.

"What the fuck, George?" I asked. I told him I'd been out frantically looking for him. He just shrugged and said he'd gone to visit his friend at the torture center again. I was seriously pissed by this point.

The next day, the Arab YPJ commander at the other base was able to arrange transportation to take us back to Derik. Benni, Amanda, and I agreed that we had accomplished what we'd set out to do in Syria, but now we were just grinding our gears, as things seemed to be going south with us tethered to George.

After a long drive, we made it back to the big YPG base at Derik where we had started our Syrian odyssey. The base was called Karacho and was bombed by the Turks in 2017 on the night Benni was making her way there on foot in order to film a documentary, but that was years later. We spent the night there, and in the morning, we went down to the border checkpoint, which was run by Assyrian Christians. They were nice guys but limited in what they could do for us. We'd been smuggled into the country, so we had no visas, and the KRG would not just let us back in. We could wait for another smuggler boat across the river, but we were told that could happen tomorrow, or it could happen ten days later. We were on Kurdish time now.

It is important to understand a little bit about the nuances of Kurdish politics here. Yes, the Kurds controlled both sides of the Iraqi/Syrian border in this particular place. However, the Syrian side was controlled by the PKK-linked YPG and YPJ militias. Meanwhile, the Iraqi side was controlled by the Kurdish KDP political party–linked Peshmerga. Because the KDP is no friend to the PKK, the border was often shut down and the guards on either side were not necessarily willing to cooperate with one another. Basically, different Kurdish factions controlled each side of the border.

We spent a frustrating day at the border checkpoint, trying to negotiate something, but we were unable to find a way to cross, despite the
guard's best efforts to help us. When we got back to Derik, there was
a pouring rainstorm, just a deluge of water being dumped on us. I told
Benni and Amanda to go straight to the YPJ house and spend the night
there, stay indoors, don't go near George. I found a place to bunk with a
young YPG soldier just across the way from them.

Drying off inside, he and I began to communicate. He was twenty at
best and a PKK member. We had a little show-and-tell session in which he
showed me the contents of his small backpack, his worldly possessions.
Mostly what he had was Apo literature, as well as pictures of Apo, one
of which he kissed right in front of me. He had been shot and had to go
to Turkey to receive treatment but was now recovering; he had a pretty
gnarly scar on his stomach. We showed each other pictures on our cell
phones. It was pretty funny because we both had pictures of guns, knives,
and soldiers. I ended up giving him my folding knife and a North Face
top, figuring he would need that stuff more than I would.

By dawn, the rain had stopped. I stepped outside, my boots sinking
into the mud. A vehicle would soon arrive to take us back down to the
border checkpoint to try to cross again. I crossed over to the YPJ building
to meet with the girls and get ready to roll out. Soon the pickup arrived,
and we were throwing our bags in the back when George spotted us. He
had been wandering around telling people that the party was going to
send him to Kobanî. He approached, trying to get me to go with him
instead of leaving. He'd thought he could capitalize on my Special Forces
background to gain credibility with the Kurds. What I later learned was
that George grew up in a very affluent family outside of Chicago. His
mother had put him in an expensive private school in Thailand (George
is half Thai, half Jewish) because she knew that such a socially inept kid
would be eaten alive in American schools. George had gone to the University of Edinburgh, but it seems that just about everything else he told

us was a lie. He was a trust fund baby running around Syria, trying to establish himself as the Lord of War, like Nic Cage's fictionalized portrayal of real-world arms dealer Viktor Bout in the movies.

George kept pushing me. I looked right at him and said, "No." All he had to do was say one more word and the consequence would be more than just verbal. I think he finally understood, because he backed down. He didn't look happy when we pulled away.

Back at the border, we trekked through the mud up to the checkpoint again, where I got to meet a Syrian Christian who called himself Rambo. He said, "Take my picture, put on Facebook, show whole world." We still were not having any luck crossing the border. We placed a call to the PKK gun runner back in Suly to see if he could work something out for us. "Sure," he said, "I got a guy." Thirty seconds later, the phone rang in the office next to where we were waiting. It's a small world.

Slowly, something that resembled a plan began to come together. Heading south, we would walk across the border back into Kurdistan/ northern Iraq. It was risky, as there were border guards patrolling the area, and ISIS was in the neighborhood as well. But it was our only course of action, aside from camping out in Derik for a month.

The border guards drove us out to a YPG base on the border. Out here, the terrain was like a prairie, just flat open fields, muddy roads, and more mud. The YPG base was a small compound out in the middle of nowhere, about a mile south from the border checkpoint. Inside, we were ushered into a common room and served chai. We had to wait for Peshmerga patrols to move on.

An Arab farmer affiliated with the YPG and the border guard called by our PKK contact escorted us as we probed the border. Our first time, we had to turn around; the Peshmerga was on patrol. We went back to the base and drank some more chai. We made a second attempt around dusk.

Humping our rucksacks and other bags, we trod through the mud. Once again, we were stymied by Peshmerga patrols. Back at the YPG base, the girls were getting upset, and I was frustrated.

The locals agreed to make one more attempt for us. Night had set in, and the red brake lights of the car in front of us bounced along the muddy roads as we were driven to another area along the border where we might have better luck. I carried my ruck as well as Benni's bag as we approached the border. The Arab looked around a bit and then led us forward.

Saddam had erected huge dirt mounds on the border, about thirty feet high. It was extremely difficult to even get on top of the berm, so one of the border guards gave us a boost. The Arab continued leading us forward as we scrambled up the side of the berm. We stayed low, so as not to silhouette ourselves against the overcast sky, slipped over the top of the berm, and then slid in the mud all the way down the other side into Iraq.

In the distance was the orange glow coming from scattered buildings that made up part of a village. I felt like I was on a combat mission again, but this time I had no weapon, no platoon at my back. To get to the village, we had to cross a huge open field. The mud squished beneath our shoes and collected on the soles. Every few steps we had to kick out our legs to shake the mud off or we would seem to be walking on stilts.

Feral dogs could be heard barking in the distance, which is a truism anywhere in Iraq, but as we approached the village, one began circling us, growling and barking. The Arab threw a couple rocks at the dog to keep it at bay. It was getting closer and closer and seemed like it might come and take a snap at us at any moment. We walked between the lonely concrete structures until, finally, a car's headlights flashed at us from a few hundred meters away.

It was our PKK linkman on the other side. We had made contact. As we approached, he popped open the trunk and got out. We tossed our bags inside and quickly shook hands with him, then said a quick goodbye to the Arab. He had to walk back across the border. We were endlessly grateful to the old man for his assistance.

The PKK driver was in his thirties, had a thin mustache, and wore normal civilian clothes. We piled into the car and departed the village, heading north on the road. The driver didn't speak much English, but as I handed him my passport for inspection at the first checkpoint, there was one thing I caught quite clearly: "No Syria."

We got the message: Don't say a word to anyone about being in Syria.

We made it through the first two checkpoints without a problem, but then we hit the big one on the way to Dahuk. When the guards examined our passports, something seemed wrong. We were asked to step out of the vehicle. We were all covered in mud up to our knees. During the ride, I had concocted a very flimsy cover story with the girls that we had been writing stories about poverty in the southern villages of Kurdistan. Who knew how long that would hold up, but it was better than nothing.

We were brought to the officer in charge of the checkpoint, who was very nice and asked us some simple questions. He wound his way back to what we were doing out there. How was it possible that we were passing through his checkpoint but had not passed it on the way to the villages, as there was only one way in or out? "Oh, I don't know," I said, "we went through the checkpoint in the early morning, and we were sleeping in the car." The Kurdish officer just laughed.

The good news was that we had made it into Kurdistan without being captured by ISIS and having our heads sawed off. The bad news was that we now had to bargain for our freedom. Some of the foreign volunteers with the YPG had been detained when they crossed back into Kurdistan, some of them afforded an extended stay in a one-star prison with captured ISIS terrorists.

After our initial interview/interrogation, we were told to sit tight in another room. I sat on the edge of a desk, smoking cigarettes with one of the border guards, trying to fish for additional information. While we were there, young men wearing desert fatigues were brought in, shivering from being exposed to the elements. They were not soldiers. There were seven of them, men in their twenties who had also made a border run. They'd left Syria to escape conscription and wore fatigues in hopes of disguising themselves as Peshmerga. I felt bad for them; they looked like they were in a shit state.

In the back of my mind, I knew that I was in a foreign country and things could get pretty bad. Still, I had a blue passport and would eventually be heading home; the question was whether it would be before or after a few months in Kurdish prison. These guys were not going anywhere; this was their home, and it was at war.

Maybe an hour or so went by before the captain of the guard called us back into his office. He asked some more questions, laughed to himself, and then said that he would release us but would send one of his guards with us to Dahuk to "ensure our safety." We got into the car with the PKK driver and the Peshmerga border guard and hit the road. The driver's words echoed in my mind: "No Syria." If they found out we had been in Syria and made an illegal border run, we were fucked.

The girls were happy to be heading to the city and the chance to sleep in a real bed for the first time in a couple weeks. I tried to dial them down a bit, feeling that we were not out of the briar patch yet. Sure as shit, when we arrived in Dahuk, the border guard began giving directions to the driver, and they were not to our hotel. We turned a corner, and our vehicle maneuvered through a serpentine made of concrete barriers toward a barren-looking three-story building. Aw, fuck, I thought. This is an episode of *Locked Up Abroad*.

We parked the car and were escorted inside. It was about midnight by this time. The Peshmerga guard handed off our passports to someone in the building. From the patches on the Kurdish soldier's shoulders, I saw that we were in the Directorate of General Security, which sounded to me like an ominously generic name. It soon became apparent that this was the *asayish*, the secret police.

We were seated in what passed for a lobby, the inner door consisting of a barred gate. Prisoners were being escorted around. The PKK driver was taken aside and strip-searched. He was the one we were really concerned with. The secret police then wanted our cell phones. I lied and said I'd lost mine in all the excitement. One of the officers on duty that night walked past us, putting on a big show of looking us up and down while holding an open notebook that had our passports taped inside. This was some Keystone Cops stuff, but hey, I wasn't going to say anything. I was a captive audience at this point, literally.

I think we all knew what was coming next. I was the first one called into the interrogation room. They sat me down on the couch beside a rather large gentleman who appeared to speak little English. A younger guy with black slicked-back hair seated in front of me spoke very good English. A young man, maybe in his early twenties, who also spoke English, leaned against the wall on the opposite side of the room but said little.

We went through the whole song and dance, as you might expect; they tried to find holes in my story, which wasn't hard. I quickly fell back on some of my peacetime detention training from the army and began demanding to see a representative from the American consulate. I rebuked all charges made against me. Such accusations could sour relations with my government! Yeah, right, as if I were so important. I was trying to save my ass, and everyone knew it.

Eventually, they got tired of me and sent me back out into the lobby. I told Benni and Amanda not to worry, that everything would be fine. They had no real information about us and were just fishing, hoping that we would inadvertently reveal something. You see, we were all hanging by a thread. We can make denials all day, but they were no doubt searching through our bags out in the parking lot right now. If they opened up my digital camera and scrolled through the pictures, they would quickly see pictures of YPG members and huge portraits of Apo. Maybe even worse, there was Benni's notebook, which she had hidden under the driver's seat, with her notes from Syria, hand-drawn maps, essentially a cornucopia of evidence if, or when, it was found.

Benni turned out to be a natural-born resister. When they got her in the room, she berated the secret police, stood up, and declared that she was on "that time of the month" and needed to go home and take a pill. The conversation was pretty much over by that point. Amanda went next, and she stuck to our story. Then they brought me back in for round two.

The main interrogator began telling me that I'd been in Syria and had met with a particular commander on the other side of the border, which I hadn't, and I told him as much. He started pushing hard, and I started pulling every card I could out of my sleeves, as I really didn't want to go to ISIS prison. I told him I was a former soldier myself and that we should be friends. I told him I was now a journalist working for a website called SOFREP.com.

The younger Kurd came up and handed me his cell phone. He said, "Pull up this website and show me one of your articles." I went to SOFREP and started looking for my articles. The first one I saw was about the YPG in Syria. No, not that one, keep scrolling down. Next article was about the YPG fighting ISIS in Syria. No, not that one, either. I found an article that was situation-appropriate, and that seemed to satisfy them for the moment.

In between my demands to speak to my consulate, the main interrogator asked if I had been on ODA 5220. "No," I replied, "ODA 5414." Clearly, these guys knew my guys. We had arrived at a deadlock. We were all sticking to our stories, and the Kurdish secret police had to make a decision—keep us in prison or get us out of their hair.

Out in the main area, the interrogator came out and informed us that we would be released and driven to our hotel. "You are welcome in Kurdistan, but please do not disturb us again," he said to me.

"NO PROBLEM," I said enthusiastically.

Several members of the secret police escorted us and our driver up the hill to our hotel. I laid a very generous tip on the driver. He had more than earned it, and I felt quite bad that we had gotten him involved in our ordeal. Inside the hotel, I sat down in one of the plush chairs in the lobby and took a deep breath. What a night. Once we were checked in, I got on the elevator with Benni and headed up to our room. "You know," I told her, "you are kind of a badass."

There are a few addendums to the Syria trip. When I got home, I found out from my ex-wife that she had been getting creepy phone calls in which someone would whisper over the phone, "Jack needs your help . . . only you can help him," and then hang up. I did a little bit of math and realized that these calls had started happening right around the time I was trying to cross back into Iraq. I figured fucking George, and maybe Havrem, too, playing games.

Working on my laptop in my apartment in Manhattan, I started getting the calls on Skype. When I picked up, someone would whisper, "Jaaaaaacccckk . . . Jaaaaccck." After a few times, I would play clips from the classic movie *Predator:* "Turn around, turn around. MWHAHAHA!" The calls stopped after that. As best as I can figure, that psycho George found my ex-wife's phone number on an old résumé that she had uploaded to a jobs website years prior and started making harassing phone calls, probably in order to put pressure on me as I was trying to exit Syria—but who really knows.

Over the years, George has remained in Syria and Kurdistan, basically just squatting with the Kurds and having them take care of him. His family back in America has essentially disowned him.

Then I found out more about Havrem. He claimed to be a YPG general but was a translator for them. He claimed to be a PKK ideologue but was a crass opportunist. His real name was Alex and he was a British national being paid by the YPG, but little of that money ever reached the volunteers that Havrem was supposed to be paying. Eventually, the whole scam got blown wide open, partly because I wrote about what he was up to. Last I heard Alex ran back to the UK.

CHAPTER 13

Dark News

I STAYED BUSY WORKING AS A JOURNALIST, EVEN WHEN I WAS not overseas. I wrote about topics that ranged from ISIS to a little-known prison riot in Panama to a history of the U.S. Special Forces. There are moments for a journalist when you know you are getting the real deal: when a Korean War veteran tells you about one of his soldiers dying in his arms, his last words "Full of grace." He said he became a Christian that day. An American who served with the Selous Scouts in Rhodesia recounted to me a counterambush in which their position was overrun by terrorists. He said he was so scared that he couldn't talk for about half an hour. A soldier who served with Studies and Observations Group doing cross-border operations in Laos during the late 1960s told me how he'd shot and killed a sixteen-year-old Vietcong in the jungle; turned out the kid had only a few bullets in the magazine of his decrepit rifle. He said he always felt bad about killing that kid.

Then there are moments for a journalist when things get way more real than you ever expected. Years prior, when I was in 5th Special Forces Group, I'd had a conversation with a guy on the dive team down the hall about how many victims of sexual assault in the military were actually male. Following up on this angle led me to one of those moments.

The army has a really cynical approach to alcoholism, suicide, and sexual assault. They have taken corporate tactics that involve "qualifying" soldiers by forcing them to undergo mandatory training, much of it via online computer modules that soldiers click their way through while half asleep. One such bloc of instruction involves training select soldiers in each unit to become advocates for victims of sexual assault. It is a well-intentioned program to inform the troops about sexual assault and to create advocates whom peers within the unit can approach about abuse. When I was in 5th Special Forces Group, a buddy in our company's combat diver team went to that training. I said to him, "Well, thankfully, we don't really have a problem with sexual assault in our unit, since we are all men." Up until recently, only men could apply to become Special Forces soldiers. The only women in our Green Beret unit were in staff and support positions. By my reasoning, we could not have much of a sexual assault problem simply because there were not many women around in the first place.

My friend just shook his head ominously. "Actually, you would be surprised how much of it is man-on-man."

"Bullshit," I replied.

"No, seriously. You would not believe how many young joes go out and get drunk, then pass out in the barracks in Korea, only to wake up with their battle buddy's cum leaking down the crack of their ass."

This was a conversation I kept coming back to as the issue of military sexual assault became a bigger and bigger issue in the media in subsequent years, but I never heard anyone talk about male sexual assault. It was always stories about men assaulting women. We even had big vinyl banners hanging up in the halls, saying that stopping sexual assault was the army's number one priority. (I'd thought winning wars was our number one priority, but I guess I was wrong.) The picture on the banner was of a female soldier.

When I set out to write a story about male sexual assault in the military, I asked a friend if he knew anyone who had been through this ordeal and if they would be willing to speak with me. To my surprise, my friend relayed that indeed he did know someone and would ask to see if they would be willing to talk. Soon, I had a name and a phone number. This is how I came into contact with Joe Barnes. Joe had been an infantryman, serving in 10th Mountain Division as well as the 101st Airborne Division where he became a sergeant. It was during a deployment to Afghanistan with the 101st that things really came apart at the seams.

I gave Joe a call. It wasn't exactly a cold call, as he had already agreed to speak with me, but you never quite know what to expect. As I soon realized, I was about to get way more than I bargained for. A lot of the things I've been through in life I can just shrug off, most of it like water running off a duck's back. But I think about Joe Barnes every day. As I write this, I'm looking over the notes I wrote from our first conversation and it is still horrifying.

Joe served in 1st Platoon, Charlie Company, 1st Battalion, 506th Infantry Regiment, a part of the 101st Airborne Division. The 1st of the 506th attempts to trace its lineage back to the famed "Band of Brothers," made famous to a younger generation by the HBO miniseries depicting American paratroopers heroically parachuting into Nazi-occupied France on D-Day and battling the Nazis. Joe told me that the unit would play the theme song from the HBO miniseries at all of their unit's events and functions.

Sergeant Joe Barnes caught up with his unit halfway through the deployment, arriving at FOB Kushamon in Patika Province, Afghanistan. He had already heard stories about one soldier in his new platoon. "I started hearing rumors about this squad leader, who they think is gay and very forceful on certain people," Joe told me over the phone during our first conversation. The squad leader in question was Staff Sergeant Jonathan Santoro. Joe, who was a big professional wrestling fan, described Santoro as being built like John Cena.

Meanwhile, 1st Platoon was rolling outside the wire on combat operations. The deployment was characterized by long-range firefights and mortar engagements. An informant would often lead the platoon to IEDs, which he was paid in cash for uncovering. Joe told me most of them were not even rigged to explode, and it felt like the informant was running a scam. For his part, Santoro was one of the most competent sergeants in the platoon. Several members of the platoon told me about how in the middle of a firefight, the remote weapon system on top of their vehicle went down, and Santoro jumped up on the roof of the truck and began firing it at the enemy manually. As weapons squad leader, Santoro not only knew his job but was fearless in combat. Despite previous reservations, Barnes and Santoro struck up a friendship.

The platoon was dependent on Santoro for their survival during a difficult combat deployment, even more so because, these platoon members reported, their platoon sergeant was regarded by many of the men as a coward. The platoon sergeant is the senior enlisted soldier, the most experienced member, often called "Platoon Daddy" by soldiers due to his important role, but not in this case. One night, I was told, their platoon sergeant boarded a helicopter at their base in the dead of night and abandoned his men in FOB Kushamon. He had quit his job, and no one even knew.

However, Joe continued to hear rumors about Santoro. "I started hearing from other lower enlisted guys that they would get drunk with this guy and then he would offer to suck their dick," Joe told me. "Like you don't have to do anything, I'll just suck you off." But Joe never witnessed any of this himself at the time.

Meanwhile, their FOB was getting mortared and rocketed all the time and they were not getting much sleep. Their new platoon sergeant showed up, Sergeant First Class Matt Mason. Almost immediately he had to begin addressing discipline issues in his platoon, including a soldier who was huffing canned air and another who was stealing mail from other soldiers.

Mason had also heard some stories about Santoro but had no proof and no witnesses coming forward to him. In a later conversation, Mason told me, "The way they made it seem was that he [Santoro] was being selected as a quality leader to take these positions and train these soldiers, which was not what was happening," Mason said. "He was not being selected, he was being fired, relieved of his duty, and sent to another place to attempt to rehabilitate him." This story got darker the more I looked into Santoro's background and was told of incidents going back many years.

One was said to have occurred while Santoro was stationed at Fort Campbell and was assigned to a funeral detail with two other soldiers. During that detail, something happened while they were all staying at a hotel, but no one knew exactly what, they just knew that those other soldiers got out of the army very quickly. Another reportedly occurred during a previous deployment to Iraq where something had happened with Santoro, which was again kept very hush-hush. And yet another occurred when just prior to being assigned to 1st Platoon and deployed to Afghanistan, Santoro had been assigned to the battalion commander, Lt. Col. Womack's, personal security detachment, which basically serve as bodyguards. While there, he was alleged to have been pressuring a private to have a sexual affair with him, and when the situation couldn't be ignored, he was fired and sent to 1st Platoon. Even Santoro's promotion to staff sergeant appeared questionable, SFC Mason told me, as he had never gone before the board, but there was his rank on his official paperwork nonetheless. For a staff sergeant, it seemed to several in the unit, Santoro wielded an almost supernatural amount of power and influence in the battalion, which was completely inconsistent with his rank.

From my first conversations with Joe, I was shocked that something like this could ever happen in the same army I served in. While we had our issues in the units I served with, I had never heard of anything approaching what Joe was describing to me. His account of when he became convinced of the rumors about Santoro was chilling: It was one day during an impromptu wrestling match on the FOB, which is a fairly common occurrence in infantry units. While wrestling on the ground on the gravel, Santoro deliberately attempted to jam his fingers up Joe's anus through his physical training shorts. Joe pushed him away and asked him what the hell he thought he was doing, but Santoro laughed it off.

Reflecting on the notes I took from talking to Joe, I began my own investigation.

I cleared off the corkboard behind my desk and began writing names down on 3x5 cards. I tacked them onto the board, fleshing out the task organization of Joe's platoon, and then charting the chain of command up to the company and battalion level. The Internet and social media make it pretty easy to track most people down. Joe was not in contact with a single member of his former platoon, but I was able to locate most of them on Facebook. I very selectively began reaching out to people in the platoon. A few I talked to were as disgusted with the situation as I was and were more than happy to help make further introductions, which is how I came to speak with Sergeant First Class Matt Mason. I was also able to speak with another important soldier in this story, Private First Class Brandon Queen.

Others were more standoffish; some in the chain of command were still in the military and spoke to me off the record, as I was able to track them down using various other means. While minor details varied, the gist of the story was consistent with all of those I spoke to. Jonathan Santoro was a sexual predator, and the 101st Airborne had conspired to cover up the abuse.

Santoro even apparently got into trouble when he left the deployment for mid-tour leave, when he was alleged to have solicited a minor, flying him out to meet him in Las Vegas. The parents reportedly decided not to press charges against Santoro, and the army again swept the incident under the rug. Back in Afghanistan, Mason was beginning to notice things.

During patrols, members of Santoro's squad would fill the role of machine gunner on Mason's vehicle and they would ask Mason if they could change squads. The platoon sergeant first thought that these soldiers simply resented Santoro's strong leadership style. But as time went on he saw "a lot of hands-on playing around, horseplay, and they did not feel comfortable with it at all. You could tell by the emotions on their faces and body language. I had to try to have him [Santoro] removed several times through the first sergeant, and he talked to the battalion command sergeant major, who said that will never happen." According to Mason, it was the battalion's command sergeant major named Judd who prevented Santoro from being removed from the platoon.

Meanwhile, soldiers in 1st Platoon, especially the ones in Santoro's squad, were, by the accounts that emerged, being terrorized. In addition to Joe Barnes's report of what occurred during the wrestling match, others told of having been groped, having had their genitals fondled, and more. The stories were beyond disturbing: Santoro would make privates sit on his lap while he groped them. He was witnessed to nibble on the ears of soldiers. A skilled manipulator, Santoro would assign soldiers he was not sexually interested in to pull tower guard duty on the base's perimeter, soldiers like Jon Jonas, because Santoro was not interested in African Americans. He was also not interested in one of the team leaders in the squad, who was a bigger guy and twenty-eight years old at the time.

Unfortunately, he was interested in smaller, younger soldiers like eighteen-year-old Brandon Queen. The twenty-eight-year-old team leader advised Queen to carry a knife around with him, saying, "Once the sun goes down, who knows where Santoro is and where Queen is, something could happen in the corner of the FOB." I gave Brandon a call and found him to be both forthright and brave in telling me his story. Most of those abused by Santoro simply wanted to disappear, but Brandon wasn't having it.

"When I first got there, he was talking about other boys, calling them deployment bitches," he told me over the phone. Santoro was known for flexing his rank in order to coerce soldiers into having sex with him. If a soldier denied him sex, he would physically punish them with so-called smoke sessions, having them do exercises like pushups and flutter kicks until they were exhausted. "Everybody knew he was gay and everyone was scared of him. Basically, he used intimidation and rank," Brandon explained.

Manipulating the guard duty roster, Santoro made sure he had plenty of opportunities with Brandon and would follow him to the bathroom and basically stalk him around the base. Santoro would also not let Brandon call home to his then wife, further isolating him. One soldier was so upset by Santoro's advances that he pulled a pistol on him and said he'd kill him. Santoro just laughed and walked away.

The officers in the unit were also of little help. The platoon leader was a lieutenant named Matt Jones, and the Company Commander was Captain Andrew Hill. Both would go to the gym with Santoro and engage in what other soldiers described as a bizarre game of grab-ass. Hill and Santoro would haze Jones while spotting for him in the gym, Santoro rubbing his testicles on Jones.

Queen told me that the situation reached a boiling point when Santoro was watching a DVD with Queen one night and he tried to force Queen's pants down to perform oral sex on him. Queen managed to wiggle away and burst out of Santoro's hooch at a full sprint. Several members of the platoon told me about how they heard Queen's boots beating against the gravel as he made his escape. Queen took the issue to his platoon sergeant, SFC Mason.

"He is a small guy, very small frame," Mason told me about the conversation he had with Queen that day. "It was basically that he was afraid—for one, to be in that building with Santoro. And that he is tired of living in fear, I guess is the best way to put it—of being groped on a daily basis. Because there is nothing he could do about it and he was scared to death." Mason was fed up and had had enough of the bullshit. He took the issue to their company's senior enlisted leader, whom Santoro was known to be very friendly with, in addition to the battalion commander himself, Lt. Col. David Womack.

It was now three or four weeks before the platoon was scheduled to redeploy back to the United States, and a commander's inquiry was initiated on the actions of Santoro. Amazingly, he was not moved out of the platoon. I asked SFC Mason why that was. "I don't have a good answer for that, it still puzzles me now," he replied. "At that point there were still guys who were actively being assaulted, sexually. It was rough times. I don't know why they didn't move him."

The platoon returned home at the end of their deployment, and the commander's inquiry somehow found no wrongdoing, and no action was taken against Santoro.

Back home, "my mental status just degraded severely. There was one point that I had stopped and picked up a sandwich at the local Walmart, and I walked in, grabbed it, and was on my way to get a drink from further in the back, and all of a sudden, like, sparks started flashing and getting weird and fuzzy and then just black. I convulsed almost and could not walk; this went on for a long time. No one could figure out what was wrong. I'm a wreck. People at work are wondering what is going on," Mason said. He was suffering from PTSD, and his unit put him on suicide watch. He was also struggling with guilt he felt about how Santoro was able to abuse the men in his platoon. Meanwhile, other soldiers in the unit were committing suicide or attempting to.

Back at Fort Campbell, Joe Barnes was struggling with feelings that the army had completely betrayed him. For complaining about Santoro he had been removed from the platoon, and Santoro ensured that he was made an ammunition NCO, a staff position where Santoro could keep an eye on him now that he was on the brigade staff as well. When the change was made, Barnes told me how "I got pulled into the 1st Sergeant's office with the guy who assaulted me. 'We need a guy in the ammo NCO position and Staff Sergeant Santoro says you are the man for the job,'" the first sergeant said to Barnes.

Frustrated, Barnes said he approached a reporter at the *Army Times* with his story. When the chain of command found out, they went ballistic.

"Sergeant Major Judd and Lieutenant Colonel Womack made me call the *Army Times* in front of them and retract. They wanted no part of me going forward with my story," Barnes said. The sergeant major and brigade commander asked Barnes why he would want to tarnish the image of the Band of Brothers by talking about Santoro. Meanwhile, he continued his new job at the brigade staff with his abuser. "When I got put in the ammo NCO position I was sitting across from him [Santoro] every other week in a brigade-level meeting. Since I was ammo NCO I got to sit across the desk from him every other week. Nobody cared, nobody gave a fuck."

The deeper I dug on this story, the more surreal it got. There appeared to be incredible failures at every level of the chain of command. Was it a confluence of bad leadership, or were these failures by design? A number of platoon members felt that to understand how this could happen you had to look way above the leadership at the platoon level and examine what was going on across the entire brigade under Lieutenant Colonel Womack and CSM Judd. At times I felt like Rust Cohle in *True Detective*, wondering if this was real or if I was losing my mind. But I wasn't going crazy, and neither were the soldiers who I was talking to about these events; it is simply that the truth is horrifying and difficult to accept.

But as Joe Barnes told me, "When it blew up, it blew up."

After the failure of the commander's inquiry to do something about Santoro, the ball got rolling again when Brandon Queen was assigned to staff duty, a mundane military chore in which a private and a sergeant basically just sit at headquarters all night in case the phone rings. Queen told the sergeant he was on duty with the entire story about Santoro in Afghanistan. That sergeant (who had not been in their platoon) hit the roof and took the issue higher.

At the same time, a new captain assumed the role of company commander over the platoon in question. The first day on the job, Captain Kyle Packard came into work and found Joe Barnes standing outside his office crying, begging him to listen to what he had to say. He did.

Packard, who had previously served in the Ranger regiment, was completely shocked by what Barnes had to tell him. He could not believe that something like that could happen in the army that he knew and loved. For that matter, neither could Barnes, up until it did happen and his chain of command sold him out.

Captain Packard pushed for a new investigation and ultimately a court-martial. Barnes told me that Packard refused to just ignore the issue and cover it up as so many others had. But now Barnes, Queen, and others began getting threatening text messages from Santoro. Barnes also believed he saw Santoro's car parked outside his residence several times. At least this time the investigation was done by the book and UCMJ action was pushed for. According to Joe and others, Lieutenant Colonel Womack and CSM Judd promised their men anything to make the issue go away, then promised they would give them anything they wanted to keep the issue quiet, and finally when none of that worked they simply vanished, leaving the unit, and leaving a trail of destruction in their wake. As the investigation continued, Santoro was eventually told to stop texting witnesses by army criminal investigations personnel.

As the court-martial neared, it was difficult for the army to find witnesses to come forward due to how damaged they were. Many were a wreck, psychologically speaking, after enduring so much trauma. Of course there was trauma from their battlefront experiences, but what was happening in the "safety" of their bases seemed, in some cases, to be even more damaging. Soldiers in the unit had gone AWOL multiple times. Others had attempted suicide. Some of the soldiers were such a psychological mess that an army physician had prescribed them Xanax, Lithium, Ambien, and other pharmaceuticals. At least one soldier attempted suicide simply because the prescription drugs were making things even worse for him. Several of the soldiers were also committed to mental institutions for weeks at a time.

Via a Freedom of Information Act request, I was able to obtain a copy of the court-martial transcript. The names of witnesses are redacted, but by cross-referencing the redacted information with the names and duty positions on the 3x5 cards up on my corkboard, I was able to reconstruct most of it. The trial began in May of 2012.

In the opening statement the prosecution said, "The accused is an experienced infantry soldier and a good tactician outside the wire; however, off mission, he was something completely different." The prosecutor goes on to describe how Santoro controlled and manipulated his soldiers, isolating them, fondling their genitals, knife-handing their buttocks, and even crawling into bed with them. However, Santoro was never put on trial for rape, only wrongful sexual contact, hazing soldiers, and drinking alcohol while overseas.

The defense countered by saying that "the evidence is going to show that some of these squad members, some of these, especially the young soldiers who had just returned from their first deployment, were confused by this blurred line between friend on the one hand, and disciplinarian squad leader who held them to the standard. They blame the post-traumatic stress, they blame their depression, they blame their anxiety on their squad leader, on Staff Sergeant Santoro. They tried to find meaning in war to meaning in their pain, in what they had to do every day, in the combat that they saw, and they blamed their stress and trauma on their squad leader because, sir, they were confused by him, because they found out that he was bisexual and because he was an easy scapegoat. They called it sexual assault and they called it maltreat[ment], sir, but you will see that the evidence supports neither."

The defense's argument was essentially that Santoro had simply been engaging in horseplay with his soldiers. In infantry units it is very common for soldiers to have impromptu wrestling matches, but these physical confrontations are a way that soldiers blow off steam and goof around. They do not involve sexual contact like knife-handing someone's ass or groping their testicles as Santoro did on many occasions. In a court of law, these distinctions were difficult to explain. From the defense's point of view, Santoro was a victim of homophobia and soldiers who were projecting their post-traumatic stress onto their squad leader.

Five witnesses testified against Santoro. What also emerges in the transcript is that platoon members were aware that Santoro had more power within their unit than a normal squad leader. He had cultivated a culture of impunity within the unit, one that was abnormal. The defense strongly implied during cross-examination that the five victims were homosexual and had led Santoro on, de facto consenting to their abuse. They also marshaled soldiers who testified in support of Santoro, maintaining that his conduct in the battlefront was exemplary, and on the base, nothing out of the ordinary.

When it came time for Santoro to testify, he denied sexually assaulting anyone, although he conceded to participating in sexualized horseplay, along with others in the platoon, including his platoon leader, Matt Jones. During his testimony, Santoro explained that he grabbed his platoon leader's genitals as part of the grooming process that seasoned sergeants put junior officers through. Santoro explained that while he was bisexual, he never groped anyone, nibbled on their ear, or offered to perform oral sex on soldiers.

During closing statements the prosecution pointed out that "if five female soldiers came in and testified about exactly what these soldiers endured, that sure as hell would be no joke to anybody in this courtroom; but these were men, these were infantry soldiers, these were tough guys." It is important to recall that this male-on-male military sexual assault took place during the days of the Don't Ask, Don't Tell (DADT) policy which was still in effect in 2010 and repealed in 2011 after the Afghanistan deployment in question.

DADT had added an additional layer of complexity to the case, and at least some leaders, perhaps wrongly, felt that they could not confront Santoro because of the policy. Additionally, the male-on-male nature of the crimes carries additional social stigma for the victims. Accusations are made that the victims are secretly homosexual and like the abuse. People as questions like "Why didn't you fight back?" despite the perpetrator being in a position of authority and being physically intimidating to young soldiers.

In this case there was also the issue that the abuse happened in the middle of a war zone in which the soldiers were conducting combat operations, and their base was being bombarded by enemy fire on a daily basis. Sexual assault may be deprioritized as an issue to deal with when facing matters of life and death every day. As the defense put it, "When you are an inexperienced infantryman doing daily patrols in eastern Afghanistan the last thing you want to do is piss off the squad leader whose job it is to keep you alive."

The prosecutor wrapped up the closing argument stating, "This case should be briefed at the sexual harassment assault response training across the army. To think that our leaders, our senior noncommissioned officers, in the most crucial leadership positions in our army, leading soldiers at the tip of the spear, are doing this to their troops? What faith can we have in our system to protect soldiers against predators when we call that a game?"

The military judge made a ruling on the case by himself, which Santoro requested. The judge took less than an hour to decide and find Santoro guilty of all charges.

During the sentencing, the soldier who had pulled a pistol on Santoro offered additional testimony about how the abuse impacted his life and how Santoro once made him drag a tow rope a mile through an uncleared field believed to be full of IEDs, when there was no reason since the vehicle he was told to move the rope to already had its own tow rope. He suspected that Santoro was "just petty enough that he was kind of hoping that I'd get killed."

During sentencing, Lieutenant Colonel Womack was interviewed telephonically, as he had now moved on to a position in the Pentagon working for the Secretary of the Army. He stated that he had known Santoro for many years, going back to when Womack had been a company commander. The two had served together in 4th Brigade for a long time. Now that Santoro had been convicted, Womack offered that he had a very low opinion of him.

The last witness called as a part of the sentencing process was an army forensic psychologist named Dr. Jeffrey Bass. Dr. Bass was assigned to the Walter Reed National Military Medical Center in a forensic psychology fellowship, where his main function was conducting risk assessments for violence and sexual violence for sanity boards and criminal cases. He had previously worked at the FBI's Behavioral Sciences Unit conducting psychological profiles and at the time of the trial was working at the NSA. His experience included conducting around 115 forensic evaluations previously.

Dr. Bass interviewed Santoro for about eight hours and reviewed all the case materials. When asked for his diagnostic conclusions, Dr. Bass stated to the court that "I did not diagnose Staff Sergeant Santoro with a mental illness, a severe mental illness, even a severe adjustment disorder. I did diagnosis him with alcohol abuse."

Dr. Bass was then asked if there were any signs of a sexual disorder. "No, there were not," he said. The psychologist also gave an assessment on how likely Santoro was to commit future sexual violence, based on his own empirical research. He assessed a low to moderate range for engaging in future sexual violence. He also assessed Santoro as having a low chance of committing violence in general in the future. When Dr. Bass subjected Santoro to the PCLR (the Psychopathy Checklist Revised), he found Santoro to be in the non-psychopathic range, scoring a five out of a top score of fifty, with the average person being somewhere between twelve to twenty-two on the test.

The psychologist then suggested a treatment plan for Santoro to undergo while incarcerated, as the judge was about to sentence him to twelve months in a military prison for the crimes he had been convicted of. "Based on your overall evaluation of Sergeant Santoro, do you believe that he could be safely managed in the community with your treatment plan?" the defense asked.

"Yes," Dr. Bass answered. "I do."

During cross-examination, the prosecution asked if Dr. Bass had tested Santoro for sexual deviancy. The psychologist had not. The problem was that Dr. Bass was part of the defense team, and Sergeant Santoro knew this from the onset, and knew that during a potential sentencing it would look better on him if he was deemed as a low risk to the community. The only other people Dr. Bass interviewed were soldiers that had been referred to him by the defense counsel. He did not talk to Santoro's mother, his ex-girlfriend, or the man that he was currently in a relationship with because Santoro himself asked him not to. The tests Dr. Bass subjected Santoro to did not account for the fact that there were multiple victims, simply assuming that there was only one data point without multiple offenses.

Dr. Bass assessed that with a treatment plan Santoro was not likely to reoffend. But was he right?

As I was about halfway through writing my article about this entire ordeal, I learned that Joe Barnes had passed away. The family kept the cause of death under wraps, but I had been told that there were some substance abuse issues. He told me himself over the phone that he felt incredibly guilty about what had happened at FOB Kushamon. It wasn't the trauma that he personally experienced that bothered him so much as it was the guilt that he should have done more to protect the privates in his platoon as a sergeant. He felt that he had let them all down.

Although I did not know Barnes aside from our phone conversations, his death hit me hard. I felt it even more important to tell his story. A lot of people talk about how many of our veterans come home and end up committing suicide or otherwise dying young. This story answers the question of why. I published the article in May of 2016.

Many 101st veterans were furious, not because of the fact that their unit had a sexual predator in the ranks, or that their chain of command covered for him, but rather that some asshole journalist had tarnished the image of their unit. Band of Brothers indeed. But on the other hand, many of the soldiers showed courage by speaking with me and going on the record to tell the truth about this incredibly difficult story. They will always have my respect and admiration. It isn't easy to choose the hard right over the easy wrong, even if it looks that way in retrospect.

I had cause to question Dr. Bass's psych eval when I was contacted by someone who was working with Santoro in civilian life. They gave me an account of behavior that convinced me that Santoro had not changed his ways. At this point, it was just one secondhand account, but I had to wonder whether it would turn out that the army not only covered up Santoro's sex crimes for years but then gave him a light sentence, an ineffectual treatment plan, and set loose a sexual predator on the American public.

Meanwhile, I noted that Lieutenant Colonel David Womack was promoted to colonel and went on to serve in the 25th Infantry Division in Hawaii. I found it interesting that Matt Jones was also promoted and served in the same unit as one of Womack's subordinates once again. CSM Judd retired out of the army. Many of the victims simply dropped off the face of the earth. Joe Barnes was laid to rest by his family and some friends he served with in the 10th Mountain Division. He had not stayed in touch with anyone from the 101st.

I've worked on a lot of stories over the years, some of them pretty grisly and dark, but this one has stuck with me. I think about Joe Barnes nearly every day.

There are some things about this case that I never got to the bottom of. There are indications that there was some kind of strange underground subculture in this unit. One soldier told me about waking up on the flight home and seeing the lieutenant sitting next to him with his hands down the pants of another male soldier. In the court-martial transcript there are other allegations and insinuations, soldiers sharing gay porn with one another via cell phone. All of this just makes cases like this tough for prosecutors and even journalists like me because the line between consensual and nonconsensual can be difficult to explain to the public.

There is also the matter of how Santoro had so much power in his unit as a lowly staff sergeant. I strongly believe that he was part of an underground sex ring that included high-ranking individuals in his unit, which would have given him a tremendous amount of blackmail material in the era of Don't Ask, Don't Tell. At least with DADT repealed, soldiers cannot be subjected to blackmail, but according to the DOD statistics sexual assault against men is a huge issue, perhaps making up as much as 40 percent of all military sexual assault cases.

I was brought back to this subject when I received an encrypted message about the command sergeant major of Special Forces Command quietly being removed from his post. The *Army Times* did a brief article on it without any explanation. I started digging around and, before long, was smack dab in the middle of another one of these military sexual conspiracies that the Department of Defense loves to sweep under the rug.

By digging through police records, trolling through LinkedIn and Go-FundMe campaigns, and developing sources, I was able to piece the story together: 7th Special Forces Group is located down at Eglin Air Force Base on the Florida Panhandle. The men of 7th Special Forces Group deploy to Afghanistan but also do a lot of meaningful work in Central and South America with and through host-nation counterparts. With that comes the prospect of being away from home in foreign cultures that are pretty fun, sexually speaking. This is a stark difference from 5th Special Forces Group, which deploys to the Middle East; in a place like Iraq, prostitution takes the form of a man pimping out his daughter or wife in an alleyway, hardly something that anyone but the most immoral person would want to get involved in, although some soldiers do, if we are being honest about it. I guess you could say that 7th Group's area of operations is just more sexually permissive. For that reason, the unit has developed a bit of a reputation.

The scandal began when 7th Group needed to hire a new civilian secretary. One officer candidly told me that he had been advised to hire the fattest, ugliest secretary possible in order to avoid future indiscretions. But he didn't follow this advice after several other officers vouched for an applicant named Jennifer O'Brien. It may not be politically correct to say so, but, according to soldiers in the unit, Jenn, as she was known, was quite prolific in aggressively seeking out sexual relationships with senior enlisted men and officers in the unit. There were even sexual encounters taking place in the offices.

It was discussed around the group headquarters that she was having workplace relationships, often with married men, but it was ignored until she came to work crying one day. At the urging of some coworkers, she revealed that she was in a relationship with a 7th Group officer who was now sending her unsolicited pictures of his genitals. Initially, she declined to name the individual, but it came out that his name was Dave Bowling.

Bowling commanded 3rd Battalion of 7th Special Forces Group and was a competent professional soldier; many of his peers credit him for doing important work in Iraq during the fight against ISIS. At the time, the U.S. military was conducting operations in Syria and Iraq, but these elements were not effectively communicating with each other. Bowling reversed this and made major improvements toward creating a unified front against the enemy. His involvement with Jenn was unexpected from the point of view of the men under his command and led his men to call him Dick Pic Six.

Things continued to slide downhill for Jenn when she got involved with another 7th Group officer. Jason Sartori had taken command of the Commander's In-Extremis Force (CIF), which is a dedicated counterterrorism and direct action element. Sartori was allegedly physically abusing his wife, so she left him. He then pursued a relationship with Jenn, and she claimed that he began physically abusing her as well. In conversations with Sartori, he vigorously denied that he had physically assaulted either woman. Jenn posted pictures in a GoFundMe campaign she started, showing scratches and bruises on her body.

Jenn was now coming to work distraught and was reported to have been smoking crystal meth. Seventh Group got a new commander, Colonel Michael Ball, who saw that something was very amiss in his group headquarters and wanted steps taken to correct the issue. Some leaders in 7th Group had been trying to initiate an investigation and get Jenn removed; it may sound sexist, but for them, it was a more pragmatic decision to remove the secretary than to attempt to remove every soldier she slept with. However, their attempts kept getting shut down by higher, and Special Forces Command told them to stand down and stop making waves. But why?

It was actually the investigation into the meth use that opened the door for some 7th Group soldiers to finally start looking at the allegations and take some action. Sartori was removed from his position pending the investigation. Jenn was removed from her position as well and had her security clearance suspended. Realizing that she might lose her job, Jenn reportedly said that she was going to take down the entire Red Empire with her, using the unit's nickname. It turned out she had a little black book, so to speak, a trove of incriminating emails, photographs, and videos. In the past, it seems, she had been able to stymie investigations against her by using this information as leverage.

Some of that leverage may have been applied straight to the top at Special Forces Command. One of the names in her little black book was Command Sergeant Major Brian Rarey, the senior enlisted man in all of

Special Forces. This would explain why Special Forces Command had refused to support an investigation.

Until the dam broke, it had been a classic case of a boys' club in which not just sexual affairs but also physical abuse had been covered up by high-ranking Special Forces members looking to hide their own dirt as well as that of their buddies, since they were all mutually compromised by this point. Jenn seemed to actively seek the sexual relationships but had been a victim of the physical abuse. On television crime dramas, sex crimes come across as clear-cut, but in reality, they are anything but, something that law enforcement officers and prosecutors know quite well.

When I asked a Green Beret who was involved in the investigation why this kind of behavior persisted in the unit, he answered bluntly, stating that the male soldiers "married young, and now their wife is fat, and they think they are a 'pipe hitter' and can do whatever they want."

Enlisted soldiers are often lectured and even condescended to by their superiors when it comes to issues like honor and integrity. For them, the actions of their leadership seemed hypocritical. Worse yet, their leaders were allowed to quietly retire as a punishment for actions that lower-ranking soldiers would be court-martialed over. And that was exactly what happened as the men associated with Jenn O'Brien quietly separated from the military.

In covering cases of sexual assault, physical abuse, and sexual conspiracies in the military, I learned that the truth is anything but easy to discern. Finding out what really happened takes months, if not years, and there are no shortcuts, no life hacks, when it comes to investigative journalism. Oftentimes it is a long boring slog toward finding some new sources, new names, someone who knows that what they witnessed is profoundly wrong and wants the truth to come out.

I also learned that not everything is black and white. Johnny Santoro was a competent squad leader and fearless in combat. He was also sexually assaulting soldiers. Dave Bowling was, by most accounts, a good man who made important contributions to our war against ISIS in the Middle East, but unfortunately, he made a mistake, one that many men are probably wishing they could reverse in the wake of the #metoo movement that has taken America by storm.

I've also learned that my sources take extraordinary risks in talking to me, which I've come to respect and hold sacred. One of my sources split up with a spouse over an argument about whether to talk to me. When I start poking around and asking questions, there are often prices to be paid. If you are not cautious in this line of work, you can really hurt some good people.

I sometimes find myself in a very dark place while working on these stories. It isn't because I'm suffering from some kind of proxy traumatic stress from talking to victims—it is something else that keeps me up at night: What really happened? Who knew what and when?

Over a drink one night, a journalist I know told me, "Everyone lies about sex and money." She wasn't wrong. In my experience, conspiracies come about because some guy did something he shouldn't have when it comes to sex or money. It is kind of a letdown for people used to reading conspiracy theory headlines. At the end of the day, they are all really banal.

Covering scandals in the military has made me an unpopular individual. People are angrier that a former member of the special operations community writes these things than they are outraged about the illegal activities. It is a bizarre dynamic, one in which we are supposed to maintain omertà. This is romanticized by soldiers and veterans who say that the first rule of fight club is that you don't talk about fight club. Personally, I have yet to find anything romantic about sexual assault or spousal abuse, but groupthink is strong in the military, and many will never break free from it. I've even been accused of trying to be a white knight, which I find amusing. My job is to be the dark knight—the white knight can kiss my Irish ass.

Some of my friends and former teammates come under scrutiny

simply because of their proximity to me. One former teammate was called into the group commander's office and shaken down on the suspicion that he'd been a source for me. He hadn't been. I understand that I'm not always an easy person to be friends with, and I've come to value those who have stood fast while others have blinked. Adversity is a great way to find out which of your friends are the real deal and which are just superficial pretenders. Real soldiers don't run from the truth, even if it's ugly.

CHAPTER 14

Humvees and IEDs

MEANWHILE, THE WAR IN THE MIDDLE EAST WAS ONLY getting more desperate. The war against ISIS was far from finished, and now I had an opportunity to cover it up close in Iraq.

Benni had been back to Iraq once to do some reporting from Sinjar, home of the ethnic minority called the Yazidi, which several of my interpreters in Tal Afar had belonged to. When ISIS invaded the city, they engaged in a wholesale slaughter. Babies had to be left in their cribs to die as Yazidi parents could only carry two children on their backs up the nearby Mount Sinjar to escape what became a full-scale genocide. Thankfully, my interpreters from my army days had both been given green cards and emigrated to the United States with their families. I was more than happy to write letters of recommendation to the State Department for them. Meanwhile, Benni had been writing stories about the mass graves she witnessed in their home city. Now we were heading back together. Our first time going there as journalists, we had made some mistakes that we were determined not to repeat. I started generating potential sources and contacts for the trip and developing everything before we arrived.

We made the most of our time there, staying at a hotel in Erbil and traveling out to various places. Benni was working on a big story about Iraqi Christians who were protecting centuries-old documents. It was a story that took us high up into dozens of switchbacks to an ancient monastery in a place called Al Qosh. Later, we examined actual Christian manuscripts at a refugee camp in Erbil that were being digitally preserved.

Another story developed when a fixer we had hired to help translate informed us that there was a big battle going down early the next morning near Kirkuk. No way were we going to pass that up. We left around four a.m. the next morning.

"Just keep driving until you get to the Daesh," the Peshmerga checkpoint guard said. I was trying to get to the front line to follow along with the Kurdish offensive outside Kirkuk on September 11. Can't really blame the guard for his concise instructions. As our car approached the front, we saw dozens of up-armored Humvees and pickup trucks. Peshmerga fighters stood around waiting for their orders, talking and smoking cigarettes. As I got out of the car and began walking down the road, a group of Kurdish journalists looked at me and began waving their hands, saying, "No good, no good!"

The puffs of smoke from either IEDs or mortar rounds rose into the air in the distance. Before even getting to the berm lines, I ran into a group of foreigners who had joined up with the 9th Brigade. They all wore MultiCam and balaclavas to conceal their identity. As I was soon to find out, one of them had already had his rifle confiscated because he was taking potshots at the Pesh, mistaking them for ISIS.

It was now about six a.m. The sun had not fully risen and burned off the cloudy haze that engulfed the battlefield. The Peshmerga's mission today was to liberate a series of villages on the outskirts of Kirkuk, pushing ISIS farther away from the city. What I had come upon was a fighting column, firing on a Daesh village called Zanghar with machine guns and tanks, while hundreds of vehicles were stacked up, ready to roll forward.

I was able to get my eyes on some of the new weaponry that the Pesh had obtained from the Germans. G36 rifles aplenty, as well as Panzerfaust and Milan anti-tank systems. One Peshmerga soldier even carried a .50-caliber sniper rifle, very similar to the locally manufactured Zagros rifle that I'd seen used by female YPG snipers in Syria months prior. The Pesh had taken their training to heart; they employed their anti-tank weapons appropriately. This was serious business, as one of the main Daesh tactics is to load captured up-armored Humvees with explosives and drive them right into the Pesh front lines before detonating.

This time, the Daesh were not putting up much of a fight, at least not with small arms fire. They abandoned Zanghar, and by 6:40 a.m., the village had been liberated. Ground troops were swarming into the village. Just before I got there, an IED went off and killed a Peshmerga fighter. One of his teammates showed me the cell phone video of a bulldozer trying to recover his body, which had been cut in half by the blast.

The sun was coming up, and the haze began to clear. With Zanghar captured, the fighting column crept forward. Peshmerga EOD teams were digging up and disarming IEDs all along the road. Sadly, the Kurdish EOD experts had little to work with besides a piece of string and a fishhook. An ambulance blaring its siren came blasting by me, picking up the wounded after IEDs were tripped and exploded prematurely.

Around this time, someone's toy airplane started buzzing overhead: a UAV, watching us from above. Benni and I were arguing because we kept getting in each other's shots.

The Peshmerga advance split into three columns, moving on different villages. I trailed behind the leading edge of the Peshmerga element, noting dozens upon dozens of disarmed IEDs. Wires to command-detonate the explosives ran up both sides of the road. When I asked about a cherry picker in their convoy, the Pesh said it was for clipping the power lines before they went into the villages. Some of the IEDs could have electronic detonators, which would set them off when they were stepped on, completing the circuit.

The Peshmerga doctor was someone who stood out as earning his pay that day. He was shouting orders, getting casualties evacuated on stretchers. After an IED went off about thirty meters in front of me, half a dozen bleeding Peshmerga were carried off on litters, while others limped toward the ambulance with the help of their buddies.

The Daesh were practicing a tactic called defense in depth. Instead of holding ground until the last bullet, they were quickly withdrawing under the Peshmerga assault, then detonating already prepared booby traps in the form of IEDs—nickel-and-diming the Kurdish fighters. Seven would die and forty-five would be injured by the end of the day.

Moving up to record a black ISIS flag flapping in the breeze, I ran into a Kurd named Qabat. He once lived in the United States, where he worked as a bank manager for many years, then he came back home to help his people fight ISIS. While we were having our conversation, IEDs were going off in front of us as well as off to our flanks. How many of them were command-detonated and how many were remote-detonated was impossible to say. Qabat went on to tell me that he worked with Americans who'd volunteered in the Peshmerga.

"Do you know Kurt?" I asked, inquiring about someone I had been talking to online for a while.

"Come on with me. They are up here."

Walking around an armored vehicle, I heard someone shout, "Hey, I know that guy!"

Sure enough, it was U.S. Marine Corps veteran Kurt and his friend, an army veteran named Joey. I had been talking to Kurt on social media since before he first joined the Peshmerga, and we had always planned to meet up in Kurdistan eventually. Of course, our conversation quickly turned to war porn: gun talk. We showed off our knives and chatted while we waited for the next advance, probably sounding like women discussing shoes and clothes. It is always nice to meet like-minded people out on the battlefield. Kurt and Joey had both done very well for themselves, but more important, they had done well in terms of helping the Kurds. Back in Sulaymaniyah, they'd taught the Peshmerga basic infantry tactics; they also got to jump into the fray during offensives like this.

Sporadic gunfire sounded amid the occasional IED blast. I had never seen fighting quite like this. The Daesh appeared weak and unable to defend their terrain. They had cut and run, leveraging their only relative strength against the Peshmerga, the same one that so many American soldiers had faced before: remote-detonated improvised explosives.

Qabat, Kurt, Joey, and I continued marching forward behind the armored vehicles. The sun was up now, and it was getting damn hot, the kind of hot you feel only in Iraq. Off on our right flank, a mass of civilians was inching toward the Peshmerga column. There looked to be about a hundred of them, some driving vehicles jam-packed with their worldly possessions. They waved white sheets above their heads in surrender. One villager was herding his flock of fifty or so sheep toward the Peshmerga lines. They were villagers from bad-guy land, trying to defect to the other side.

The Pesh set up their anti-tank weapons and security positions oriented toward the civilians, not willing to risk believing the Daesh were not mixed into the group. The Asayish, the Kurdish intelligence officers, then showed up in balaclavas to begin interviewing the villagers to see who was or was not an ISIS collaborator. In a face-to-face meeting with one of the Asayish a few days later, I found out that some of the villagers were, in fact, collaborators. Sadly, one of the civilian vehicles hit an IED on the way to surrender to the Peshmerga. The blast took off a woman's arm and killed her baby.

Overall, I was quite impressed with the planning and preparation that the Peshmerga put into the offensive. The refugee situation slowed them down a bit, but they responded and quickly regained their momentum. Taking a break while we waited, I sat down on the side of the road, but the vehicles were moving again shortly. A Peshmerga officer walked by, looked at me, and said, "Come on, let's go and finish this!" It is hard not to respect that type of leadership. Even the doctor, who later took IED shrapnel to the forehead, bandaged himself up and continued to do his job that day.

General Ja'afer, the Kirkuk sector commander, told me later in an interview, "We are not the army. We are Peshmerga. We don't say go, we say come."

Pounding down another bottle of water, I took the officer's advice and kept moving with his men. Joey, Kurt, and I were walking forward, talking casually, when it came out of nowhere. Black smoke shot up into the air about a hundred meters in front of us. The size of the blast made it seem a hell of a lot closer.

"Stay down, stay down," Kurt warned. "Some stuff is going to come back down on us."

Sure enough, something zinged into the grass a few meters to my right. It turned out that there was an outhouse up ahead. The Peshmerga were not taking any chances, so they'd lit it up with machine-gun fire. It turned out to be another IED. Fed up with the situation, the Peshmerga called in their bulldozers and began making new roads on the fly so that they did not lose their tactical momentum on getting waylaid by IEDs.

There was one more village to capture before the day was done: Hasan Sha-lal. I climbed into the back of a pickup truck and got a ride up to the village. As we cruised by, the ground was on fire around us from the massive IED that had gone off. PKM and DShK gunners were laying down suppressive fire on Hasan Sha-lal, prepping it for the ground assault force. The Pesh again used their bulldozers to make a new road up to the village and then occupied the high ground on a hill adjacent to it. With overwatch in place from two angles, dismounted Peshmerga soldiers entered and began clearing the village.

With the task mostly completed, I rode in the back of the pickup as we drove into the village on the main road and up onto the hill. I would be lying if I said that my pucker factor was not a little high at this point.

On top of the hill, a Peshmerga officer stood alongside an observer from the PKK, distinguished by his OD green uniform and sash belt. The officer was on the radio and looking through binoculars. A few puffs of smoke in the distance signified coalition air strikes that they had coordinated.

Trotting down the hill, I went inside some of the houses in the villages. They appeared lived in but were sparsely furnished. There probably had not been more than thirty or forty people living there, at least until they left and surrendered to the Peshmerga. Now it was a ghost town.

Bulldozers came in and started flattening the village. It was a type of scorched-earth policy to prevent the Daesh from coming back in and occupying the buildings. Walls were knocked down, and roofs caved in under a haze of smoke. Another Peshmerga officer saw me and said I needed to go back up the hill for my own safety. He said that radio intercepts had indicated a suicide vehicle en route to our location. Not seeing much need to push my luck, I walked back up the hill and drank some water while the village was being razed.

It was a long, difficult day for the Pesh, but they had accomplished their mission and once again disproved the myth that ISIS was some unbeatable, magical Islamist force that will sweep across the entire Middle East.

That wasn't the end of that trip. I still had a sit-down interview with Kurdistan's elite counterterrorism group, or CTG, which ended up becoming a long-form article. Like everything in that part of the world, truth is stranger than fiction, with operations happening that the public has little if any knowledge of. CTG worked closely with the SAS, Delta Force, and the CIA to kick down doors and roll up bad guys.

After wrapping things up in Suly, Benni and I made the trip to Qandil, the PKK stronghold in northern Iraq. Back in the 1980s, the PKK had taken refuge in this mountainous valley, digging in with a series of tunnels and underground bunkers. After some coordination, we were granted permission to visit. At that moment, Qandil was under attack from Turkish air strikes that were killing people every few days. According to the Turkish media, a battalion of Turkish Special Forces soldiers was involved in a massive ground assault there as well.

A local from Qandil came to pick us up in Erbil. All we had in terms of contact information in Qandil was a name: Havel Zagros Hiwa. We stopped at a small shop alongside the road for a typical Kurdish lunch of kebabs and flatbread before continuing on. Eventually, we came into a wide-open flat expanse that led up to the mountains. In the middle of this bowl was a lake that shimmered in the sunlight. We were in another place, another world. After a few more hours on the road, we went up a series of switchbacks, maybe twenty-five of them, into Qandil. On the way, we passed a PKK shrine to several martyrs who had been killed in a Turkish air strike.

Several PKK guerrillas waited at the top of the switchbacks, manning a checkpoint. They wore OD green jackets and baggy pants. Like most guerrillas, they sported thick bushy mustaches. Our driver just said one word to them, "Zagros," and we were ushered through the checkpoint without further delay. Just a few minutes down the road, Havel Zagros stood alone, waiting for our arrival.

As we shook hands and said hello, I noticed that Zagros was dressed like the other PKK members but spoke impeccable English. He didn't look like most of the Kurds I'd met, and I suspected he was originally from Iran. We drove to a local house that Zagros had arranged for us to stay in for a small fee. We sat while tea was brought for us and talked about our trip to Rojava in Syria.

Zagros nodded and told us that he wanted to go there and fight, but the party would not let him. As a PKK spokesman with strong language skills, he was a valuable asset—at least that was what I took away from his words. I next told Zagros that based on my assessment, I did not think that the YPG and YPJ could win in Kobanî, but thankfully, I was wrong.

He smiled and told me that when you believe so strongly in something, it binds you together with your comrades. It is true that the Obama administration eventually green-lit U.S. air strikes in Kobanî to support the Kurds, but it was still primarily a YPG and YPJ victory. They had fought tooth and nail against the so-called Islamic State. They had also paid a steep price for it, with many guerrillas killed in the process.

Zagros informed us that he would be more than willing to show us the sites of the air strikes in Qandil but that we had to wait. A Turkish drone was overhead, scanning for targets, and he didn't want us caught in the cross fire. He sounded a bit paranoid at first, but every so often you could indeed hear a faint buzzing sound outside, coming from overhead. I was now on the other side of things, the drones looking at me as a potential target rather than providing real-time intelligence for my unit, like when I was in the army.

We toured the site of an air strike, a village that had been full of civilians who had nothing to do with the PKK. The Turks either didn't care or were punishing the local people for tolerating the party, hoping that they would turn against the guerrilla group. The homes in this part of the world are made out of cinder blocks, and after a few hundred-pound bombs had been dropped, the area was littered with what looked like gray LEGOs, with the cinder blocks tossed everywhere. Benni and I made video recordings of the wreckage. I felt awkward, as if I were walking on someone's grave. In a very real way, I was.

In between visiting the sites of air strikes or taking a trip to the martyrs' cemetery, we had to wait around because the drone could be overhead, potentially spotting for incoming aircraft. In these moments, we had time for some in-depth conversations with Zagros. He was a quiet intellectual, one with an AK-47 slung over his back.

Unlike many Americans, Zagros didn't shout or try to force his opinion on others. He calmly explained what the PKK believed and was very thoughtful when answering questions. While I am not an ideologue myself, I found parts of the PKK's political philosophy to be fascinating. As Zagros told us, the PKK first came into existence during a bipolar worldview consisting of capitalism and some variation on socialism or communism. However, their belief system evolved to keep pace with the times.

"Abdullah Öcalan realized that something has gone wrong, that

Marxism has some, shall we say, shortcomings and there are some problems with the tenets," Zagros told me. For instance, Marxism led to a dictatorship of the proletariat. The party also began to understand that society was more diverse than was outlined by Marxism's strict class struggle between workers and aristocrats. The third issue was the notion of a nation-state. The PKK realized that even if they did have a nation, that did not necessarily equate to freedom. With this in mind, Öcalan began to concentrate his ideas on the community rather than on the state.

With this came the idea of the democratic nation and/or democratic confederalism. "In democratic confederalism, the borders are untouched, but communities can relate to each other," Zagros said as we sat on the carpet of the house we were staying in. "They self-rule, they can manage their own affairs." I asked what the role of the state would then be. "The formula he [Öcalan] came up with then is the state plus democracy. Democratic confederalism is, let's say, the political and social organization of the community outside the state, but we don't ignore the state or try to eliminate it because it has a historical basis," as well as relating to other states. From this point of view, the state would gradually lose its importance.

It sounds beautiful, even utopian, but is it realistic? Currently under way is such a system in development almost as a political experiment, in northern Syria, what the Kurds call Rojava. The Kurds are interested in nothing less than a complete paradigm shift, one that they know will take decades at best. The political project of Rojava draws upon at least forty years of the PKK's political struggle.

"A generation has to sacrifice itself so that a new generation can live and have a free life," Zagros explained.

While left-wing and right-wing movements across the world currently seem determined to repeat all the mistakes that society made a hundred years ago, the PKK is one organization genuinely trying to apply new ideas and, furthermore, trying to grant human beings more freedom rather than trying to take it away. It struck me that what they are trying to accomplish in Rojava could one day serve as a template for what indigenous Middle Eastern democracies may look like.

For me, the trip back to Iraq was a surreal experience. The future we had been promised was to look like something out of a science fiction film, but in reality, it looked more like the Spanish Civil War. Kalashnikovs and drones, clearing operations and scorched earth. Special operations for low-intensity conflicts, all in a part of the world that most Americans can't begin to understand. When we left Qandil, we drove past the soaring mountains under clear blue skies. I sat quietly, watching the scenery, asking myself a lot of questions about our world and about our future.

CHAPTER 15

Another Surreal Journey: Meeting President Assad in Damascus

BY 2016, THE SYRIAN CIVIL WAR HAD MATURED SINCE THE last time I was there, and I would soon be face-to-face with one of the main players in the conflict, President Bashar al-Assad.

The number of foreign players attempting to put their thumb on the scales was difficult to keep track of. Both the CIA and the Department of Defense were now running programs in Jordan and Turkey to train, advise, and assist various rebel groups before sending them back into Syria. After ignoring ISIS for a long spell, the U.S. government was pursuing a two-pronged policy in Syria: The CIA was trying to oust Assad, while the DOD was trying to defeat ISIS. Meanwhile, Assad was fighting ISIS. Turkey was supporting ISIS, but American soldiers ran a logistical node in that country to supply anti-ISIS fighters. I'm not sure if there is a fancy political science term for all of this, but what we called it in the military was a clusterfuck.

I had written some work about American covert action programs in Syria and how they were not working properly, which caught the attention of some in the Syrian government. After shunning the international media, viewing them as co-conspirators in Western plots, the Syrian government was now going to host a seminar for Western journalists in Damascus. Ostensibly, this would begin opening the door to a new level of transparency by the Assad regime.

I flew to Beirut in October and met up with Benni and a photographer friend of ours named Joey who had also been to Syria previously with the Kurds. Walking around the streets of Beirut, seeing teenagers driving around with the yellow Hezbollah flag flying from their car window, we had to wonder what we were in store for. We were heading into Syria under the auspices of the regime with about forty other journalists. How was this going to play out?

The next morning we met up outside a hotel with the other journalists who had been invited to the conference. They represented a mix of mainstream media outlets and smaller publications, like mine. There were also some freelancers in the mix, like Benni and Joey. An older gentleman appeared in cuffed pants, loafers, and a black jacket buttoned up at the neck. He looked like the type of dude who would get busted by NYPD for beating off in Central Park behind a tree. Who he was would remain a mystery for the time being.

Suffice to say, I had my concerns about this arrangement. A busload of Western journalists driving into a war zone like Syria seemed like a recipe for disaster. We were the wet dream of any of the regionally located terrorist organizations, who would have an opportunity to kill us all or take us all hostage in one fell swoop. Traveling on your own in these parts of the world can be exhausting, but you are completely self-reliant, developing your own sources and logistics. You are in the driver's seat. This time I just had to let Jesus take the wheel and hope everything turned out okay.

On the bus ride to Syria, a younger female journalist quizzed me on a hundred different things about the military. She wrote for one of those lefty outlets that wasn't really my cup of tea, but she had her heart in the right place. At the border, we got off the bus and had our passports checked, then we drove through some rocky terrain into the night and arrived at a customs checkpoint outside Damascus. Our passports were collected, stamped, and returned to us. From there, we were driven into the city and to our hotel.

After checking in, I didn't see the female journalist who had questioned me on the bus. By the time we'd arrived in Damascus, her employer had fired her for seeming pro-Assad by attending the conference. I find such notions presumptuous. I've never been pro-Assad. I just recognize that not every action taken against a dictator is necessarily a pro-America policy move. Like many of my peers, I had direct experience in the country next door to Syria to prove it. I was going there to report on the war, not to be a stool pigeon for Assad.

As the conference began, we listened to panel after panel discuss various aspects of Syrian civil society and the war. We quickly learned that we should not call it the Syrian civil war, because really, it was a foreign conspiracy against Syria. The truth is somewhat more complicated. Blaming foreign outside actors is a typical way to defer responsibility and shift the blame for the policy failures of others, denying that there is an indigenous anti-government movement. On the other hand, with dozens of countries mucking around in Syria's internal affairs, it was no wonder that the Assad government viewed the entire conflict through this lens.

At the end of the day, we were permitted to roam around Damascus on our own. Now, I'm pretty much a poster boy for Western capitalism, but I have to say that Damascus is a beautiful place—an Arab city that is neither ruined, like I experienced in Iraq, nor commercialized with fast-food restaurants, the way I saw in Kurdistan or, worse, the ultra-artificiality of Dubai. While on the streets one day, we met with a young woman named Rania who ran a Facebook group called Humans of Damascus. It was a chance meeting that turned out to be quite insightful, as she shared her love for the city, walking it on foot, taking pictures, and sharing them with the world on social media.

Back at the conference, things were beginning to grow stale. One speaker was a Syrian who had just flown in from Moscow and treated us to an indescribable litany of conspiracy theories that was impossible to make any sense of. A woman on the panel told us that there was no mistreatment of Kurds in Syria because her name sort of sounded Kurdish and that had never been a problem for her. It's like saying being Black Irish means you know what it is like to be African American and living in Alabama in 1954. The gentlemen who ran the conference even told us that there were still six Jews remaining in Damascus and that this showed significant dedication of the minority group toward the Syrian government.

That day, one of the conference organizers pulled me aside for a moment. "Tonight, I'd like you to come with me and meet with the president," he said.

Well. Okay, then.

This was an unexpected but welcome opportunity. I was to head up to the presidential palace that night with a small group of journalists and members of Western think tanks. That night I waited in the lobby until a small fleet of black sedans arrived to pick us up. I ended up in a car with Dexter Filkins from *The New Yorker*. Despite my work as a journalist, I don't run in the same social circles as other journalists and generally don't get to meet them, so it was an interesting experience to hear about others' work.

The cars drove us up a hill to the presidential palace, where we were greeted by a young woman who I knew worked for the first lady, Asma al-Assad. She ushered us up marble steps and through the front door into an atrium. Thus far, I had not seen any security and found it interesting that we had not been searched or patted down. The young woman then told us that we could proceed up the steps behind her and meet the president. I headed up first.

I had been expecting to meet with some kind of protocol officer before being brought into an office to meet President Assad, but the woman was speaking literally. At the top of the steps, I heard someone say, "Hello, welcome!" I looked up and saw President Assad reaching out to shake my hand. I thanked him for meeting with us. The six of us Americans walked into a sitting room and sat down with Assad.

He was rather informal, pleasant, and encouraged us to ask anything we wanted. From the perspective of the Syrian government, he did quite well as he made his case for the regime, defended their choices in the war, and attempted to clarify his role in the government. The journalist from *The New Yorker* asked how he felt about the media calling him a war criminal. Assad was dismissive, saying that he was just being cast as the villain in a media narrative. "There is nothing personal, I am just a headline," he said.

Anne Barnard of *The New York Times* attempted to press Assad on the disappearance of persons who criticized the regime. President Assad danced circles around her questions as she mentioned incidents, saying that he needed to see evidence, that there were no facts, that he would need time to look into specific claims. She looked quite frustrated by the end of their conversation, not that I could blame her.

Waiting for the right moment, I asked what postwar Syria might look like and if stitching the country back together would even be possible after it had experienced so much trauma.

"I would say it should not go back as it was before, it should be better," Assad said in reference to the Syrian government. "Because you had many flaws regarding this issue, because we have been influenced by the Wahhabis for the last forty years. Of course, there was also tolerance and all these good things, that's true. But the Wahhabis influenced our moderate part of society, becoming day by day more fanatic. That is what we have gotten rid of in the crisis. The whole society was moving right by fanatics; now the society is moving left. The middle was becoming more conservative; the conservative became fanatics. The fanatics became extremists, and extremists became terrorists. Now the whole society is without the incubator. Without the incubator, you will not have Syrian extremists, so you had this before the war but not during the war.

"The incubator was the society, because when you talk about terrorists, you do not generate that inside a computer, it is not a video game. You generate it in a family, in a neighborhood, in a school. Now, in the West, they are concentrating more on the mosque. Actually, eighty percent of the recruitment happens on the Internet. Now the incubator is social media, because most of the people, they make dialogue with one every hour, let's say on social media apps. This is the incubator." President Assad's technological metaphors for politics and social matters related back to his interest in computers. As president, he played a big part in bringing the Internet and 5G to Syria (which, ironically, became the double-edged sword that helped create the jihadi incubator he spoke of in Syria). A self-described "computer nerd," he commented after the interview that he did not like video games but had an RSS feed that kept him updated on new gadgets, and he discussed new medical devices with his friends, although he no longer had the time to practice medicine himself.

Assad made some salient comments about the need to construct a new type of Syrian national identity. The average person doesn't realize it, but the state is essentially a playground for leaders to conduct these types of social experiments. We are individual case studies in these experiments, our personal and political identities crafted by powerful forces circling above our heads. However, as our interview came to a close, I could not help feeling that although Assad was very polished, he was underestimating how difficult it would be to put Syria back together. The Syria that had existed in 2012 was now dead and would never return.

What will take its place remains to be seen.

With the conference over, we had a few days to work on our stories. Many of the journalists in our group opted to go on a government-sponsored tour of Aleppo. Benni and I planned to work on some stories about recently liberated neighborhoods in Damascus, which turned out to be an adventure in and of itself. First you needed to be assigned a minder from the government's media affairs office. Next you needed to obtain permission from the ministry of defense, since they actually controlled the neighborhood, called Katsia.

I arrived at the media affairs office with Benni, Joey, and our minder. A Syrian colonel welcomed us into his office. Two Caucasians sat on couches across from us, staring at us with blue eyes. They wore woodland camouflage fatigues without any patches or insignia. The colonel began talking to us, telling us how journalists had lied to him in the past and how unfairly Syria had been treated in the media.

I turned and looked at the archaic desktop PC sitting in the corner of the room. On the screen was a news site in Cyrillic, a video of Vladimir Putin at the top of the webpage. I turned and looked at the two guys sitting across from us. They hadn't said a word.

The colonel inquired about the indigenous population of America. I assumed he was talking about the American Indians and asked through the translator. Yes, those were the people he was referring to; he asked me for more information about them. Given our limited time, and speaking through a translator, I made some rather simplistic statements about the differences between the Plains Indians in the American West and those found where I grew up in the Northeast.

"Do they have their rights?" he asked me.

"Yes," I answered. "They have the right to vote, are full American citizens, and they even have their own land."

He continued, undeterred. "I want to ask you, on behalf of all of the Syrian people, that you should give the Indians their rights."

It was pretty hard for me not to roll my eyes. This is a classic Russian propaganda technique known as "whataboutism." When pressed on important issues, the Russian government will attempt to divert attention back to you. For instance, when challenged on human rights issues, the Russians will simply turn around and say: What about all the black people shot by American police officers? When asked about their invasion of Crimea, the Russians will respond: What about America's illegal invasion of Iraq? And so on.

This wasn't my first exposure to Russian propaganda. I once received an email from a woman named Natalie who claimed to be working for Interpol and wanted to leak important information about the CIA trafficking weapons from Bulgaria to Syrian rebels. The email used all the right buzzwords; it said everything, but it also said nothing. I had a friend trace the email and found that it had originated in St. Petersburg. This is part of a technique that Russian intelligence calls reflexive control theory.

The two Russians sitting across from me had obviously been coaching the Syrian colonel, who could not have been a more obvious puppet. Nonetheless, he granted us permission to travel to Katsia, and we thanked him for that. The Syrian government had promised that this was a new era of transparency and cooperation with the press, and despite the bureaucracy, it seemed that they were attempting to follow through.

The three of us and our minder drove to the outskirts of Damascus, passing through the military checkpoints that dotted the entire city. When we got to the last checkpoint, we pulled over, and the minder got out to talk to the guards. We must have sat there for half an hour before I got out to see what was going on. The minder was having some kind of back-and-forth with the guards.

What I discovered: It was a special day. We could not access Katsia today. We could have if we had come yesterday. Maybe if we showed up tomorrow, things would be different? I asked the guard through our minder why we couldn't go into Katsia when we had permission from the ministry of defense and we were told that the local sector commander had said no media was allowed in Katsia today. I asked for the name of his sector commander. He didn't appear to know. I asked where the commander's office was so we could go meet him. The guard didn't seem to know that, either.

As it turned out, the so-called Syrian military guards in these neighborhoods were really just rebel militia dudes who had cut some kind of backroom deal with the regime in exchange for amnesty. The regime had bigger priorities in places like Aleppo than screwing around with these yokels and making sure that the rule of law was fully enforced. The result was a situation where it looked like the Syrian government was the authority when it really wasn't.

We had our minder call back to the Syrian colonel at the ministry of defense and explain the situation. Goshdarnit, he remembered now that in fact we couldn't go to Katsia today. So sorry!

I found the whole situation exhausting and frustrating. We had spent days being lectured at the media conference about the lies of the Western "corporate" media and the international conspiracy against Syria, but when we tried to do our due diligence in the country, we got shut down. Then the Syrian government would whine that no one was telling their side of the story.

The next day we hired a taxi to drive us back to Lebanon. On the long ride, I contemplated some of the things I had seen in Damascus and the real reasons for the conference, which had been hosted by the British Syrian Society. The Brits have always had a knack for parlor room intrigue. While sitting in the lobby of our hotel one day, I noticed a member of the backbench of the British parliament (meaning he didn't need his government's permission to attend the conference, because his wasn't an elected position) having a sit-down meeting with the embargoed head of Syrian military intelligence. The British backbencher was himself a former MI-6 officer. The conference provided an excuse to get foreigners into Syria for high-level meetings, facilitating back-channel communications.

In Beirut, Benni and I spent a day walking around the city, sitting next to the sea, before she caught a flight to Italy. I flew out the next morning with a layover in Amman, Jordan. Waiting in the terminal for my flight to New York, I ran into the odd-looking British guy who had been with us at the conference, the one who looked like a public masturbator. As it turned out, he was in the business of what he termed "insurance plus."

That was a clever euphemism for what most of us would call an international arms dealer.

CHAPTER 16

No Matter Which Way You Have to March, It Is Always Uphill

THERE IS SOMETHING DARK ABOUT BEING AN INVESTIGA-
tive journalist. You spend days, months, and sometimes years studying a
certain subject, jumping through all kinds of hoops to get people to talk
to you. You have good workdays, bad workdays, and worst of all, those
moments between stories when you are looking for something to write
about. Without the chase, life just seems to be lacking something; there
is nothing to get excited about. Some journalists work in a newsroom. I
work alone.

Each story you write causes some kind of controversy; sometimes
it is a minor one. Sometimes no one cares aside from those who closely
follow, say, the Syrian civil war, Special Forces training, or some other
specific subject. Other times the story bumps up into the national news
service and your work is reported on Fox News or CNN. Each story leads
to more people hearing about you, more potential sources, who in turn
reach out to you because they see that you are not afraid to confront difficult issues.

And each story you work on seems a little darker than the last. SEAL
Team Six war crimes in Afghanistan, sexual assault in the army, officers
involved in sexual blackmail, soldiers shot up and blown up, the Pentagon desperate to gloss over what really happened. But you keep writing,
because you believe in telling the truth. After breaking each story, you tell

yourself that now you want to write some positive news about the military, because our troops are out there doing great work every day. That's a fact.

But people reach out, asking for help. You're the guy on the telephone with a woman who was violently raped, the female soldier being stalked at night by her supervising officer. You can't look away, so you keep researching, you keep writing. Another story goes out, and more people get angry at you for telling the truth. Now you're infamous. Over the years, I have had both close friends and acquaintances part ways with me because of my work. Where does it end? Do I keep working as an investigative journalist until everyone turns their back on me? Do I end up dead in a ditch, a future I've been told is mine more than once?

The most insulting thing is that some people think I do this job for the money. It would be hilarious if it weren't so sad. If you want to make money, go into finance. If you want to be well liked, become anything but a journalist. There are so many jobs out there where you can make more money doing less work with less headache.

In today's media environment, more and more credible people are turning away from careers in journalism, since clickbait, fake news, and "content" are of more value to employers and readers alike than facts and careful reporting. When your work just isn't valued by the market—a public largely consumed by outrage rather than facts—a lot of reporters move on to careers where they can make money and provide for their families. Who can blame them? There is nothing romantic about being a starving artist. Being a journalist often involves a lot of work to report facts to a public that often doesn't want them.

A welcome respite came from a trip I took in 2017 to the Philippines in order to cover that country's special operations units. With the elections of Rodrigo Duterte in the Philippines and Donald Trump in the United

States, it seemed that we would be entering a time of hostile relations with the Philippines and an overall period of isolationist policies. But blood is thicker than water, as they say, and the military-to-military relationship between our countries goes back about a hundred years. America does have friends and allies around the world, and some of the best are found in the Philippines.

Not only was it nice to be able to write about some of the positive work being done by the Philippine special operations soldiers and their U.S. Special Forces counterparts, but it was nice to get out of the sandbox (the Middle East) for a while. Besides, there was a whole other war out there that rarely got focused on—the one in Southeast Asia.

I had the opportunity to meet with members of the Philippine Scout Rangers, SEALs, Special Forces, Light Reaction Regiment, Special Action Force, as well as the marines. At one point, I sat across from a Light Reaction Regiment operator at a restaurant where we tried in vain to escape some of the humidity. He was smoking a cigarette while we discussed his unit and their operations. He was a quiet man, quick to tell me that his job was to execute the mission rather than complain about the burden of his responsibilities, and just as quick to credit other special operations and conventional forces for their contributions to the fight against the many threat groups facing the Philippine armed forces. When I asked about a rumor I had heard regarding his unit conducting a high-value target strike mission disguised as a wedding procession, he smiled a little bit. That's when I knew I was on the right track.

In a previous interview, I had talked to General Danilo Pamonag, the current Philippine SOCOM commander who had commanded the Light Reaction Regiment on two separate occasions. We talked about how the human and geographical terrain of the Philippines makes for a difficult operational environment for their special operations units. "The biggest challenge we have as special operators is how to sneak into the operational area, because every time we move out of our camp, the civilians would always see us, hear the noise of our vehicles, and blood is thicker than water, so they will try to pass on information that there is military going," Pamonag said. Sometimes those passing on information are enemy agents, other times just family members communicating with one another, but either way, the cat is out of the bag and word gets to the enemy. "It is the hardest part of our mission, finding our enemy and putting our troops there undetected," the SOCOM commander elaborated.

When the Light Reaction Regiment deploys by airplane or boat, they are often observed disembarking at the airport or the wharf. Within twenty-four hours, everyone knows that a new special operations force is in town. Operators are airborne-qualified but hesitant to infiltrate the target area by parachute, because they will be noticed in the air and the enemy will close around them. Meanwhile, those troops will have little access to mutually supporting fire from other units or air support. Helicopters offer another alternative, but the noise of the rotor blades tips off hostiles.

"You have to strike a balance between mass and mobility. That is how we tailor-fit the TTPs [tactics, techniques, and procedures] we use. We study the enemy first," explained the Light Reaction Regiment operator sitting across from me in the restaurant. I will call this Filipino operator Harold. In 2014, Harold was deployed to the island of Sulu with the 1st Light Reaction Company. He had recently come back from training in Australia with the Special Air Service Regiment and then almost immediately deployed to Sulu. First LRC was preparing to be redeployed home when an intelligence officer came to them asking if they would like to roll out on one final hit before leaving.

The target was number seven of the Abu Sayyaf target deck: Sihata Latip. Wanted for kidnapping twenty-one people in Malaysia in 2000, he went on to conduct a string of kidnappings in the Philippines over subsequent years. As the Philippines got better at countering terrorism, the Abu Sayyaf Group was cut off from overseas international terrorist finance networks, particularly those originating in Saudi Arabia. In order to make up for this loss in income, they engaged in kidnapping for ransom as their livelihood.

"Right then and there, we decided we were in, payback is a bitch," Harold said.

Intel had been monitoring a motorcycle gang and discovered that Sihata Latip was running a gambling ring based around motorcycle drag races in Sulu. They estimated that there would be approximately fifty civilians at the next drag race, along with Latip and an Abu Sayyaf bodyguard.

"It took us a week to plan, rehearse, and execute the mission," Harold said. The Light Reaction Regiment operators knew that this capture/kill mission could not be run in a conventional manner because the target would be tipped off by someone the moment the 1st LRC's vehicles rolled out of the gate of their base. Instead, they developed a more unconventional tactic, utilizing a Trojan horse as an infiltration platform.

"We dressed up like we were going to a Muslim wedding. We rented out a local jeep, dressed it up also. So we decorated it exactly the way it was supposed to look. It would be suspicious if it were a truck full of men, so some of us dressed up like females." The wedding procession also included a Light Reaction Regiment operator dressed as an imam. Their SAW gunner had to carry a bulkier weapon and drums of linked ammunition, so he was disguised to look like a pregnant woman.

Finally, on the day when Latip was to be running his gambling ring at the drag race, the LRR men were ready to deploy. The first snag occurred when Harold realized that the SAW gunner had not shaved that day. He wore an open-faced head scarf, as was the cultural tradition in Sulu, and would make for a rather unconvincing woman. "You still have your goatee, you motherfucker!" Harold scolded him as they were about to roll outside the wire. The SAW gunner had a moment of inspiration when he saw a female soldier on the base walking by with a fan. He asked to borrow it to hold in front of his goatee.

Finally, the two-jeep convoy departed. The SAW gunner fanned himself continuously throughout the fifteen-kilometer movement, hiding his facial hair. Proving that Murphy's Law was in full effect, one of the two jeeps broke down halfway to the target. On the radio with the intelligence officer, Harold had to decide if they could complete the mission with thirteen operators instead of twenty-four. With only two enemies to deal with on target, Harold decided that his remaining thirteen men would be up to the task.

When they arrived at the drag race, the LRR operators identified their high-value target and quickly approached him. Weapons were drawn out from under wedding clothes and brought into action. "But apparently, in the crowd there were a lot of armed dudes, ASG and MILF guys betting on the race," Harold said. "A supposed mission of capture or kill turned into a big firefight." Bedlam broke out, with civilians fleeing in all directions. Latip went for a concealed weapon, and one LRR member quickly killed him. Abu Sayyaf Group and Moro Islamic Liberation Front terrorists were now engaged in a firefight with the thirteen LRR operators. One of the operators was shot in the neck and killed. The two bodies were quickly loaded onto the jeep.

"Since we had the body, the guys [enemy] were still trying to go after us, shooting us. So it was a hot extract." Their jeep was shot up and running on flat tires as they quickly got off the X and to a safer area, just as five tanks belonging to the Marine Corps arrived to back up the LRR's mission. Years later, an intelligence officer explained to Harold that if not for the marines launching to protect the LRR, they all would have been killed, as the enemy was quickly massing their forces on the small LRR team.

"I think it opened the door to do more covert missions," Harold said, stubbing out his cigarette.

In the press, Latip was reported as killed in some hazy military-police operation or by unnamed security forces.

The Light Reaction Regiment simply dipped back into the shadows and awaited their next mission. This was standard operating procedure for the LRR. While I was conducting that interview, a different company from the same unit was in Bahol, hunting insurgents. The media reported the enemy as killed by the Scout Rangers, because that was what the military told them. In the more recent siege of Marawi, it was reported that the terrorist leading that attack was killed by a machine gunner in an armored vehicle, but those in the know, know. He was taken out by an LRR sniper.

During my time there, I kept hearing about Regional Affairs or RA. I took this to be a euphemism for a Philippine intelligence service. Eventually, I asked and was laughed at. "No, man," a contact told me, "that's you guys." In Iraq and Afghanistan, we used the acronym OGA to describe that particular governmental agency. They maintained a counterterrorism operations center (CTOC) in the Philippines and worked with two battalions of the police Special Action Force (SAF). SAF is interesting in that it is a police unit that can conduct unconventional warfare. Officially, they conduct just about every mission you can imagine. The first example of the SAF working with RA that I am aware of goes back to when a former SAF officer told me that the Americans had asked him to raid the Iraqi embassy for them just prior to the invasion of Iraq. The Americans offered him straight cash for this task, but he said he wanted training and equipment for his men. Soon he was visiting Range 37 at Fort Bragg. I believe the reason for working with the SAF is because they are a police unit that can execute arrest warrants at any time, while the military is hamstrung and prevented from going after enemy targets during peace negotiations.

I spent my days in Manila interviewing important personalities in the Philippine special operations community, got snuck onto a military base by one Philippine operator by ducking down in the back of his truck as we went through a checkpoint, knocked back a few drinks with American soldiers at a nightclub, and had a few interesting dinners. It is times like this that being a journalist is really fun and exciting, as you have to rely on your own resources and wits, digging up secrets, and finding things that are unexpected. If you get into trouble, this isn't like being back in the army when you had the option of calling in a air strike or being extracted out of a firefight by black helicopters.

The adventure wasn't quite over, though, as the next leg of my journey was down to Zamboanga and then the island of Tawi-Tawi, where I had to be escorted around by a squad of Philippine marines due to security threats. From there it was off to Seoul, South Korea, to do some reporting from the DMZ. It was the height of another flare-up between the North Koreans and the American government, but in Seoul I sat at a beer garden with Korean hipsters drinking and singing melancholy love songs while playing the acoustic guitar, unconcerned by the Armageddon that Fox and CNN kept telling us was coming. Sometimes I feel like it is useless to watch television news or read newspapers because they just feed us one crisis after the next while the reality is usually completely different.

CHAPTER 17

Controversy and Upsets

THIS IS A PERIOD OF HISTORY IN WHICH AMERICANS ARE grappling with the issue of identity. We're fortunate to live in a country where our Maslow's hierarchy of needs is satisfied, the secondary effect being that people express themselves in new and different ways, some of it good, some of it bad. We have open conversations about issues of race and gender, but there is an undercurrent of tribalism setting in as people revert to their primary loyalties and see themselves as one identity or another rather than as first and foremost an American.

Military veterans like me face a schism, pulled between two worlds. There is who we were, and then there is who we are today. Many former soldiers see themselves as having peaked at the ripe old age of twenty-one; now they are not as cool as they used to be. After flying around in helicopters and gunning down terrorists, what do you do for an encore? It is kind of like walking on the moon. After that, what do you do with the rest of your life?

I was lucky to find a job with SOFREP and have the opportunity to report on our military all around the world. I was also very lucky to have a daughter and be a big part of her life. Not everyone is so fortunate.

Professionally, I have always faced the problem that people generally see me as a former Special Forces soldier rather than a journalist. The fact of the matter is that I have not been a member of the special operations community since 2010, when I left the military. Part of it is my own fault. The website I've written for the last seven years is called Special

Operations Forces Report. While my biography could emphasize my journalism and academic background, instead it focuses on my eight years in the army. The reality is that I'm not in the military anymore, a fact that every veteran has to reconcile with eventually.

These dynamics lead to a split among veterans as well. One group integrates back into the world, goes to college, finds a normal job, and raises a family. Another group becomes professional veterans, spending the day posting memes on the Internet and writing misspelled political diatribes to social media followers. They end up like John Goodman's character in *The Big Lebowski*, a parody of themselves. In my post-military years, I've had a foot in each world. I've tried to commit myself to writing serious journalistic work, but at the end of the day, a lot of people just see me as a former snake eater.

This perception issue is why I have been so controversial among special operations veterans. As one of my Ranger instructors once said, if you're a good patrol leader, putting a boot in people's asses, you might get a negative peer evaluation. A lot of folks just won't want that boot there. Some veterans feel that someone like me should simply be a cheerleader for the special operations community. If only that were possible. When you get phone calls from crying women or soldiers who can't get the inspector general to investigate corruption, you are a pretty shitty journalist if you don't listen. You're probably a pretty shitty person, for that matter.

At the end of the day, you can't make everyone happy, and why would you even want to? Part of being a man means that you make enemies because you stand for something. This is my mantra and my religion. The truth is horrifying, and people will hate you for telling it. If you want to be popular, you have no business being a journalist. Find something else to do if you want to be well liked.

In 2016, three Green Berets were murdered in Jordan. Matthew Lewellen, Kevin McEnroe, and James Moriarty were Special Forces soldiers detailed to the "interagency," or IA, mission. This is another cute acronym that means the same thing as "Other Government Agencies" or "Regional Affairs." I had written extensively about this mission, code-named Timber Sycamore, and what a mess it was. In America's desperation to find a viable partner force to help oust the Assad regime, we had begun training and arming unviable partners. The same American general who called it wrong in Libya called it wrong again in Syria. The IA mission saw Green Berets forced to work with Arab militias who they knew were jihadists. The soldiers dragged their feet as much as possible while assigned to these CIA programs because none of them wanted to be responsible for training terrorists.

On November 4, 2016, Lewellen, McEnroe, and Moriarty were driving up to King Faisal Air Base, where they worked, when one of the Jordanian gate guards, Ma'arek Abu Tayeh, opened fire on them. A firefight ensued, and the three American Special Forces soldiers were killed. The Jordanian government quickly said that the Green Berets tried to run their way through the gate without stopping and the guard simply did his job. My sources said otherwise, and I published stories stating that. The Jordanian government then claimed that one of the Green Berets had an accidental discharge with his weapon, leading the guard to believe that he was under attack. My sources called bullshit and said that it was a planned and deliberate attack. Our men were murdered in cold blood.

Thanks to James Moriarty's father fighting tooth and nail to have the truth come out, the government of Jordan finally released the CCTV footage of the attack, but only after Abu Tayeh's trial was over. The video evidence showed the world what many of us already knew—it was cold-blooded murder. The American soldiers had taken cover, put their hands in the air, and were trying to communicate to Abu Tayeh that they were friendlies, but he kept shooting them.

To this day, we don't know the true motivation of the shooter. Likely, it is something the Jordanian government wants to keep under wraps for political reasons. With ISIS dying off in Iraq and Syria, they may look to move into Jordan, and contrary to what many believe, the Jordanian government and the royal family's hold on power is much shakier than most realize.

A year later, two Green Berets, Dustin Wright and Bryan Black, along with two support soldiers, La David Johnson and Jeremiah Johnson, were killed in an ISIS ambush in Niger. Most Americans woke up that day to headlines about the firefight and asked themselves, Where is Niger located, and why in the world do we have soldiers there? I had been monitoring the situation there, as I had been told to expect a military coup in that country within a year or two by a gentleman who had been in and out of that country over the last few years. The ambush came as a surprise, and I found myself trying to juggle various sources on the set of a television show. Thankfully, I had a staff of incredible writers, like Derek Gannon at SOFREP, who were able to work on the story. Before the remains of the soldiers had even been recovered, the Pentagon was plotting to throw our boys under the bus and blame the entire fiasco on the ODA. The Pentagon also put out a story saying that the Special Forces men had been on a training mission at the time. We called bullshit. Then they said that actually it was a recon mission. That was also bullshit.

As in Jordan, we were getting multiple cover stories, each one changing as quickly as the previous one fell apart. Once again, we supported the soldiers on the ground and would not allow the bureaucracy to cover up the incident and tell the American people lies about what happened. Today's military is extremely corporatized and emphasizes a risk-averse zero-defect environment. To this end, the Pentagon was saying that ODA did not properly fill out a risk mitigation worksheet. If soldiers were honest with risk mitigation, those worksheets would render any operations and much of training impossible, because there is too much risk. This is the hypocrisy of being trained and deployed but not allowed to do a job because if something goes wrong, it might jeopardize some officer's career progression. The military today prioritizes careers ahead of victories.

As with the incidents in Benghazi and Jordan, debate about the Niger ambush continued until video footage emerged in early 2018. One of the soldiers in the ambush had been wearing a personally owned GoPro helmet camera. The ISIS terrorists captured the video footage and used it in a propaganda film. In March, I was made aware that this propaganda film was circulating on the Internet. The footage I saw was graphic and disturbing.

The question was: What do we do with this footage, if anything? Ultimately, we decided that we should not allow ISIS to craft the narrative. The Special Forces and support personnel in Niger fought bravely and right up to the bitter end. We edited the ISIS propaganda out of the footage and ran it so that people could see what really happened. The result was absolute chaos as people sought to shoot the messenger. We were accused of callously exploiting our fallen soldiers for profit. Those who don't know how news agencies or Internet marketing work came to believe that we were getting paid per click on the story, which was factually inaccurate. That's not how it works, and none of us saw any increase in salary. That wasn't the point.

I've received death threats from Special Forces soldiers. One even described in gruesome detail how he hoped my daughter would be murdered while I watched. Other Special Forces veterans initiated a silly campaign to have my Special Forces tab revoked. Most of it was nothing more than veteran anger and virtue signaling, which came across as typecast from the beginning. This is how social media works in the twenty-first century. People engage in groupthink to create a consensus morality. If you step outside of their moral guidelines, they use shaming techniques to disconnect you from your network. They took their shots, but by this point I was on scarier lists than theirs.

There were very real and valid concerns about the video footage, and it is horrible to watch, which I understand. But then it gets to the point where angry people are just venting on social media without really understanding why we decided to publish, or republish rather, that video footage. Special Forces is a very insular community, and they would rather eat their own than confront difficult issues. Much of the anger was likely related to military veterans trying to work through their own issues and confront many of the horrible things they had witnessed in combat. In the end, it turned out that the Pentagon had been lying all along to the family members about some aspects of the ambush and how some of their loved ones had died. After the helmet-cam footage was published, the Pentagon was forced to revise the report and tell the families the truth.

Beyond that, Special Forces has also failed to acknowledge that the operational environment has fundamentally changed. Today, just about everyone has a camera and a phone in their pocket, even in third-world countries. Gone are the days when you can deploy small groups of soldiers into austere environments without creating a signature or being discovered.

Others, like the late great Tom Greer, who wrote *Kill Bin Laden,* were attacked for airing uncomfortable truths. One of my favorite comments on this subject was actually from an SAS operator, who said that when an officer writes a book, it is called a memoir, but when an NCO writes a book, it is called an exposé. There is a double standard, and powerful individuals want to control the overall narrative and claim credit for operations without people like me getting in their way.

I've often found it amusing that a retired officer can walk into a six-figure job with a think tank or lobby group that actively campaigns against our own government and foreign policy, something that no one bats an eye at. If a sergeant gets out of the military and writes a book or starts a company that sells Ranger T-shirts and coffee mugs, it is treated as a scandal.

You can't be an investigative journalist covering military special operations while also being a gentleman in good standing with all of your former brethren. It just doesn't work. You can't serve both masters. This is a dynamic that other journalists have grappled with in the past, coming to realize that they can't be friends with politicians while also reporting on them in an unbiased manner.

Special Forces is who I was, not who I am. There are a lot of great guys out there who are still grappling with this identity issue. It is literally a struggle of life and death when you consider the high number of veterans who commit suicide. Evolve or die. We don't have a choice in the matter.

EPILOGUE

MARRIAGE IS WHAT HAPPENS WHEN TWO WORLDS COLLIDE, which was perfectly evident at my wedding. We looked out over the East River back at Brooklyn on a beautiful day in October. Benni's friend Maria was marrying us while we stood hand in hand, my daughter right alongside us and handing us the wedding rings. My mother, stepfather, and sister were all there, having been able to put up with all my shit for so many years and still be happy for me, maybe even relieved, that I was marrying Benni.

Benni's family is from Northern Italy, and mine is from New York. Her childhood friend from Italy was her maid of honor. My best man was Jim West. Benni is a feminist. I'm basically a poster boy for American hegemony and global capitalism. I love the U.S. Constitution, cheeseburgers, and cold beer. My friends are a bunch of ex–Special Forces, CIA, and military intelligence weirdos. Hers are journalists and activists.

There is a theory about counterinsurgency: When you walk a mile in the enemy's shoes and share the same life, the enemy becomes more like you, and you become more like them, which nullifies the insurgency. I'm sure there is a metaphor about marriage in there somewhere.

Together Benni and I had been smuggled into Syria, detained by the secret police, marched into battle with the Peshmerga, and toured through Beirut and Damascus. It was time to make it official. The day was a huge blur of conversations, pictures, and handshakes. I think my daughter stole the spotlight, though—she seemed to make her way into every single one of our wedding photos.

There wasn't any time for a honeymoon to Nepal, though. A day after the wedding, I was on a plane to Serbia to finish filming the television show I was working on about Nikola Tesla for the Discovery Channel. The day after I flew out of New York, Benni was flying to Afghanistan to finish shooting her documentary about women in war zones. This was the life we chose, and we also chose each other. Life has been a crazy, unexpected ride for both of us.

And not everyone has made it.

In 2017, my old teammate on ODA 5414, James Hupp, took his own life. I flew to Ohio for his memorial service. It was the first time in eight years that many of us from the team had seen one another. A few of the guys were still in the army and deployed abroad, but five or six of us made it. It was a sad way to have a small team reunion. Some of the guys had fallen on hard times, gotten involved in drugs, and faced some dark moments before reaching down deep and pulling themselves through. We were all in shock that James Hupp was the one who didn't make it. He was the strong one, the guy with a good head on his shoulders.

Suicide is a strange thing. Those left behind wind up with more questions than answers. When a larger-than-life guy like James dies, you have to ask yourself why you are still here. I wasn't the toughest or the smartest, I was just average. So many highly competent soldiers have been killed in this war. Others came home but couldn't survive as civilians. Why me and not them? This was the first time I had ever questioned whether joining the military had been the right thing for me to do.

Years ago, when I got out of the army, I received word that my old platoon sergeant, Jared Van Aalst, had gone on to become a Delta Force operator and had been killed in Afghanistan by friendly fire. Van Aalst was undoubtedly a more talented soldier than I ever was.

One thing I do know is that Jared Van Aalst and James Hupp would not want me sitting around feeling sorry for them or for myself. Some veterans whine about Memorial Day, saying it is a time when we're all supposed to be sad, quietly drinking in solitude, as we remember our lost friends. I cannot for one moment imagine my lost teammates wanting this; they would want me to have a BBQ with my family. If they thought I was drunk in a bar by myself instead of spending time with my family, they would slap me in the face, and rightly so. Our war dead want us to live our lives as a way to honor their sacrifice, not revel in or glorify the loss we feel.

Looking back on it all, I can't believe how lucky I've been. Sure, there was some skill involved, some smart decisions made, but more often I was just one of the lucky ones. I served eight years in army special operations with barely a scratch on me. I integrated back into civilian life, attended college, and found a job, not without difficulties, of course, but I was still incredibly fortunate. I've also had people taking care of me and watching over my shoulder, even when I didn't realize it at the time, people like Van Aalst, Jim West, and a few others mentioned in this book.

Something else I've grown to appreciate over the years is the leadership that I worked under in Ranger Battalion and in Special Forces. In my work as a journalist, I've uncovered the dark side of the military enough times to become cynical. I've fallen from the special faith that exists between a soldier and his army. I no longer believe. However, when I look back at Squad Leader Ken, Platoon Sergeant Van Aalst, ODA Team Leader Marcus, and Team Sergeant Michael, I realize how incredibly fortunate I was to have ethical leaders. At the time, they may have come across as strong or even harsh, but they were fair and made sure I stayed on the right path. Now that I've seen what it looks like when soldiers are left unsupervised and unaccountable, I appreciate these men even more.

Meanwhile, our war in Afghanistan has stretched into infinity as our government prosecutes it in a manner that is immoral and unethical, deploying America's young people to that country over and over without any strategic end game in mind. American soldiers are dying in that country for no reason. If we had a fifty-year plan for Afghanistan and accepted that the campaign would take that long, then it might be understandable, but in the absence of any real plan and with our politicians desperate to kick the can down the road, we just repeat the same deployments, pretending that we will get a different result, while the generals promise us that we are making real progress and that the war is about to turn a corner. These swivel-chair generals are moral cowards and should be named as such.

In Iraq, we pulled out on Obama's orders and shut down our human intelligence networks in that country. Then ISIS came to town, and we sent the troops right back into theater in a classic case of shortsightedness. Had the Pentagon not forced our junior officers to send up false reports about the progress of the Iraq government, perhaps this would not have happened. Instead we wished upon a star and forced our military to lie to our policy makers about the ground truth.

Officers show up in Afghanistan or Iraq and report their host-nation partner force as being untrained and in the red. By the end of the deployment, the partner force is trained and in the green. The next American unit shows up and starts the cycle all over again, with the locals magically back in the red. Then someone like ISIS shows up, and the real report card gets issued. Americans would be disgusted and outraged if they really understood what was going on over there. I am glad that I no longer have to participate in perpetuating this fraud against the American people.

I've mentioned how I've always felt older than I actually am. Now in my mid-thirties, I feel as if I've lived several lives already, and here I am writing a memoir, a privilege usually reserved for retiring professionals. I find my thoughts wandering to issues of mortality, the fading of certain skills with age, how the young must replace the old, and humankind's ancient and petty quest for immortality. I would think that these are topics people don't normally contemplate until they are twice my age. What men fear the most is the fading of their own skills. What soldiers fear the most is quitting, failure, and being ostracized by their peers. I've been there and back several times. I hung up my rifle when I decided to become a father, and I have never regretted it.

I'm not the same man I was fifteen years ago or even four years ago. Why would you want to remain static? The interesting aspect of human experience is our ability to change. If we remain in the same rut, then there is little difference between us and inanimate objects.

You might leave the military physically, but it takes much longer for the mind to accept this reality. I've now been out of the army as long as I was in, and it is only in the last few years that I've fully come to terms with the fact that I'm not a soldier anymore. I now live a profoundly different life. You wake up one morning and you realize that you don't have anything left to prove behind a gun. You don't have to prove to anyone how tough you are; it doesn't matter anymore, because you know who you are and what you've done. Your coming-of-age story is over and now it is time to live your life.

Recently, I went to visit my old team sergeant Michael. Not quite a year after we attended James Hupp's memorial service, suicide struck again: Michael's brother killed himself, leaving behind a fourteen-year-old son. Michael took custody of the boy and adopted him. When I arrived in the airport, I was greeted by my old friend, his new son, and four of his five daughters. We spent the next couple of days playing laser tag, watching movies, going to the arcade, and making a trip to the Dinosaur Cafe. I pumped tokens into a *Jurassic Park* arcade game with Michael's seven- and nine-year-old kids until we beat the game.

Michael told me that the only time his new son cried was when Michael told him that he would be leaving North Carolina and moving in with him. He gave the kid five minutes to pull it together and get in the car. He told him that he was sorry, but his childhood had been cut short, and today he had to be a man. After four and a half minutes the boy got up, went to the bathroom, and then got into Michael's truck. Truth be told, the two of them are lucky to have each other. And I'm lucky to know them.

Your thirties, forties, and fifties are the good old days, not when you're a twenty-year-old foot soldier in a war you don't really understand. Some of my teammates had a hard time after the military; some even did hard time in the clink. Some got involved in drugs. Many had a long hard road to pull themselves out of that hole. Michael runs a limo company. My old Ranger buddies became cops, one transports organs, another works for Veterans Affairs. My old sniper partner Joe lives in Europe with his wife. My ODA team leader has had a successful career in the military and will likely make colonel. Some of you might cross paths with him at a GORUCK event when he has you doing flutter kicks in the East River.

All of our lives have changed drastically.

And yet you hold your daughter a little bit tighter than the average person. She falls asleep in your arms while you sit on the train, watching New York pass by as you head back to your hometown. You hold her tighter because you know what is out there. People pass you by like ghosts, blissfully unaware of the horrible things you've seen. And you know that this is for the best. People shouldn't have to live with that monkey on their back every day, the way many veterans do.

War is an intoxicating drug, one that fills our lives with purpose and meaning. The calls and emails still come from old friends, asking me when I will be back. But I no longer feel the need to run where the action is. As I finish writing this account, I sit in a small square in Sardinia, looking out over aquamarine waters where my daughter is swimming. I can't help but reflect on how lucky I've been. My story is only halfway over, and the end of the book may be the end of the first chapter. The war isn't going anywhere, and there will always be another one. But today I'm not running toward war.

Not unless, of course, there is a good story to chase.

GLOSSARY

15-6: informal military investigation

18B: Special Forces weapons sergeant

3/75: 3rd Ranger Battalion, 75th Ranger Regiment

5TH SFG: 5th Special Forces Group

AA: assembly area

AAR: after-action review

AQI: Al-Qaeda in Iraq

BCP: border control point

C-17: U.S. Air Force transport aircraft

CENTCOM: Central Command

CERP: Commander's Emergency Response Program

CHU: containerized housing unit

CIA: Central Intelligence Agency

CONOP: concept of the operation

CTG: counterterrorism group (Kurdish)

DD 214: the form you get when you are discharged from the army

DOD: Department of Defense

DShK: Russian heavy machine gun

EOD: explosive ordnance disposal

F3EAD: find, fix, finish, exploit, analyze, and disseminate

FARP: forward air refueling point

FOB: forward operating base

FTX: Field Training Exercise

GPS: global positioning system

GWOT: global war on terror

HAHO: high-altitude high-opening

HALO: high-altitude low-opening

HHC: Headquarters and Headquarters Company

HVT: high-value target

IA: interagency, as in joint interagency missions carried out by U.S. special operations and the CIA

IED: improvised explosive device

IMT: individual movement techniques

ISA: intelligence support activity

ISIS: Islamic State of Iraq and the Levant

ISR: intelligence, surveillance, reconnaissance

JDAM: joint direct attack munition

JSOC: Joint Special Operations Command

JTAC: joint terminal attack controller

LLC: limited liability corporation

LMTV: light medium tactical vehicle

LOA: limit of advance

LRC: Light Reaction Company (Philippines)

LRR: Light Reaction Regiment (Philippines)

LRSC: long-range surveillance company

LZ: landing zone

M9: Beretta pistol

MBITR: small military radio

MEV: medical evacuation vehicle

MH-60: medium-sized army helicopter flown by special operations aviation

MK47: belt-fed machine gun

MOD: ministry of defense

MOS: military occupational specialty

MRAP: Mine Resistant Ambush Protected vehicle

MRE: meal ready to eat

MSS: mission support site

NCO: noncommissioned officer

NCOIC: noncommissioned officer in charge

OD: olive drab

ODA: Operational Detachment Alpha

OGA: Other Governmental Agency, a euphemism for the CIA

OPCEN: operations center

OPSEC: operational security

PKK: Kurdistan Workers' Party, Partiya Karkerên Kurdistanê

PMT: pre-mission training

POW: prisoner of war

PT: physical training

PTSD: post-traumatic stress disorder

PVS-14: night vision device

Q-COURSE: Special Forces Qualification Course

RA: Regional Affairs, another CIA euphemism

RFS: released for standards

RIP: Ranger Indoctrination Program

ROE: rules of engagement

RPG: rocket-propelled grenade

RRD: regimental reconnaissance detachment

RWS: remote weapon system

SAF: Special Action Force

SAW: squad automatic weapon

SEAL: sea, air, and land

SFAS: Special Forces Assessment and Selection

SOCOM: special operations command

SOF: special operations forces

SOFA: Status of Forces Agreement

SOFREP: Special Operations Forces Report

SOG: Studies and Observations Group

SOP: standard operating procedure

SR-25: semi-automatic sniper rifle

SSE: sensitive site exploitation

SVBIED: suicide vehicle-borne improvised explosive device

SVD: Russian sniper rifle

SWAT: special weapons and tactics

SWC: Special Warfare Center

T-10C: military static line parachute

TMC: troop medical clinic

TOC: Tactical Operations Center

UAV: unmanned aerial vehicle

VA: nickname for our platoon sergeant whose last name was Van Aalst

XO: executive officer

YPG: Kurdish male militia in Syria

YPJ: Kurdish female militia in Syria

ACKNOWLEDGMENTS

I would be remiss if I did not take a moment to thank the many people who made this book possible. First, thanks to all the people who tried to shoot me or blow me up but failed—without you this book would have been one chapter long and written by someone else. I'm forever in your debt.

For many years I had resisted the idea of writing a memoir, but once I'd interviewed Kris Paronto I began to change my mind. Kris was incredibly open about his own perceived moments of weakness. I found that incredibly refreshing and realized that you can write your story without all the pretenses that often come with the military memoir. At his book signing I met my incredible editor, Natasha Simons, and we got to talking. She then introduced me to my agent, Alec Shane, at Author's House. Without these two incredible people, none of this would have been possible. They've humored me, mentored me, and put up with me. I'm forever grateful to them for their friendship and guidance through this process. I also want to thank Hannah Brown and everyone else at Simon & Schuster who helped support this effort.

This book contains many recollections from my time in the Army, and I especially want to thank the Rangers and Green Berets I served with, especially the "Glory Boys" of 1st Platoon, A/co, 3/75 and the "Wedding Crashers" of ODA 5414. Being your teammate and playing some small role in these storied organizations was an honor. Your continued friendship means the world to me. We had some great times as soldiers, but now getting to watch you guys get married, have children, and find success has been even better. I wish I had the space to thank each of you individually, but you know who you are. I also want to thank the heroes of Tal Afar ISWAT, who fought from their hometown to Anbar to Baiji to Mosul and finally back home. You've succeeded against all odds.

I want to thank everyone I work with at NEWSREP. We have an amazing team of writers, copy editors, editors, marketers, webmasters, sales people, and so much more. I specifically want to thank Alex, Jason, Brandon, Vasilis, Cris, Ian Scotto, Scott, Nate (who also edited several of my novels), Matthew, Steve, Nick, Jamie, Kurt, George, Stavros, Iassen, Joe, Eli, Dan, and so many others who have passed through our doors at various times over the last six years. We have a great team. I feel like many of you have had to ride the lighting with me more than once.

Other friends and colleagues I need to thank include Mike in the PI, Zagros in Kurdistan, photographer pal Joey, Quentin in Switzerland, Brad Hoff, Dennis in Italy, Dale Comstock, John Stryker Meyer, my good friend Jim West, Brett Jones, James Moriarty, Sam Faddis, Eeben Barlow, Mike Vining, Jeff Medley, Scott, General Pamonag, General Sabban, Larry Laveron, Jim Morris, Hershel Davis, Bob Charest, Mark Boyatt, Taffy Carlin, Peter Nealen, Manuel, Salil, Marty Skovlund, Leo Jenkins, Marc Lee, J.T. Patten, Tony, Joshua Lees, Josh Bell, BK, Danny, Lorenzo, Chuck Rogers, Sarah, Richard, and many others who cannot be named here.

I also want to take a moment to thank my sources, the people who have spoken to me over the years often about incredibly sensitive subjects and at great personal risk to either their careers or in some cases even their physical wellbeing. Some people believe that the truth wants to be free, that it is only a matter of time before the facts present themselves to us as a matter of some metaphysical determinism. I don't believe any of that. The only reason why we know the truth about certain matters is because you had the courage to speak up about it. Thank you for trusting me.

ACKNOWLEDGMENTS

Most of all I want to thank my family for supporting my endeavors over the years, including this book. I'm grateful to Benni for reviewing some aspects of this book but more so for sharing some of these adventures with me. In so many ways, this book is really for my daughter, in the hope that one day she reads it and understands why I couldn't explain some things to her when she was a little girl. Hopefully this book will answer your questions if I haven't. Thank you Mom and Irv for your continued support and always looking out for me. Thanks Robin, Russ, Jacob, Claudia, Bob, and Stephen. Anne and Paco, congratulations and thank you for your support.